IMAGES
of America

TROY'S LITTLE ITALY REVISITED

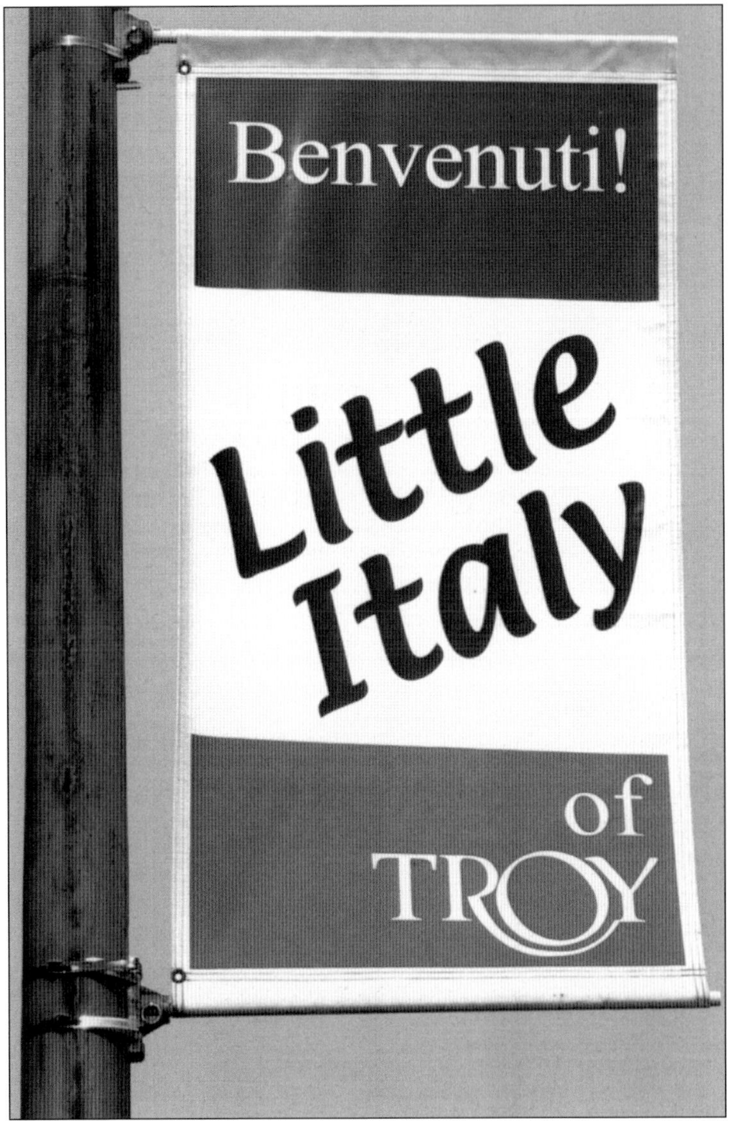

Green, white, and red street banners—bearing the colors of the Italian flag—welcome visitors to Little Italy. The banners were an early project for the newly formed Friends of Little Italy, formed in 2002, and help identify neighborhood boundaries. This photograph was also the first in a series of postcards that marketed Troy's Little Italy as an ethnic tourist destination. (Photograph by Denise Saint-Onge.)

On the Cover: Central Troy and Little Italy are seen from a point at the top of the western section of Prospect Park—located on Troy's Mount Ida. At 240 feet above sea level, Mount Ida is the most prominent geographic feature in the city and offers a view of much of the city center, its southern neighborhoods, the Hudson River, and the land beyond. Youngsters would often sit along the top of the parkland and identify their specific neighborhood block. The park was accessed via a back road, off Hill Street, but adventurous youngsters preferred to climb the slopes just a few feet from their property. Jerry Favata, seen in this 1954 photograph, is a lifelong Troy resident and volunteer supporter of Troy's Little Italy. (Courtesy of Jerry Favata.)

IMAGES
of America

TROY'S LITTLE ITALY REVISITED

Michael A. Esposito

ARCADIA
PUBLISHING

Copyright © 2015 by Michael A. Esposito
ISBN 978-1-4671-2370-9

Published by Arcadia Publishing
Charleston, South Carolina

Printed in the United States of America

Library of Congress Control Number: 2014959573

For all general information, please contact Arcadia Publishing:
Telephone 843-853-2070
Fax 843-853-0044
E-mail sales@arcadiapublishing.com
For customer service and orders:
Toll-Free 1-888-313-2665

Visit us on the Internet at www.arcadiapublishing.com

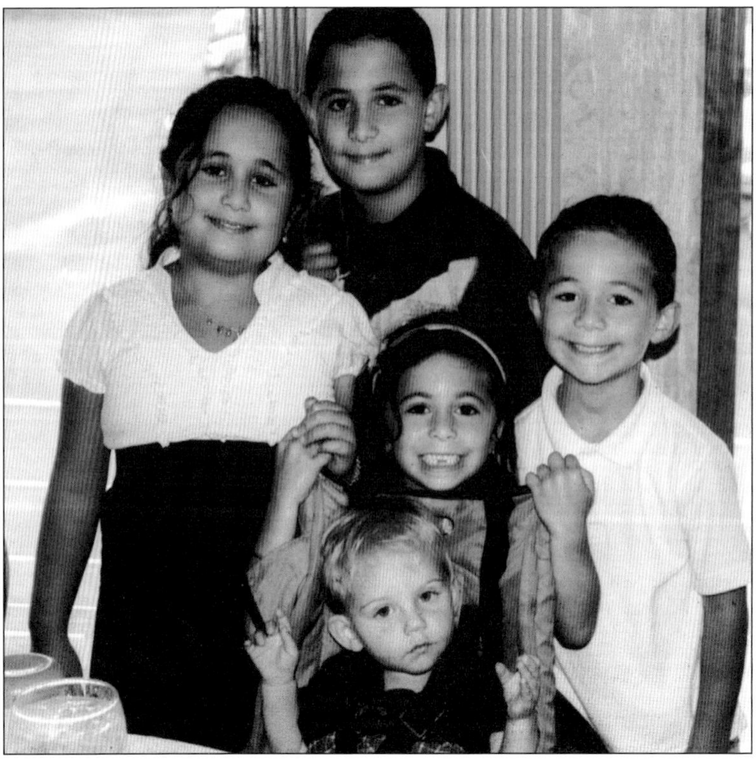

This book is lovingly dedicated to my grandnieces and grandnephews. Pictured here, from left to right are (first row) John Anthony Gorman; (second row) Madeline Ieraci, Alaina Ieraci, and Michael Ieraci; (third row) Vincent Ieraci. (Author's collection.)

Contents

Acknowledgments		6
Introduction		7
1.	What the Neighborhood Offered	9
2.	The Hill	21
3.	Beyond the Hill	37
4.	Community Partners	63
5.	Our Great Good Place	75
6.	Catalyst for Change	95

ACKNOWLEDGMENTS

Many people made this compilation possible. The photographs are treasures loaned to me by family, friends, and neighbors and from the archival collections of the Rensselaer County Historical Society (RCHS), St. Mary's and St. Anthony's churches, the Italian Community Center, the Troy Youth Association's CYO Center, and Joseph's House & Shelter. Local directories available at the RCHS and the Troy Public Library and the personal stories people shared about their families and growing up in Little Italy provided the content for the captions that accompany each photograph.

I am grateful to my friend Marion Field, editor of the *Little Italy Newsletter*. The great care she exercised in selecting and organizing the contents of each issue provided documentation of the history of our neighborhood association. Thanks also goes to Anasha Cummings, Andrea Daley, and Joe Gorman for sharing their computer skills on technical matters during the process of compiling this book and to Kathy Sheehan, Rensselaer County historian, for her research assistance. It has been a pleasure to work with the staff at Arcadia Publishing, especially my editor Sharon McAllister. Arcadia gives many people an opportunity to write about the communities they love.

Finally, a special thanks goes to my mom, Antoinette Terribile Esposito, for her inspiration and encouragement. She was my primary source of information and a great research assistant. She lived her 96 years as a resident of Little Italy and loved Troy and her neighborhood.

Introduction

A few weeks before the manuscript for this book was submitted to Arcadia, one of my heroes—former governor Mario Cuomo—passed away. During the days that followed, it was comforting to reread speeches he compiled for his book *More Than Words*. Among them was his address to the National Italian American Foundation dinner in 1990, on the topic of ethnicity and the pride he had in his ethnic roots. He said, "We should use our history as a basis for making sure that we Italian Americans continue to make a difference in this society—that we involve ourselves in furthering those policies that embody what the Italian journey into America has been all about—opportunity, hope, equality, compassion, social justice, freedom." That Italian journey to Troy was essentially the same journey made by the several million countrymen who settled in America between the late 1890s and the 1920s.

A significant part of the history of Troy and its neighborhoods is the story of the diverse ethnic groups that immigrated to our city, often living on specific blocks for generations. They sought opportunities not available to them and looked forward to a better future for their children. They knew they would work long hours and life would not be easy. They would have to prove themselves, and they would have to understand a new language. The US Census Bureau reported 465 Italian immigrants in Troy in 1900. They lived primarily on William Street, south of Ferry Street, in small brick homes—sometimes 12 to a building. By 1910, it reported the foreign born Italian population in Troy at 1,462; by 1920, at 1,412; and by 1930, at 1,883.

The Centennial Jubilee program of the St. Anthony of Padua Shrine Church reports that Rev. Giovanni Santoro ministered to 23 Italian immigrant families—the first parishioners of the church established in 1892, in a small building at 106 Ferry Street. In 1905, the growing congregation purchased the Unitarian church at the corner of Fourth and State Streets. Members of the early Italian community, like other ethnic groups, organized social clubs as a way to preserve their culture and traditions. Attorney Philip Cirillo, a 1911 Albany Law School graduate, organized the Cristofo Colombo Club, located on Congress Street. Neighbors also remember the Frosolone Club, the Cervinara Club, the Sons of Italy, and the Knights of Columbus.

The Italian Welfare League, an early mutual aid society, sponsored the organization of the Italian Community Center (ICC), which opened in February 1935 at 191 Second Street. Many prominent Italian immigrants, including Dr. Michael E. DeLuca, a 1911 graduate of Albany Medical College, restaurant owners Mario Ciccotti and Joseph Manori, and businessman D.A. Fazioli, were early officers. The formation of the ICC was a significant achievement for the growing Italian immigrant community. From the time of its inception, the Italian Community Center Charitable Foundation has had a distinguished history of charitable contributions to the Troy community, offering support for Italian immigrants and Italian American families, organizing *festas*, and working toward furthering Italian culture and traditions.

Strong ties to family and neighborhood, as well as associations through church and social organizations, helped maintain the value system that sustained the early immigrants and protected *la via vecchia* (the old way). World War II and its aftermath would bring about significant changes to *la via vecchia*, as would the shift from cities to suburbs that was brought about by changing lifestyles and the urban renewal projects that affected life in Troy's older neighborhoods. As a result, Troy's population has deceased from approximately 70,000 to less than 50,000 in the past few decades.

Fourth Street businessman Rocco DeFazio formed the Friends of Little Italy in 2002 and championed the idea of celebrating neighborhood history. Two years later, the first New York State Little Italy Heritage Tourism Conference was held in Troy. The Honorable Sergio Vento, Italian ambassador to the United States, was invited by Sen. Hillary Clinton to the conference. He reminded attendees of "the power of memory as a formula for a great project." The collective memory of those who grew up in the old neighborhood plays an important part in today's planning efforts, and in the following year, our neighborhood group, Troy Little Italy, was formed. A year later, the South Central Neighborhood Watch was established.

During the past dozen years, many creative, energetic, and generous people have worked hard and intelligently to help stabilize the neighborhood. Their goal is threefold: to establish Little Italy as an ethnic tourism destination, restore Troy's historic Hill Street marketplace, and make the neighborhood safe and clean so it will be a place where people will want to live, work, and visit. Our continuing story can be encouraging to organizers in other older neighborhoods in various stages of revitalization. Those who went before us inspire us, and we celebrate our past and have faith in our future.

One

What the Neighborhood Offered

The 1881 G.M. Hopkins text, *City Atlas of Troy*, provides a good representation of what Little Italy and the area now known as South Central Troy were like when the earliest Italian immigrants arrived. The area contained seven churches, three synagogues, eight schools, several dozen businesses, public buildings, and two parks. Many people could walk to jobs at the utility company, ironworks, foundries, coal and lumberyards, garment shops, and several breweries. The New York Central & Hudson River Railroad complex, along the Hudson River, included an engine house and freight station. The Troy & Boston Railroad Company owned property along the river, north of Adams to Washington Street. Railroads provided many jobs for unskilled immigrant laborers.

While not specifically identified on the map, dozens of small stores along Fourth Street offered convenient shopping for residents. It was a neighborhood of ethnic diversity, as evidenced by synagogues, French, German, Irish, and Italian Catholic parishes, and Episcopal and Presbyterian congregations—including an African American congregation on Liberty Street. The Washington Park neighborhood was home to many affluent citizens and business owners. Much of the area east of Third Street was home to mill and factory workers and shopkeepers. According to 1880 census data, the total population of the First, Eighth, and Eleventh Wards was 12,162. The city's population was reported at 56,747, of which 16,938 were foreign born. Of that number, only 26 were reported as being Italian born.

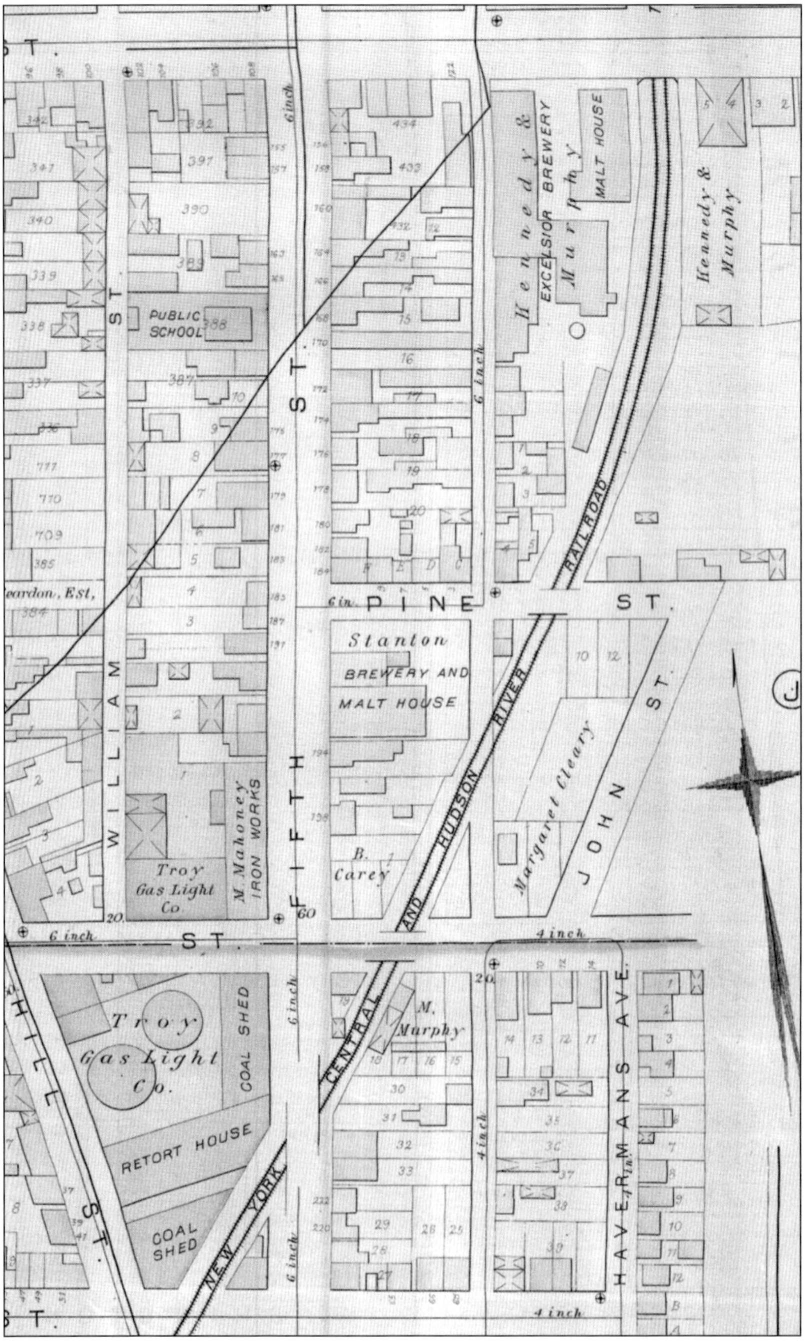

City Atlas of Troy shows Little Italy's northeast neighborhood, from Ferry to Washington Streets, and the route of the New York Central & Hudson River Railroad. Also identified are the Kennedy & Murphy Brewery and Malt House and John Stanton's Brewery and Malt House. Col. Stephen J. Schuyler started the first brewery in Troy in 1793. By 1890, there were nine breweries in the city. On the corner of Fifth and Liberty Streets is Michael Mahoney's Iron Works. The Troy Gas Light Company complex is on Hill Street, between Liberty and Washington Streets. Mount Ida lines the entire eastern side of the neighborhood. (Courtesy of Rensselaer County Historical Society.)

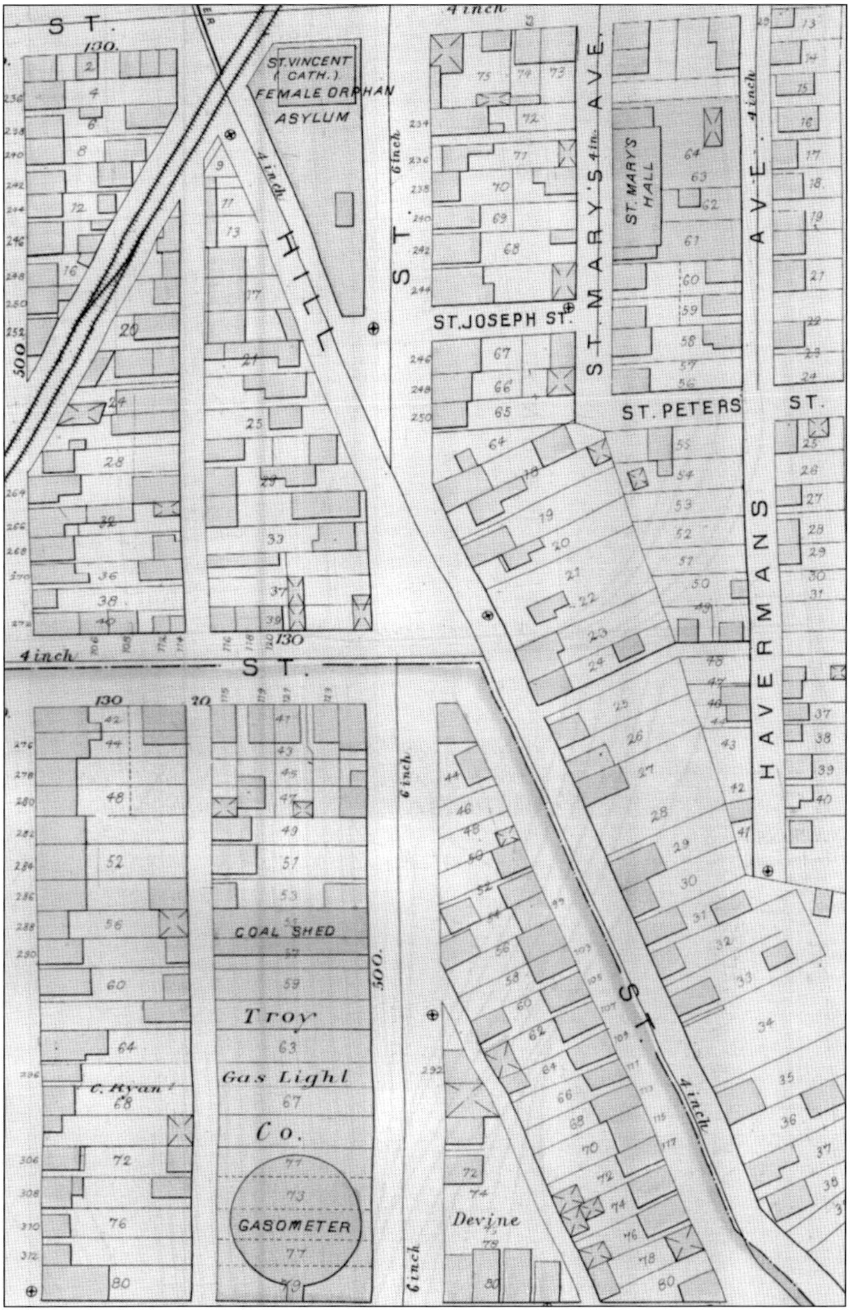

The most prominent site in Little Italy's southeast neighborhood, from Washington to Adams Streets, is the round building identified as the "gasometer" at Fifth Avenue and Jefferson Street. The Troy Gas Light Company owned a considerable number of vacant lots adjacent to their Gasholder House. Located a few blocks north is St. Vincent's Female Orphan Asylum, situated at the original site of the Troy Hospital. Just east of the orphanage is St. Mary's Parish Hall. Most of the lots on this map are 25 feet wide by 130 feet deep. John E. Van Alen for Jacob I. and Matthias Van der Heyden, who owned two large farms north of the Poestenkill at the time, surveyed the South Central area in 1793. (Courtesy of Rensselaer County Historical Society.)

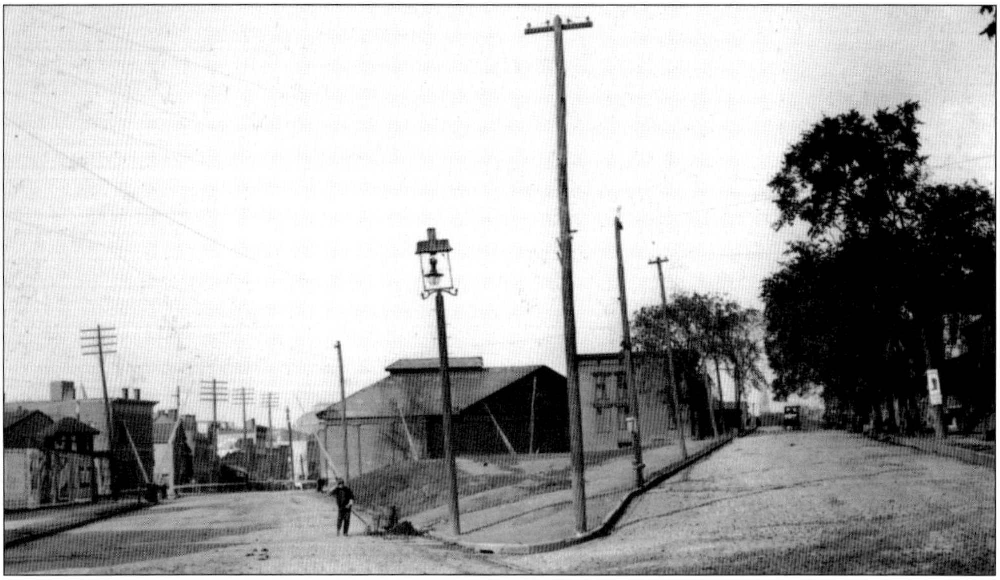

The c. 1900 photograph was taken at the junction of Hill Street and Fifth Street (now Fifth Avenue), looking north. The street above the junction is Washington Street. In 1854, Rev. Peter Havermans built Troy Hospital, the first hospital in New York State outside New York City, at the corner of Fifth and Washington Streets. Several years later, when the hospital relocated to Eighth Street, the building was used for the St. Vincent's Female Orphan Asylum. (Courtesy of Sam Chiappone.)

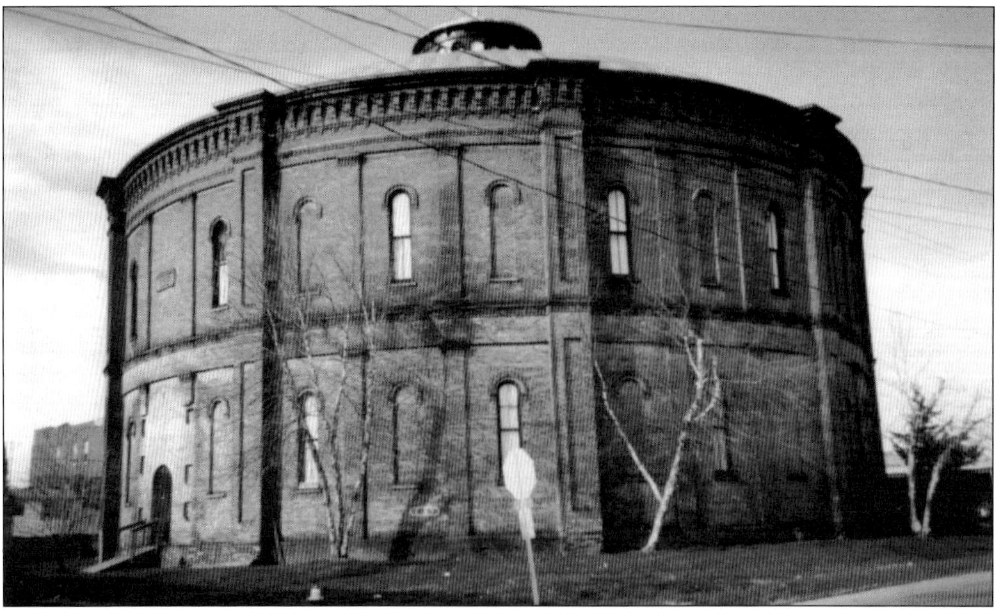

The Gasholder House on the corner of Fifth Avenue and Jefferson Street was built for the Troy Gas Light Company between 1873 and 1875, under the direction of Frederick A. Sabbaton—a prominent gas engineer. The building stored manufactured coal gas until it was needed to illuminate streets and buildings in Troy. The Gasholder House was added to the National Register of Historic Places in 1971. A sectional drawing of the building is the logo for the Society of Industrial Archeology. (Author's collection.)

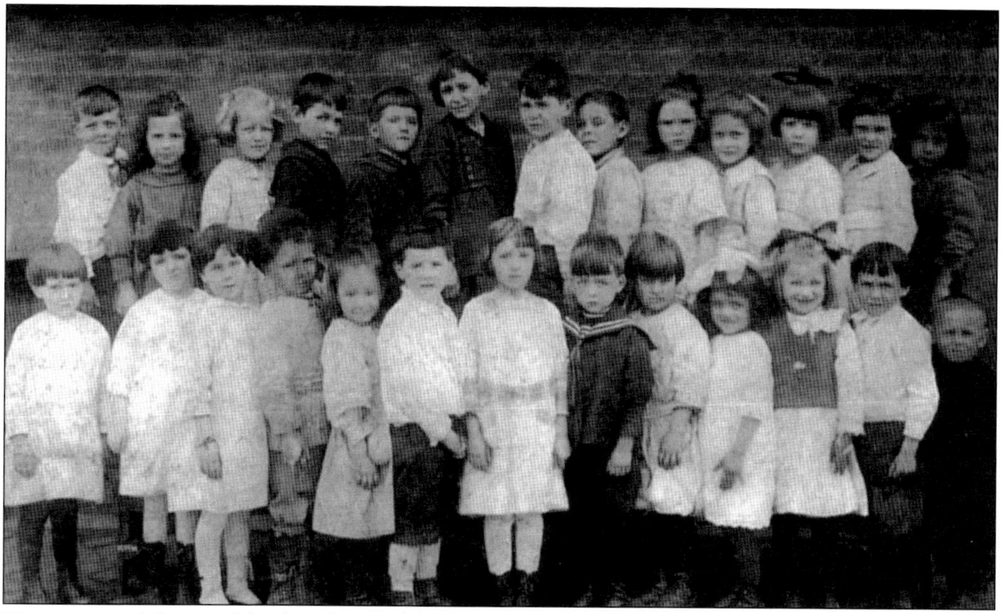

Youngsters of the neighborhood, possibly the first class assembled at the St. Anthony of Padua parish school, gather for a class photograph. Realizing that education and Americanization were important for children, Rev. Metello Galante acquired the abandoned Public School No. 8, located at 1471 Fifth Avenue just south of Ferry Street, and opened an elementary school in 1916. (Courtesy of St. Anthony's Church Archives.)

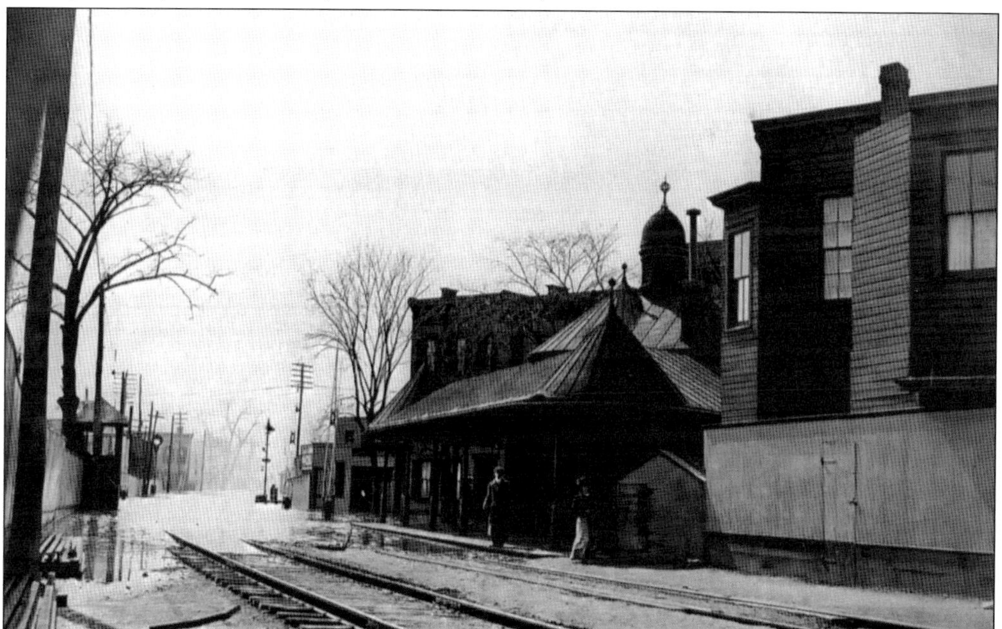

This is the trackside view of a platform station used by passengers who would board the popular Troy-Albany Belt Line—a local train service discontinued in the 1930s. The structure on the raised wooden platform contained a small room used by a ticket seller. The building was located on Third Street, below Adams Street, and is now the site of the Eleventh Ward's World War II memorial. (Courtesy of Robert Caprara.)

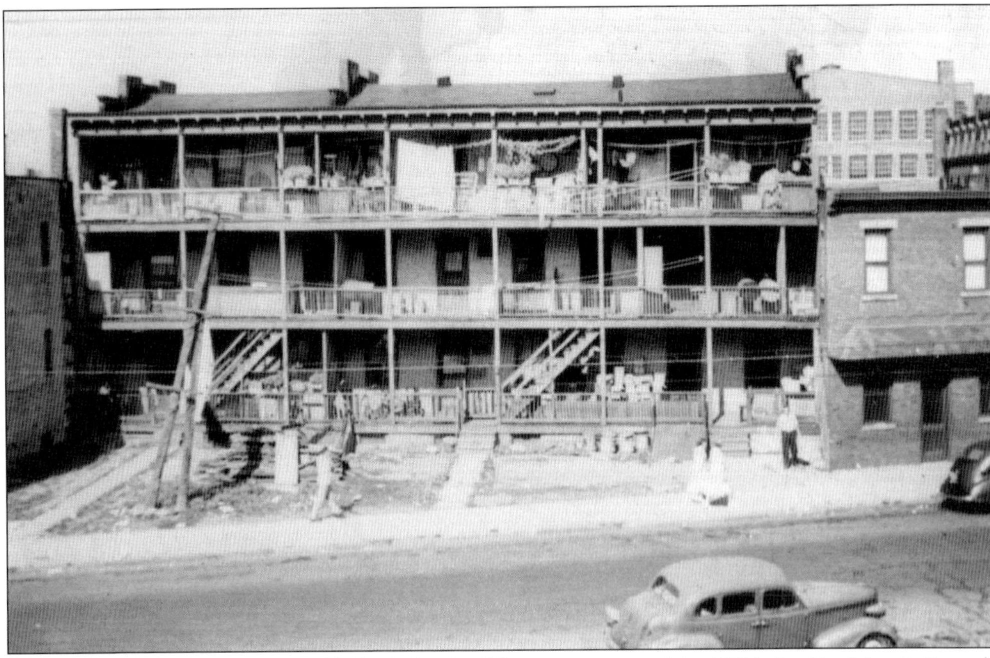

Rev. Peter Havermans originally had this building constructed in 1854, for St. Mary's Female Orphan Asylum. In 1869, it was sold to James Moran, who rented rooms to Irish immigrants. By 1912, the property, home to Italian immigrants, was resold to Joseph Geraci and later, to Gennaro Riggione. The building was demolished in the mid-1960s. (Courtesy of Leonard DeMeo.)

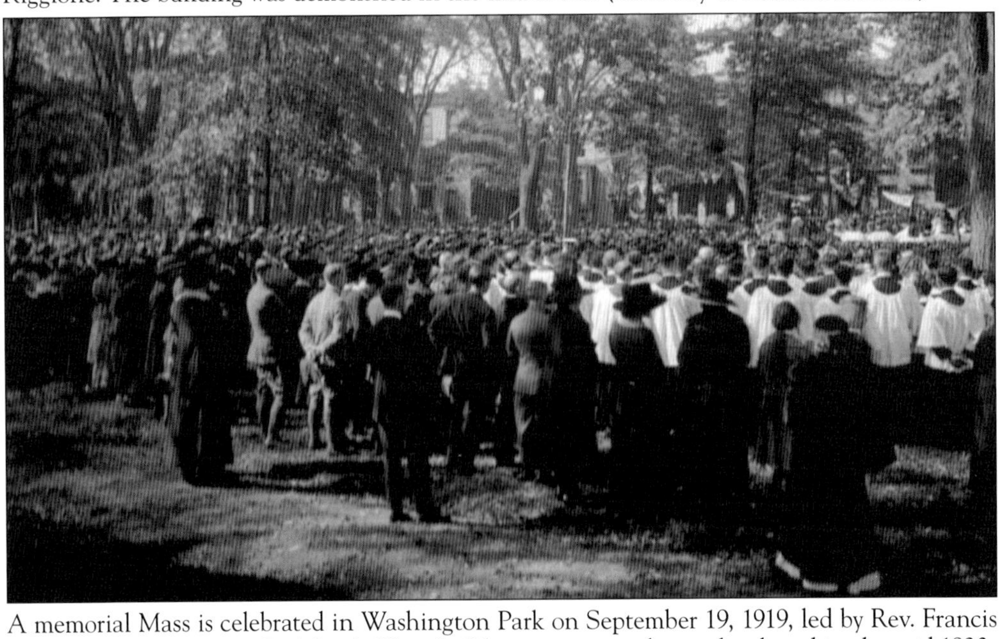

A memorial Mass is celebrated in Washington Park on September 19, 1919, led by Rev. Francis Kelly, assistant pastor at St. Mary's Church. The two-acre park was developed in the mid-1830s as the centerpiece of an exclusive residential area, following a precedent set in the state with the establishment of Gramercy Park in New York City. By 1864, owners adjacent to the park agreed to pay a special assessment to maintain the park and follow regulations regarding its use. (Courtesy of the Boland family.)

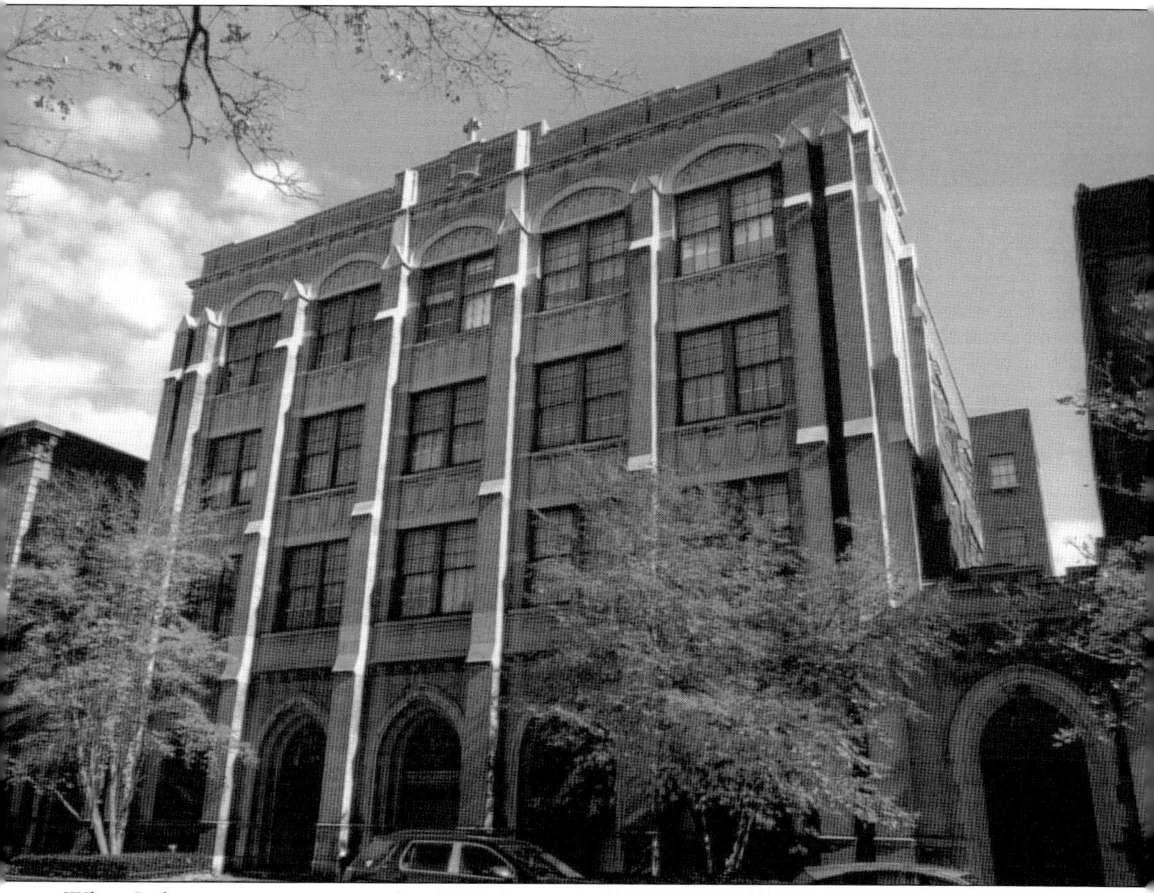

When Italian immigrants arrived in 1900, there were four private schools in the neighborhood: St. Mary's, St. Lawrence's, St. Jean's, and LaSalle Institute. St. Mary's school was located in what is now a three-story residence at 185 Third Street. The building in the photograph, the "new school" at 216 Third Street across from Washington Park, opened in 1917 with 612 pupils and served the parish until it closed in 1975. The building was renovated and converted into a residential unit called Park Place Apartments. St. Lawrence's school, which closed in 1960, was also converted into apartments. St. Jean's School, which closed in 1934, was a day care center for many years and is now a private residence. Adaptive reuse has preserved many fine historic buildings in the neighborhood. (Photograph by Andrea Daley.)

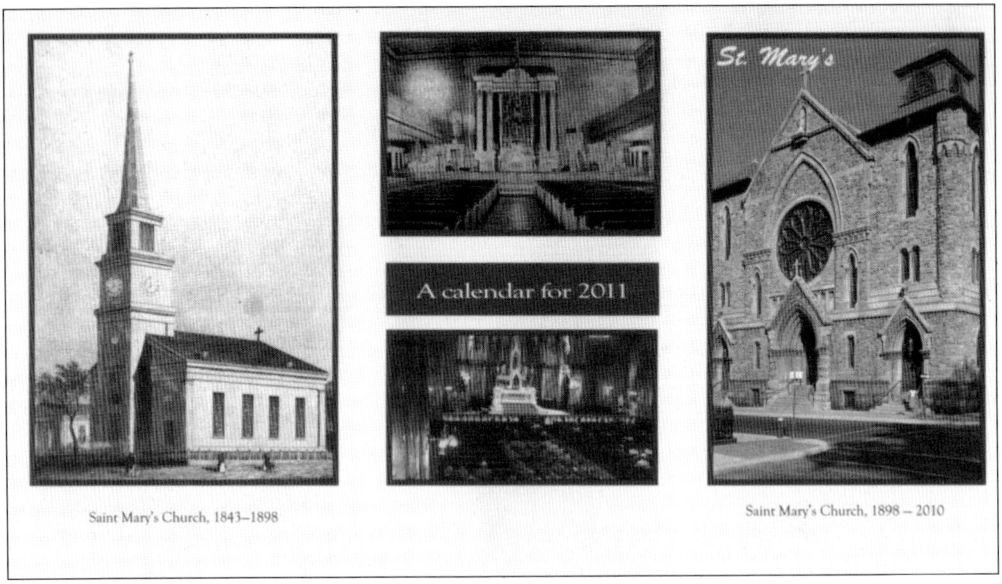

A church for St. Mary's parish has stood at the corner of Washington and Third Streets since 1842. The first church was replaced by the present structure, dedicated in 1904 and placed in the National Register of Historic Places in 1973 as part of the Washington Park Historic District. Pictured is the cover of the Historic St. Mary's Parish Calendar, which was issued when the church closed in 2010. (Photograph by Tracy Thomas.)

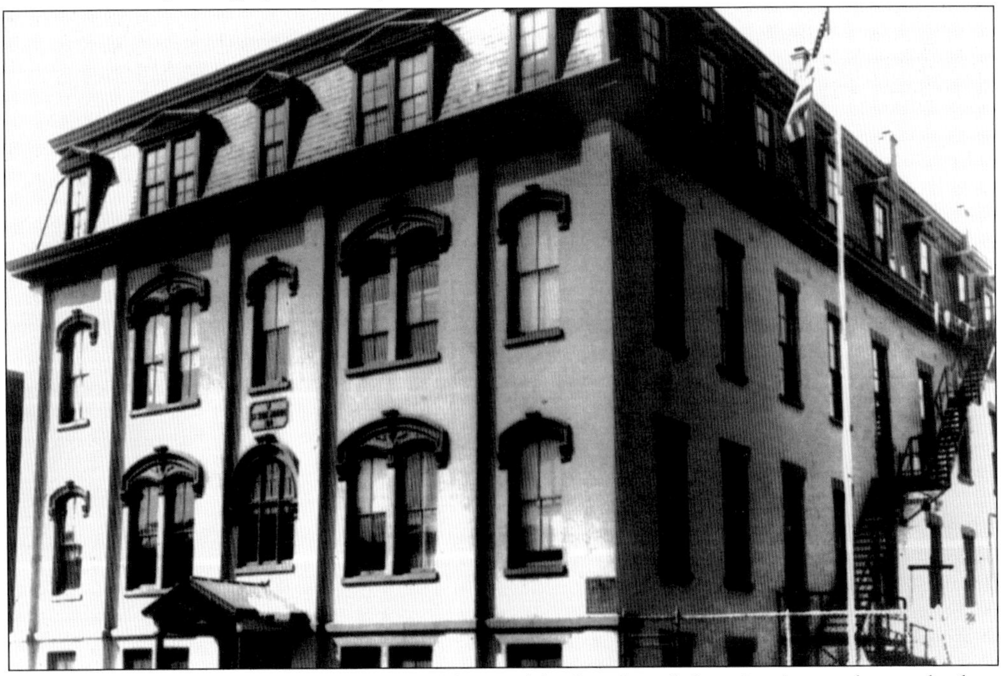

The LaSalle Institute was an integral part of the neighborhood until the school moved to a suburban campus in 1965. The school was administered by the Christian Brothers, a religious order dedicated to educating Troy's working-class young men, and organized by Fr. Peter Havermans in 1850. The building was demolished in the late 1960s, though its gymnasium is now home to the Troy Youth Association's Catholic Youth Organization (CYO) Center. (Courtesy of LaSalle Institute.)

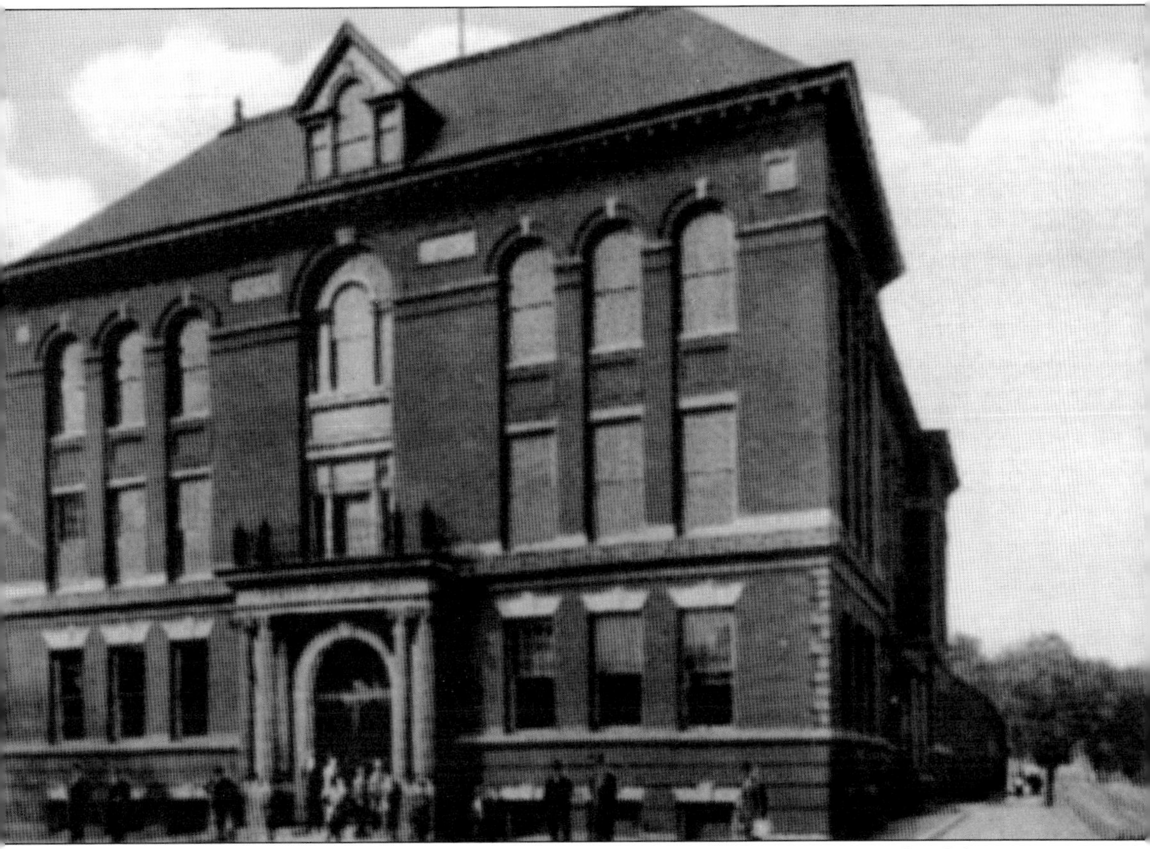

Public School 10, built in 1898 by Troy architect Marcus Cummings, is an example of the many handsome, stable area buildings renovated as housing units. The former school, located at the corner of Third and Adams Streets, was built to consolidate three public elementary schools—those of the First, Eighth, and Eleventh wards—into one structure. School 10 Apartments, owned by the nonprofit Troy Architectural Program (TAP, Inc.), is an affordable apartment community with 20 units. The building was added to the National Register of Historic Places in 1994. Behind the apartment building is Leslie's Garden, a beautifully landscaped urban garden dedicated to the memory of Leslie Adler, a longtime advocate for quality housing. (Courtesy of Troy Public Library.)

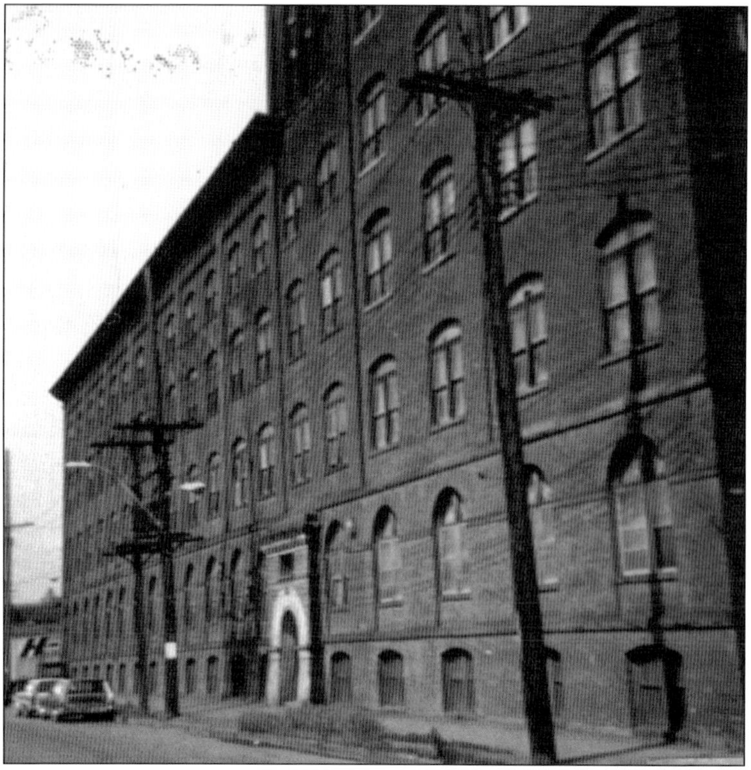

One of the largest commercial buildings in Troy was C.F. Conkey's brick malt house, located on the southeast corner of River and Adams Streets. A portion of the building housed the International Shirt Company from 1893 to 1906. It has also been the site of the Troy Underwear Company (in 1906), Tiny Town Togs (from 1935 to 1975), and is presently home to the Old Brick Furniture Company. (Courtesy of Rensselaer County Historical Society.)

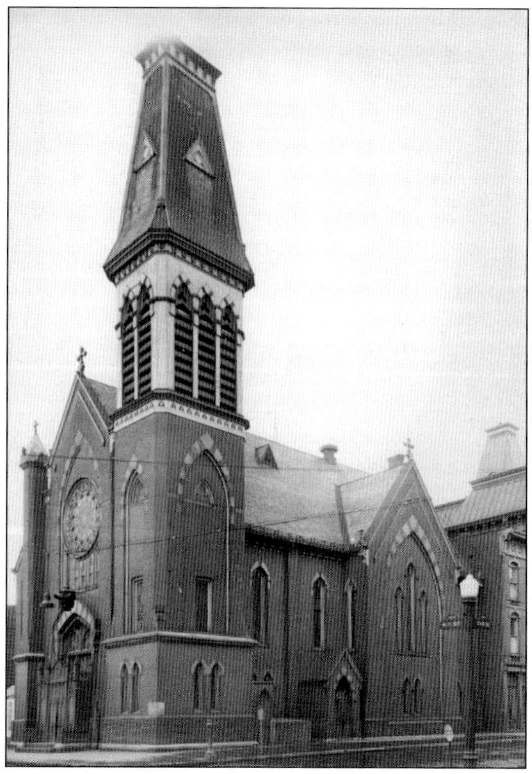

The Unitarian Society sold this building, located at the corner of Fourth and State Streets, to Rev. Giovanni Santoro in 1905. After extensive renovation, the worship site opened to Troy's Italian Catholic community as St. Anthony of Padua Church. The church was demolished in 1964. In May 1965, the parish congregation moved into its new church on State Street. (Courtesy of St. Anthony's Church Archives.)

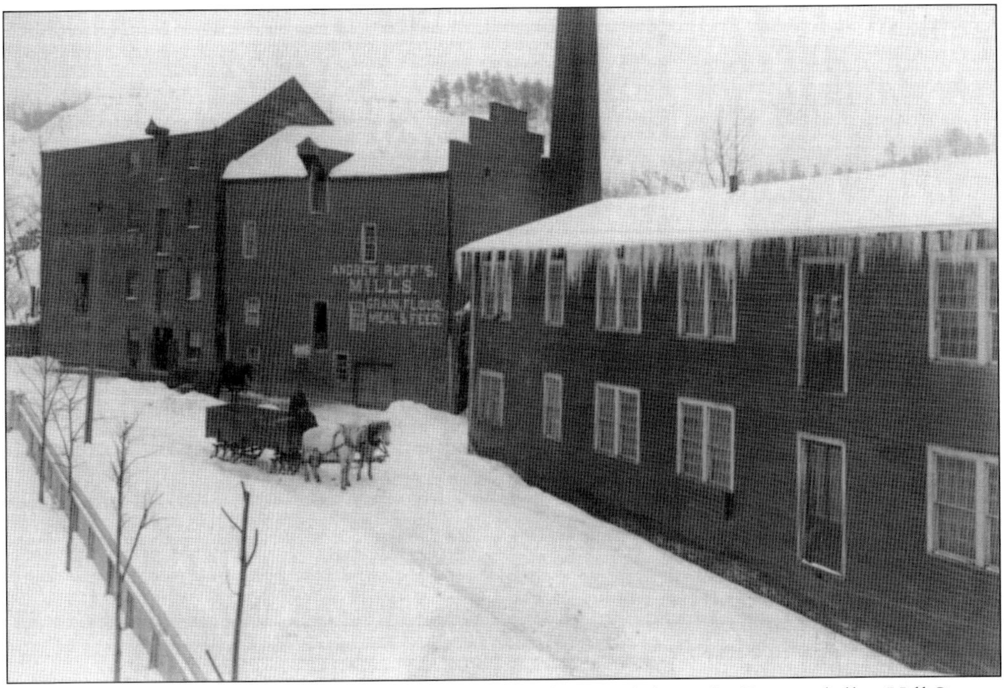

The grain mills of Andrew Ruff & Son, which opened in 1875 along the Poestenkill at Hill Street, can be traced to one of Troy's earliest and most successful industries. Northern New York's first mill for the manufacture of paper was established in 1792 by Mahlon Taylor and built on property adjacent to that later purchased by Ruff. (Courtesy of Rensselaer County Historical Society.)

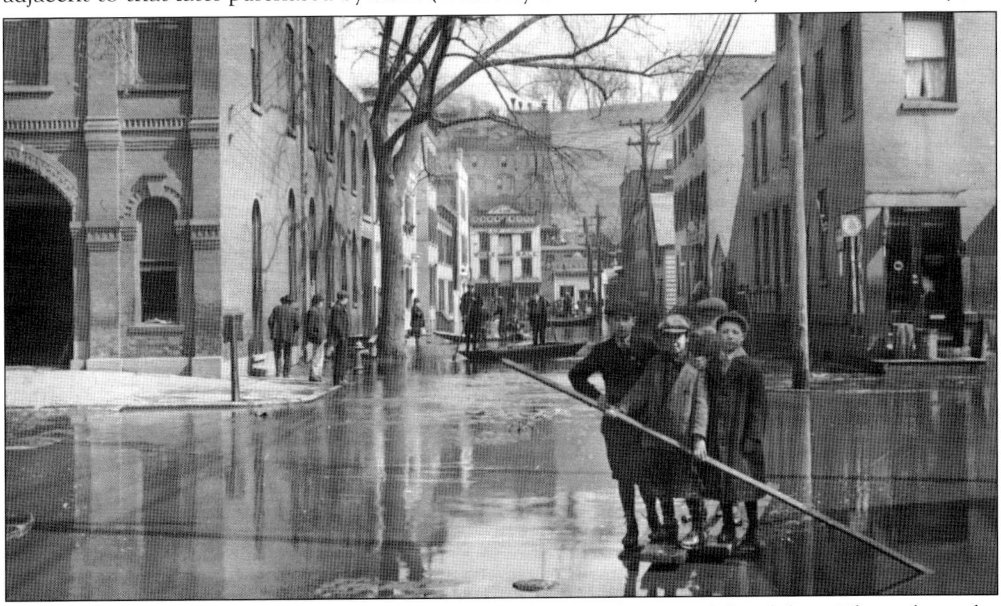

A sizeable portion of the city along the Hudson River is in a designated floodplain. Throughout the city's history, there have been several major floods, including the flood of March 1913—pictured here at the corner of Third and Division Streets. The river crested at 29.7 feet. The building at left is the Washington Volunteer Fire Company. It is now the site of the First Ward World War II memorial. (Courtesy of Sam Chiappone.)

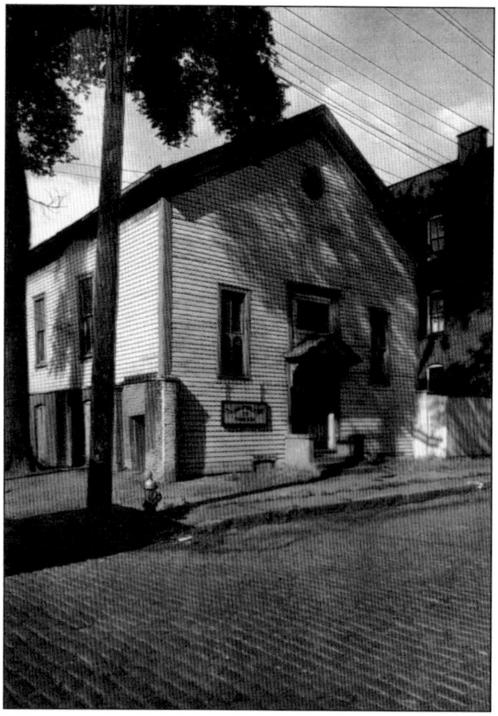

The Liberty Street Presbyterian Church—located at the corner of Liberty and Church Streets from 1840 to 1963—was a black congregation. In 1865, its first pastor, Rev. Henry Highland Garnet, was invited by Pres. Abraham Lincoln to address the US Congress. The church was active in the Underground Railroad movement and the site of abolitionist meetings, as well as a draft riot in 1863. (Courtesy of Rensselaer County Historical Society.)

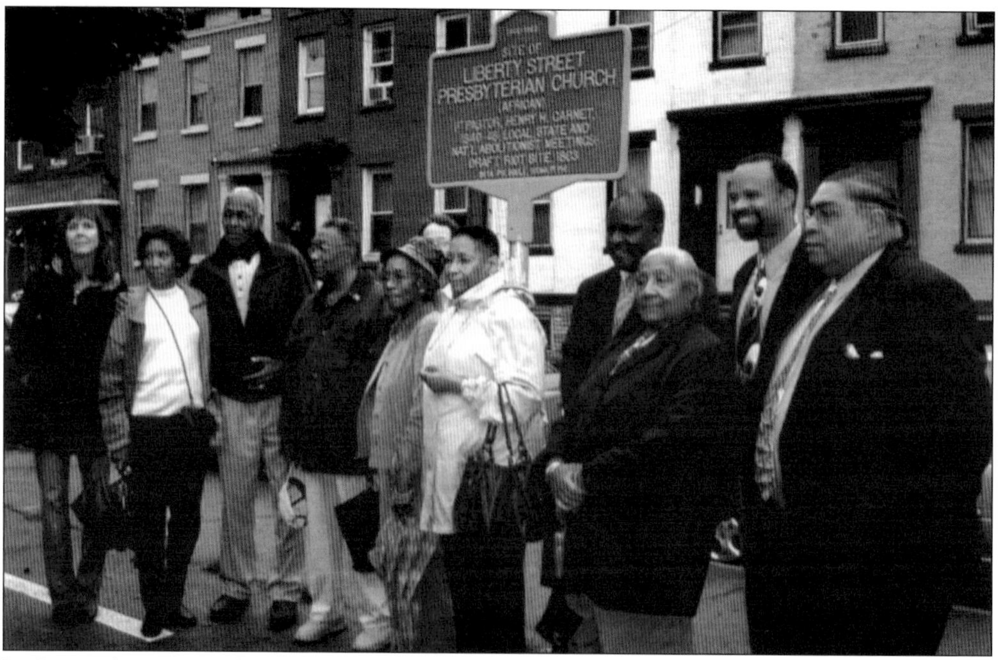

In September 2006, a historic sign presented by Beta Psi Boule, a chapter of Sigma Pi Phi, an African American Greek lettered organization formed in 1904, was dedicated at the former site of the Liberty Street Presbyterian Church. From left to right are Rev. Beth Illingworth, Marilyn O'Dell, William "Billy" Harrell, DeWitt T. Murray, Kathy Sheehan, Juanita Stenhous, Bernice Morehead, Janice Daggs, Leroy Twiggs, Stephen J. Tyson, and Carl Trantham. (Photograph by Dorcas Rose.)

Two

The Hill

In the late 1960s, the neighborhood of Little Italy referred to as "the Hill" was demolished for a proposed north-south arterial highway project that was later abandoned. Over 500 people had to move, and 100 homes and a dozen garages were demolished.

The neighborhood contained modest two-story brick homes, constructed around 1860, on streets nestled along the western slope of Mount Ida's Prospect Park. It was a stereotypical blue-collar neighborhood: stable, peaceful, and clean. Homes were owner occupied and the pride of ownership was evident in the care given to each piece of property. While backyards were relatively small, many homeowners made room for a fruit tree or grape arbor and vegetable garden. Working women were primarily employed in Troy's garment industry, while the men worked with the steel mills and railroads or as tailors, shoe repairmen, or fruit peddlers. Neighbors were respectful of each other. Children played along the slopes of Prospect Park, in the public market on Hill Street, or on the streets of the small, closely knit neighborhood. Youngsters were also only a few blocks from the local elementary schools. People did much of their convenience shopping on Fourth Street and from peddlers who sold their goods door to door.

The city lost a treasured, valuable old neighborhood, but life on the Hill is remembered in the collective memories of its families.

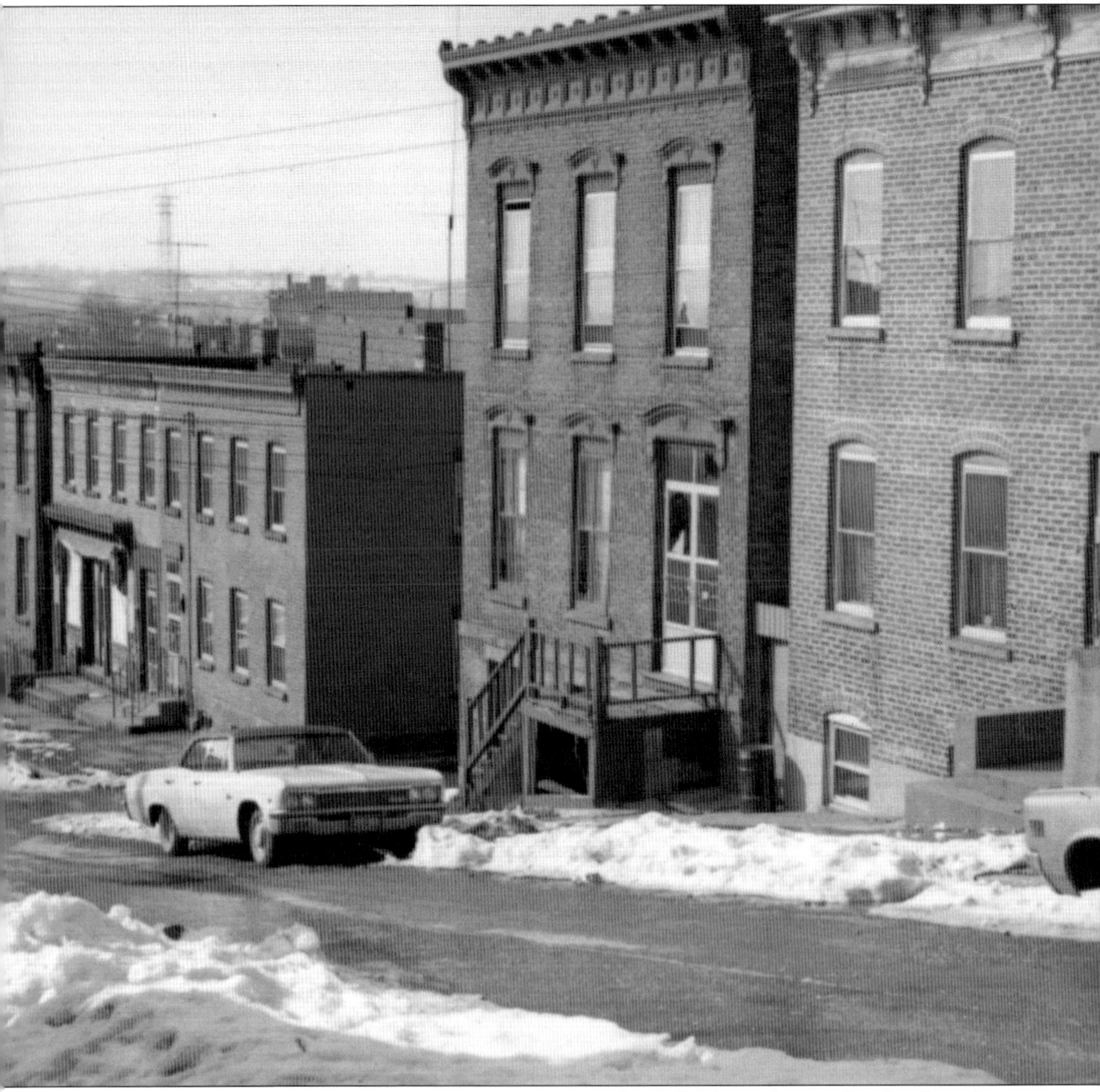

This 1960s photograph shows typical residences on the Hill, along the north side of Washington Street. From left to right, a with house number and owner or tenant identified, are: 504, Margaret Kennedy and Anna Burke; 506, Luigi Bottillo Grocery Store (first floor), Lucia Miele (second floor); 508, Victor and Catherine Speciale (first floor), Joseph and Mary Special (second floor); 550, Sheryl Cummings (first floor), Steve and Anna O'Neil (second floor); and 552, Nicholas and Victoria Mantello (first floor), James and Theresa Mantello (second floor). The homes were built between the Civil War and the 1880s. By the early 1970s, most of the buildings in the neighborhood were vacant and awaiting demolition. (Courtesy of Leonard DeMeo.)

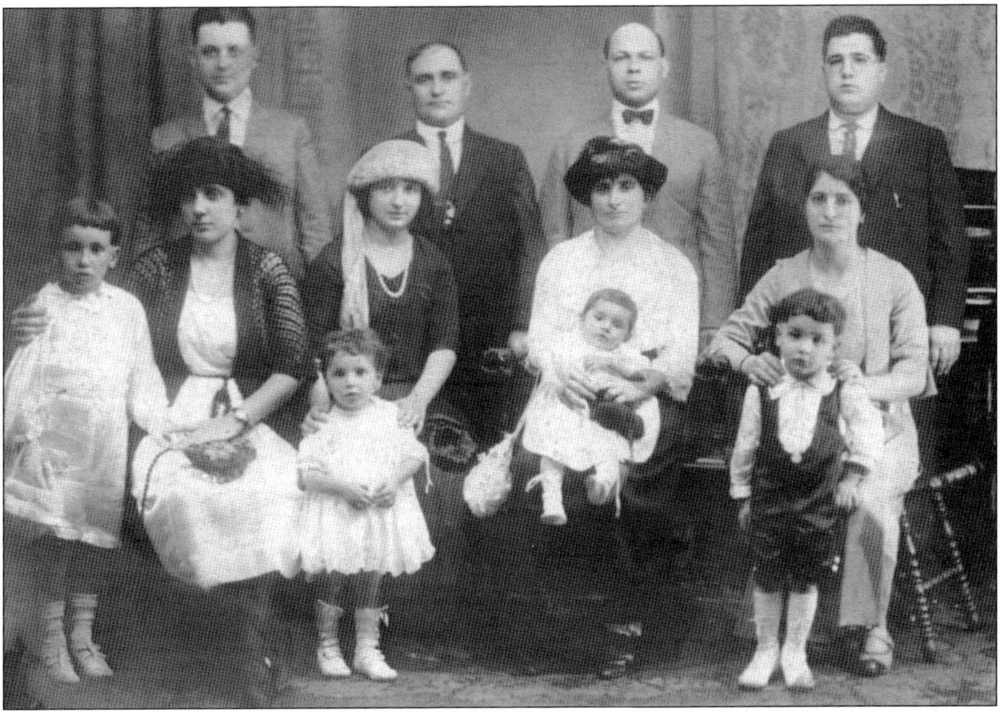

Immigrant families from the Calabria region gathered for this 1927 photograph. The adults are, from left to right (first row), Donata Mele, Elizabeth Gaglardi, unidentified, and Elizabeth Bevevino; (second row) John Mele, Francis Gaglardi, Dominick Bevevino, and unidentified. Elizabeth Bevevino is seen with her son Bruno, but the remaining three children are not identified. (Courtesy of the Bevevino family.)

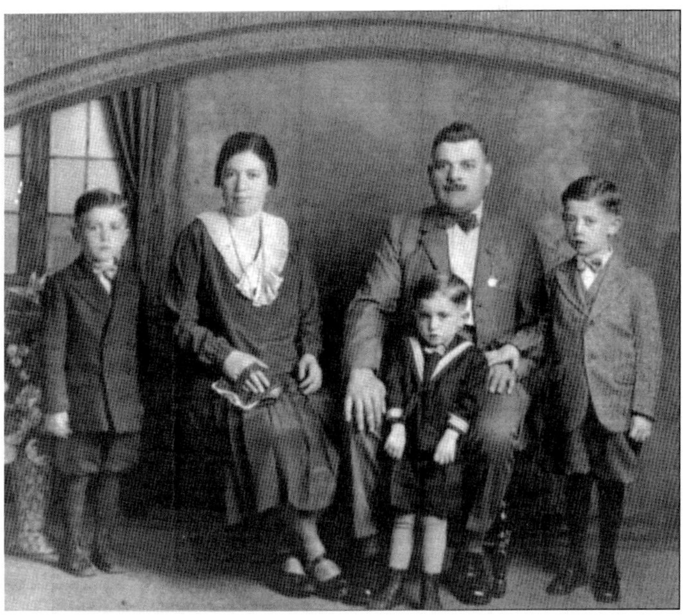

Several families from the village of Candela, located directly south of the city of Foggia in Italy's Apulia Region, settled in Troy's Little Italy in the early years of the 1900s. Among them were Antonia and Germano DeMeo, pictured here, who came with their three sons (from left to right), Rocco, James, and Anthony. A fourth son, Leonard, was born several years after this 1923 studio portrait was taken. (Courtesy of Leonard DeMeo.)

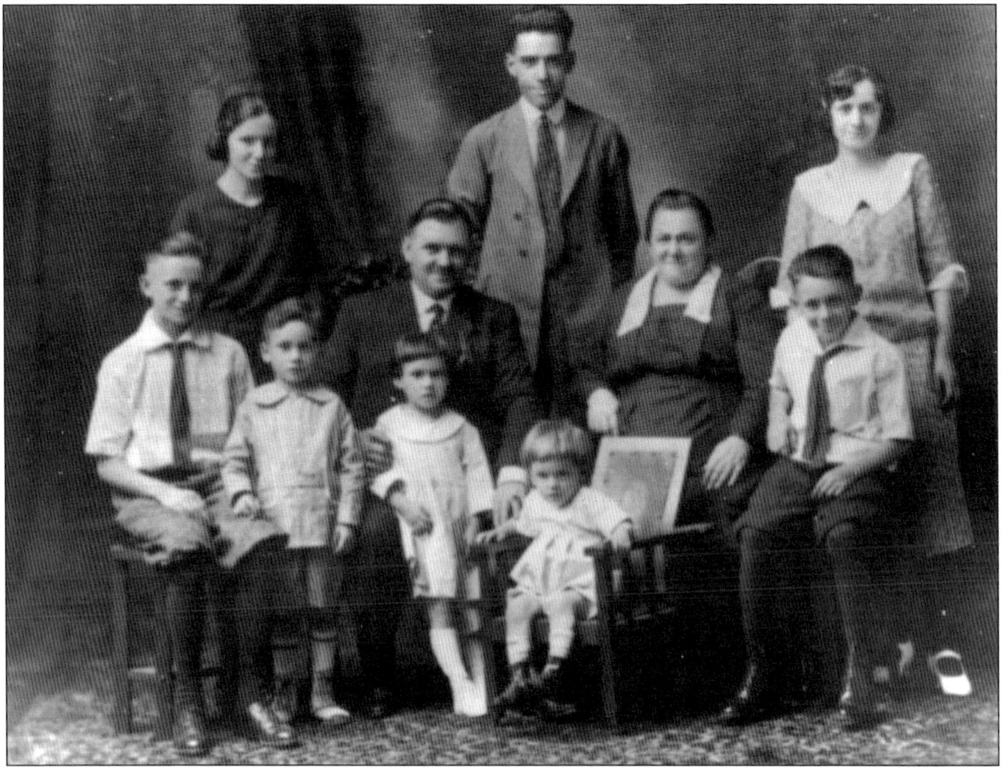

The family of Rocco and Dorothea (Favorita) Teta of 551 Washington Street gathers for a studio photograph. From left to right are (first row) William, Mary, and Nicholas; (second row) Alfonso, Rocco, Dorothea, and Anthony; (third row) Grace, Michael Saracino, and his wife Lucy (Teta) Saracino. Rocco, a shoemaker by trade, emigrated from the village of Candela, Italy, with his wife and four of their seven children: Lucy, Grace, Alfonso and Anthony. William, Mary, and Nicholas were born in Troy. (Courtesy of Philip Teta.)

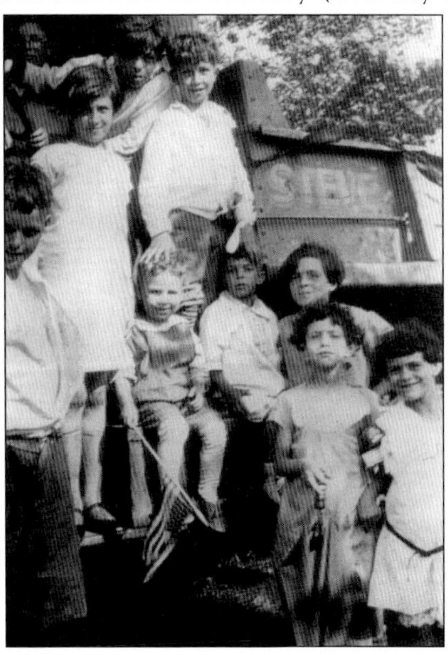

On the July 4, 1928, Havermans Avenue youngsters pose by neighbor Steve Valente's truck during a picnic for a photograph. From left to right are (first row) Dominick Piscitella, Jeanette Teno, and Mary Piscitella; (second row) Katherine Manno-Renna, Dominick Dinovo (holding the flag), James Teno, and Rose Consuelo; (third row) two unidentified youngsters and Samuel Dinovo. (Courtesy of the Dinovo family.)

A 1928 Fourth of July picnic brought friends of the Dinovo family together at 41 Havermans Avenue to for an Italian American–style celebration. From left to right are Sebastiano Piscitella, Francis Cirillo and son, John Teno, Nicolo Pagage with son Michael, Samuel Dinovo with son Manny, and Michael Manno. Manno and Cirillo were laborers, Teno was a moulder, and Palage was a tailor. (Courtesy of the Dinovo family.)

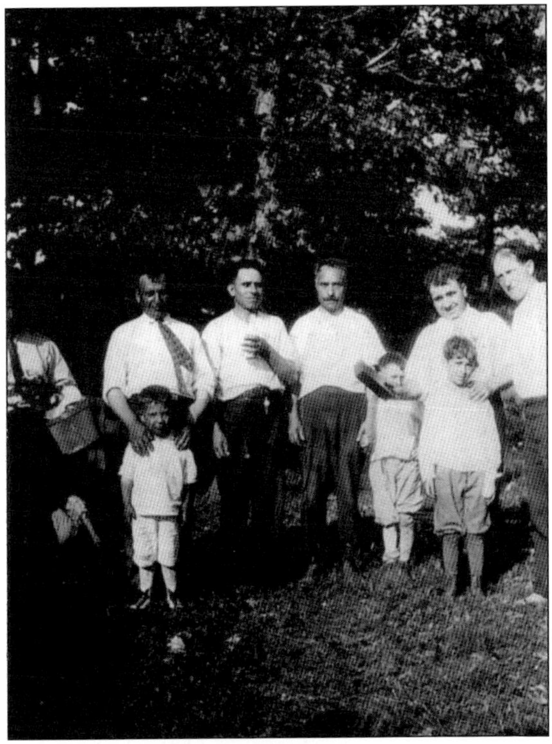

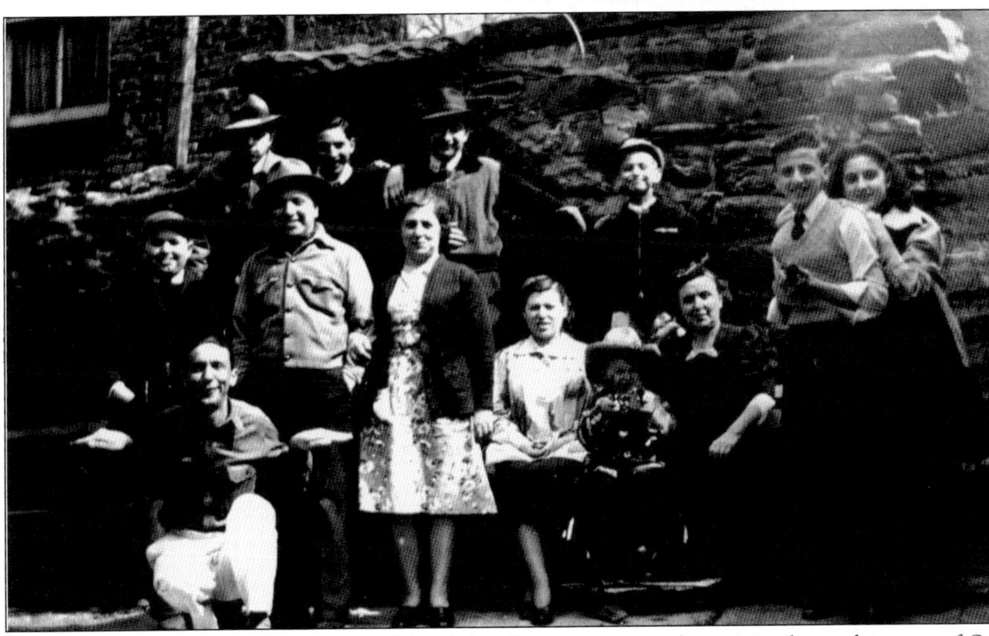

The Visk (Americanized version of *Visco*) family was among the original parishioners of St. Anthony of Padua Church and lived at 12 Liberty Street. From left to right are (first row) Anthony Visk, Esther (LaPosta) Visk, Francis Visk, and Rose (Visk) Pascarell; (second row) Guy A. Visk, Guy Visk, Sr., Mary (LaPosta) Visk, James Pascarell, and Marie Paladino; (third row) Anthony G. Visk, Anthony Morris Visk, Luciano Tornicasa, and Michael "Mickey" Visk. (Courtesy of Rosanne Milo.)

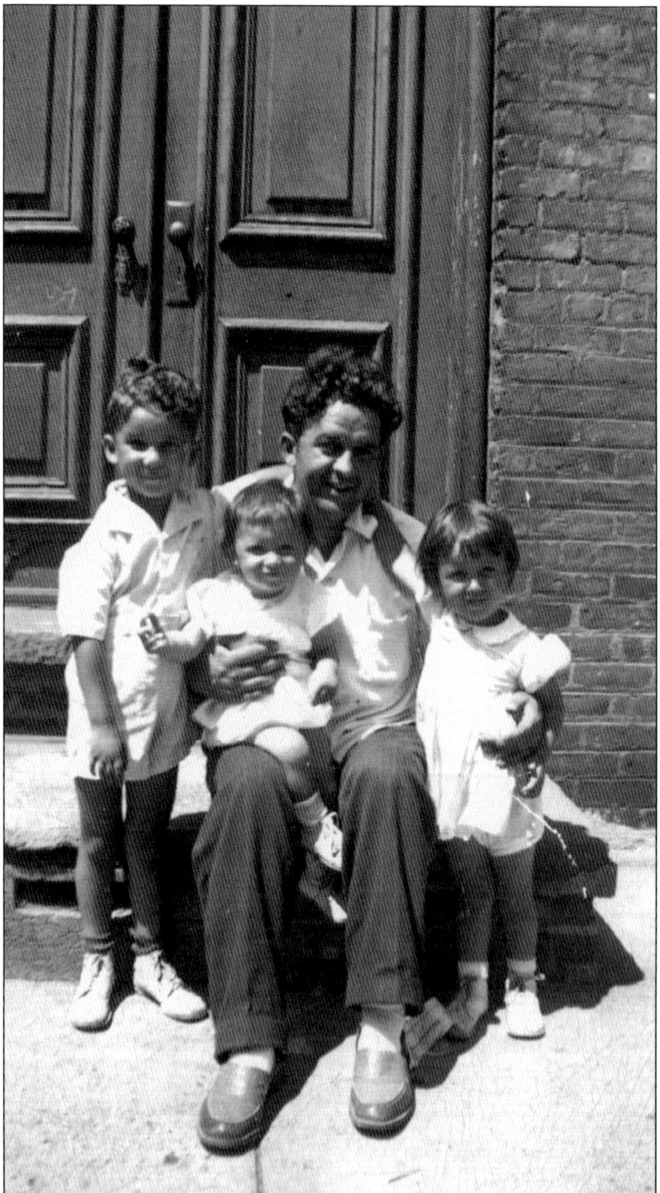

Michael Esposito Sr. is seen here, enjoying a sunny day on the stoop with his three children (from left to right) Michael Jr., Carmella, and Nancy outside their residence at 30 Havermans Avenue. Michael and his wife, Antoinette, were typical of the neighbors residing on the Hill. They grew up in the neighborhood, married, and raised their family in an apartment rented from Antoinette's father before buying a home around the corner. "Espo" sold fruits and vegetables from his truck, a 1940s era 3/4-ton Dodge pickup with built-in wood framing, awnings, and spaces for bins, bushels, and sacks brimming with produce. Antoinette worked at Tiny Town Togs, a children's dress manufacturer. After the birth of her first child, she was a homemaker until Michael's death at age 35. To support her three children, she returned to Tiny Town Togs and eventually retired from Cluett-Peabody. Antoinette, a lifelong resident of Little Italy, died at age 96. (Author's collection.)

The children of Giuseppe and Nunziata Esposito made weekly visits to their parent's farm on Sherman Avenue. From left to right are (first row) Michael Esposito and Frank Colvin; (second row) Antoinette (Terribile) Esposito, Giuseppe, and Madelyn (Esposito) White. (Author's collection.)

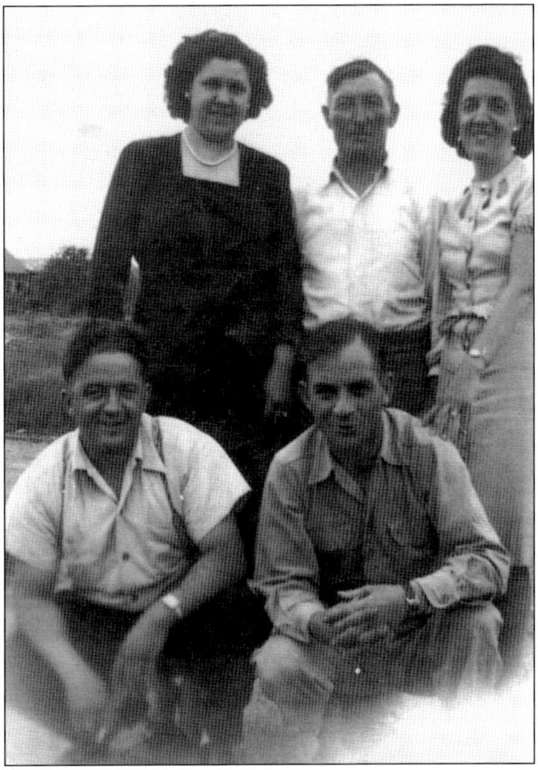

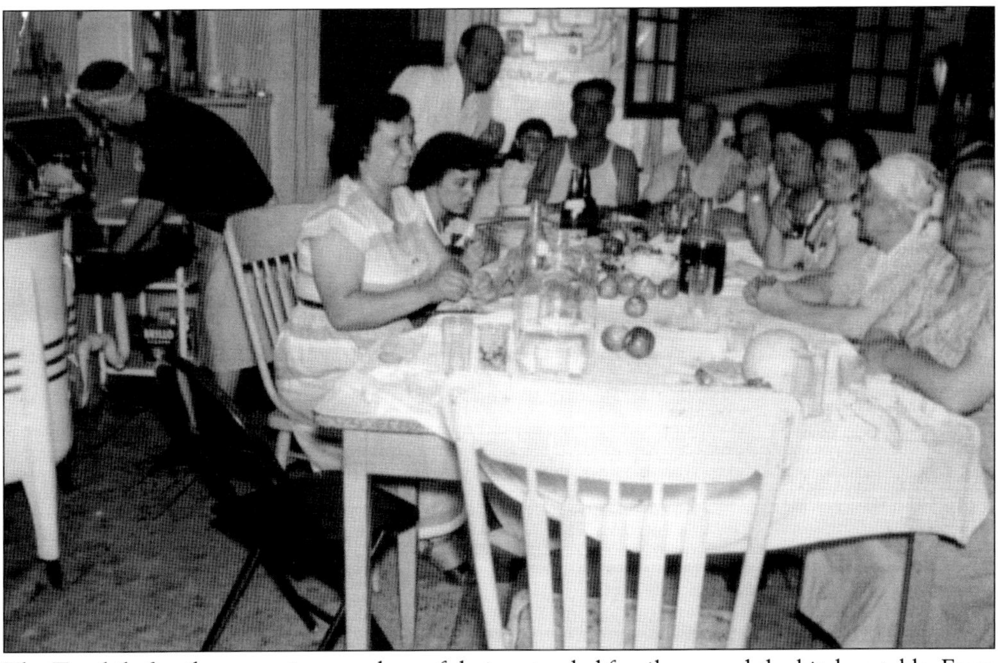

The Terribile family entertains members of their extended family around the kitchen table. From left to right are Dorothy Terribile, Antoinette (Terribile) Esposito, Francesca Vitriola, Nicholas Cavallo, Carmella Esposito, Michael Terribile, Joseph Sanalitro, Carlo Vitriola, Josephine Sanalitro, Josephine Vitriola, Michela Comegna, and Assunta Cavallo. (Author's collection.)

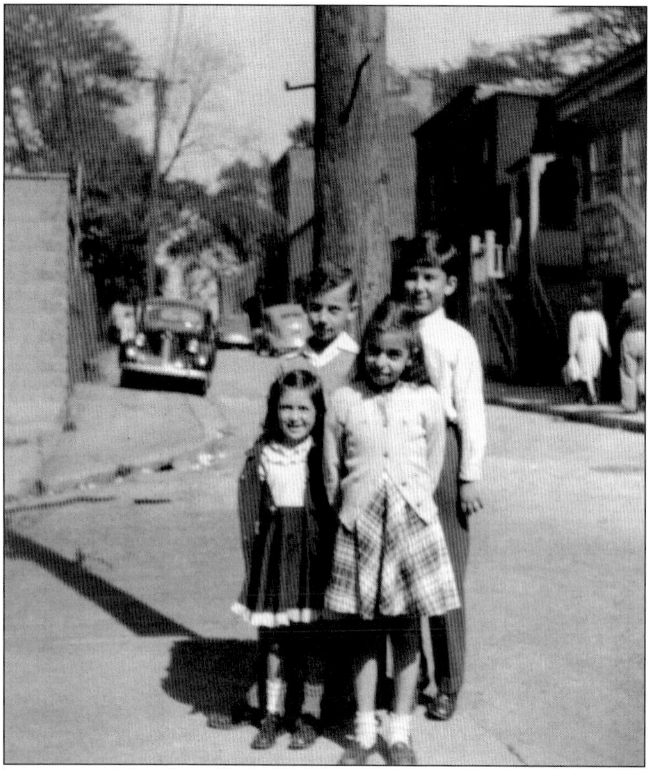

Standing on the corner of Washington Street and Havermans Avenue are, from left to right, (first row) Carmella Esposito and Geraldine Campese; (second row) Robert Winchell and Michael Esposito. In the background of this photograph, facing north toward Liberty Street and the western slope of Prospect Park, which was often used as a short cut to Congress Street and the Mount Ida neighborhood, is a view of Havermans Avenue. (Author's collection.)

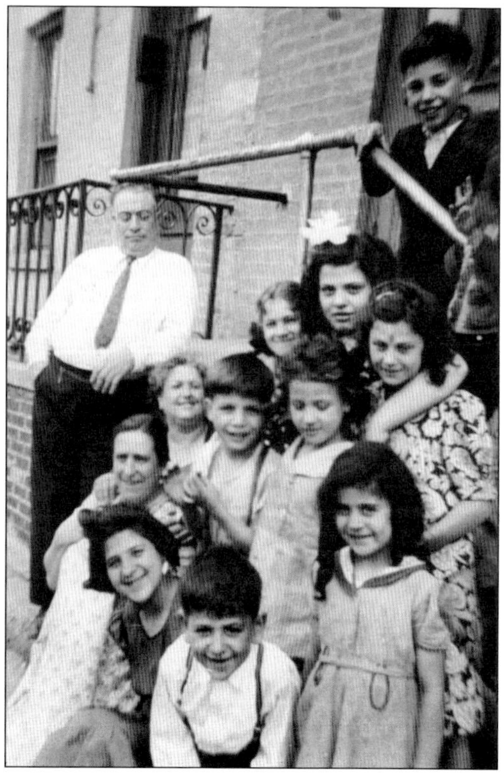

St. Mary's Avenue youngsters gather for a group photograph outside the Melia residence at 21 St. Mary's Avenue. The three adults at the left of the photograph are Anthony Melia, Katerina Montello (foreground left) of 19 St. Mary's Avenue, and Erminia Furciniti (foreground right) of 20 St. Mary's Avenue. In the first row of children are, from left to right, Elizabeth, Francis, and Mary Furciniti. Madeline Pascarella, with a bow in her hair, stands in front of Leonard DeMeo who is at the top of the stairs. (Courtesy of Joan French Furciniti.)

The terraced vegetable garden behind the Havermans Avenue residence of Leonardo and Philomena "Minnie" Dinova is the setting for this 1944 photograph. From left to right are (first row) Michael and Manny; (second row) Philomena, Antoinette, Minnie, Frances and Nicholas. Missing from the photograph is eldest son Samuel, a decorated survivor of the Battle of Saipan who was serving in the Pacific at the time. (Courtesy of Michael Dinova.)

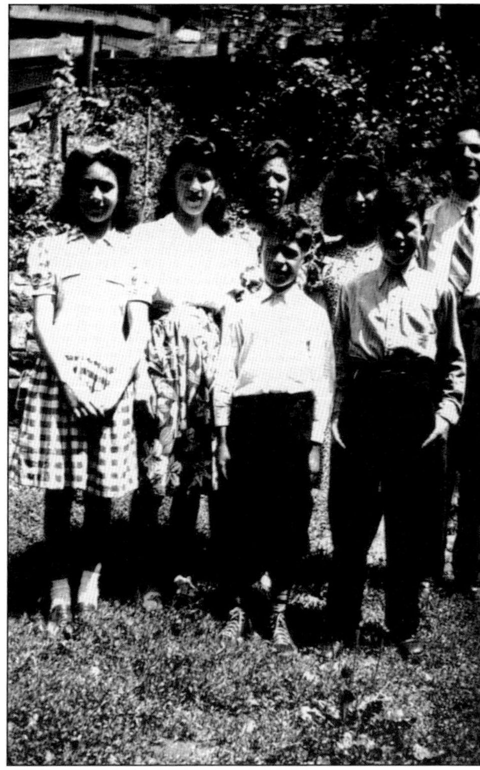

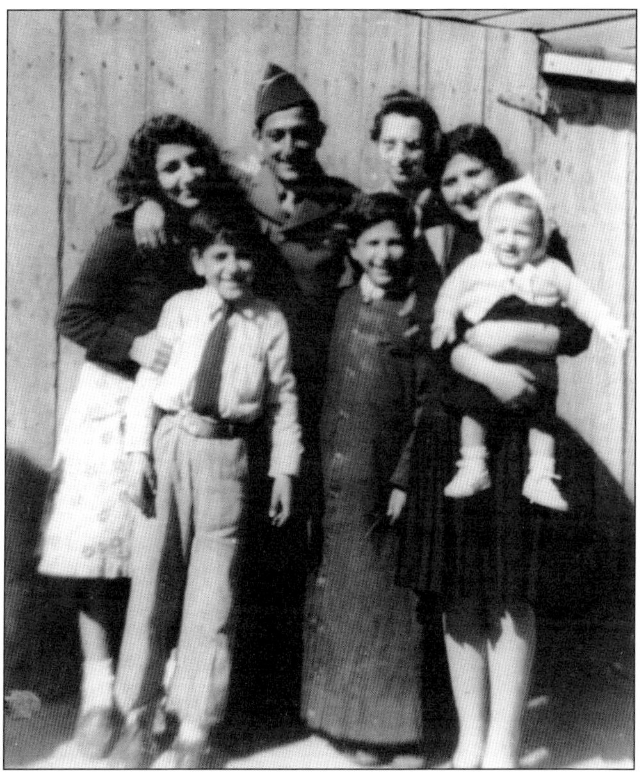

In this September 1945 photograph, the children of Vito and Ermnia Furciniti welcome their brother John, a returning GI, home during leave. In the front row are, From left to right are (first row) little brothers Francis and Anthony and sister Elizabeth with her son Edward; (second row) John's sister Mary, and John and his wife Mary (Melia) Furciniti. John had three additional brothers: Vito, Nicholas, and Gerald. Gerald, an infantryman in World War II, was killed in the line of duty while in Belgium in October 1944. (Courtesy of Joan French Furciniti.)

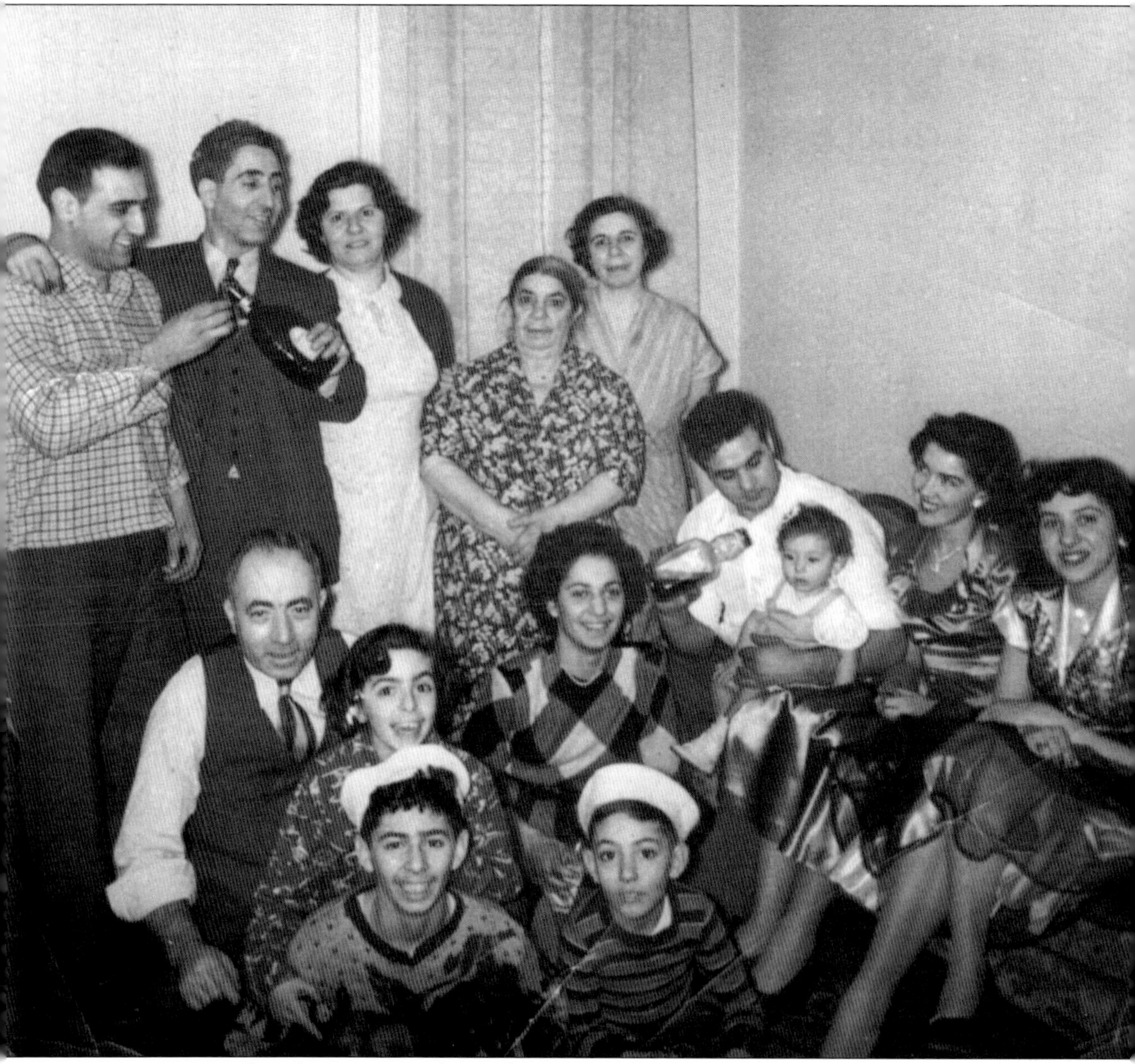

Visiting grandmother was a Sunday tradition for members of the Greco-Valenti-Campese families. Seated on the couch to the right are, from left to right, Joseph Campese holding Elizabeth Valenti, Ann Campese, and Grace Campese. Pictured on the left side of the photograph, from left to right, are (first row) Patrick and Joseph Valenti; (second row) Frank Campese, Geraldine Campese, and Mary Sally Greco; (third row) Nicholas Campese, Joseph and Victoria (Rachiela) Valenti, Catherine Rachiela, and Mary (Rachiela) Campese. The Rachiela sisters—Antoinette, Mary, and Victoria—lived within a few buildings of each other on Havermans Avenue. (Courtesy of Geri Campese DeSeve.)

Friends Betty Jane Bruno (left) and Carmella Esposito enjoy a day of roller-skating on St. Mary's Avenue. After stepping into the skates and turning a key to lock them in place, the fun begins. St. Mary's Avenue was only two blocks long. (Author's collection.)

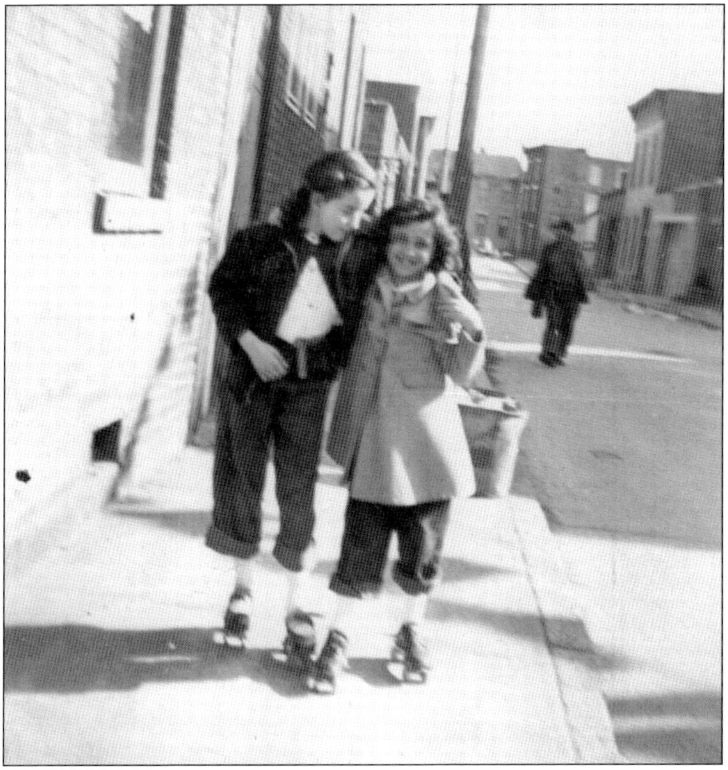

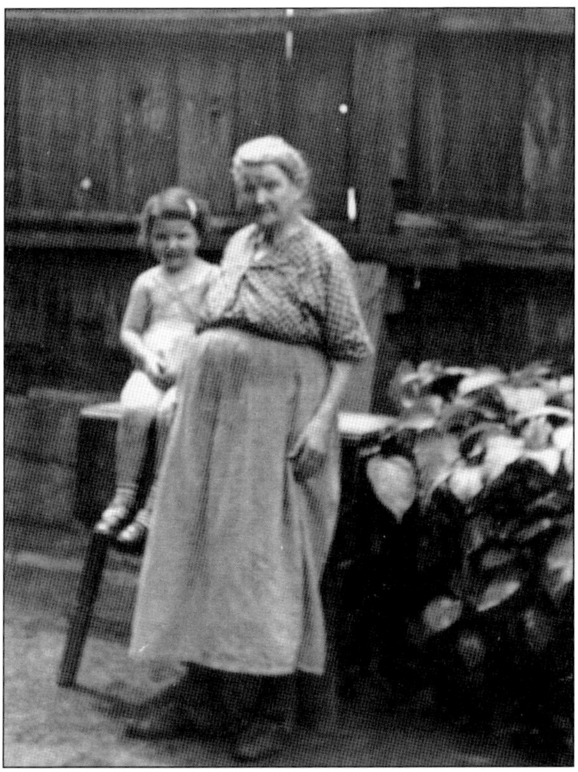

Margaret Mary Brennan and her young granddaughter Margaret (Brennan) Dessinger relax in the backyard of the Brennan family home, located at 32 Havermans Avenue. As a young woman, Margaret spent many years in the service of a wealthy Washington Place family. She and her husband, John, a mason, emigrated from Ireland. They were the parents of three sons—Thomas, John, and Daniel—and a daughter, Mary. (Courtesy of Margaret Brennan Dessinger.)

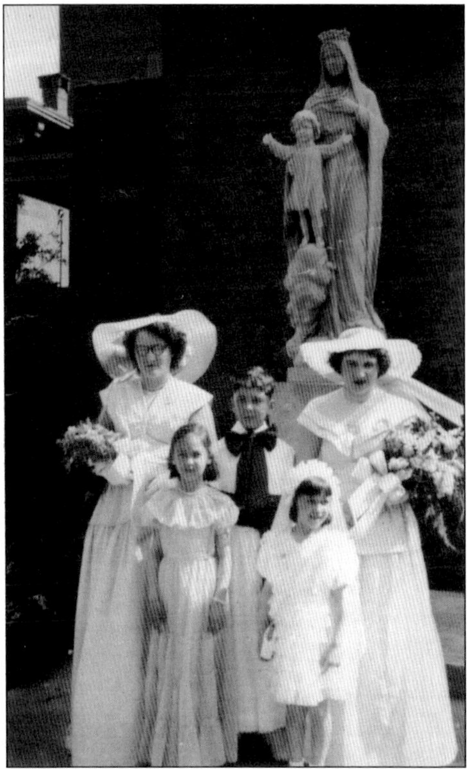

Pictured from left to right are (first row) Nancy and Carmella Esposito; (second row) Mary Ann Gazalone, Michael Esposito, and Margaret DeBonis. They pose at the statue of Mary and the Christ-child—located in the small pocket park on Washington Street between Church and Third Streets. The photograph was taken at the conclusion of the 1950 May Day Procession, an event sponsored by St. Mary's Parish that attracted several thousand spectators. (Author's collection.)

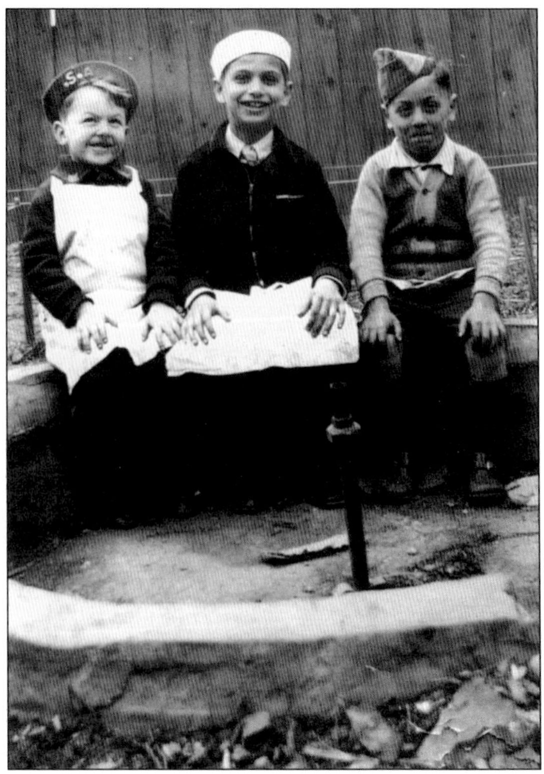

Seen here, from left to right, first cousins Frank LaPosta Visk and Michael Visk, with friend Louis Marchese, take a break from an active day of play to be photographed in the backyard of the Visk residence on Liberty Street. Each of the boys wears a different Armed Services hat to show support and respect for the troops. (Courtesy of Michael Visk.)

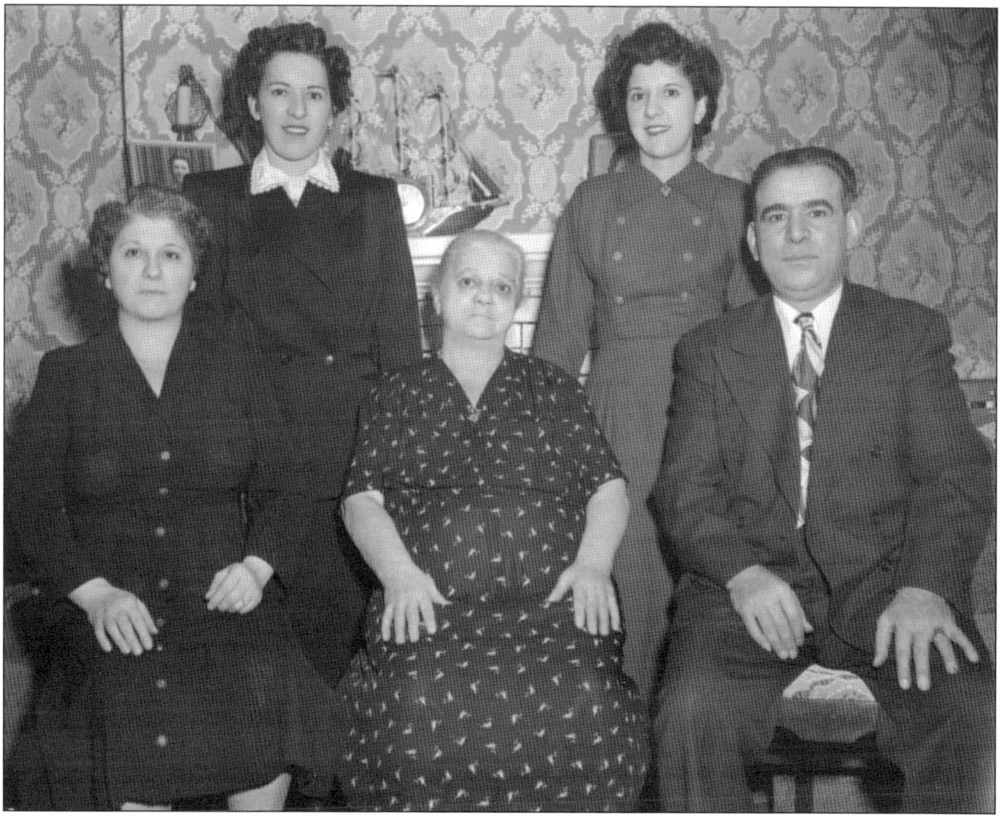

The Terribile family owned 30 Havermans Avenue since Nicola and Antonia (Favorita) Terribile purchased the building in 1918, several years after they emigrated from the village of Candela, Italy. Pictured from left to right are (first row) Clara (Comegna) Terribile, her mother Michela (Favorita) Comegna, and her husband Michael Terribile; (second row) Michael's sister Dorothy Terribile and his daughter Antoinette Terribile. (Author's collection.)

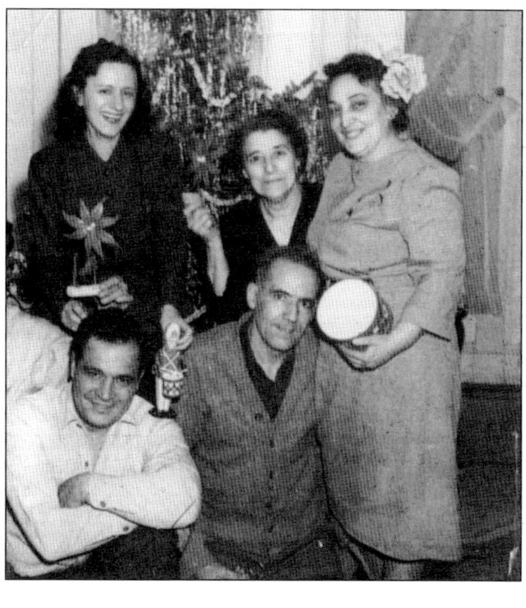

A Christmas gathering of family and friends is the setting for this photograph from the Saracino home, located at 551 Washington Street. Seen here are, from left to right, (first row) Jerry Pitanillo and Michael Saracino; (second row) Lucy (Teta) Saracino, unidentified, and Anna Reo. (Courtesy of Catherine Pitanillo Kuentzel.)

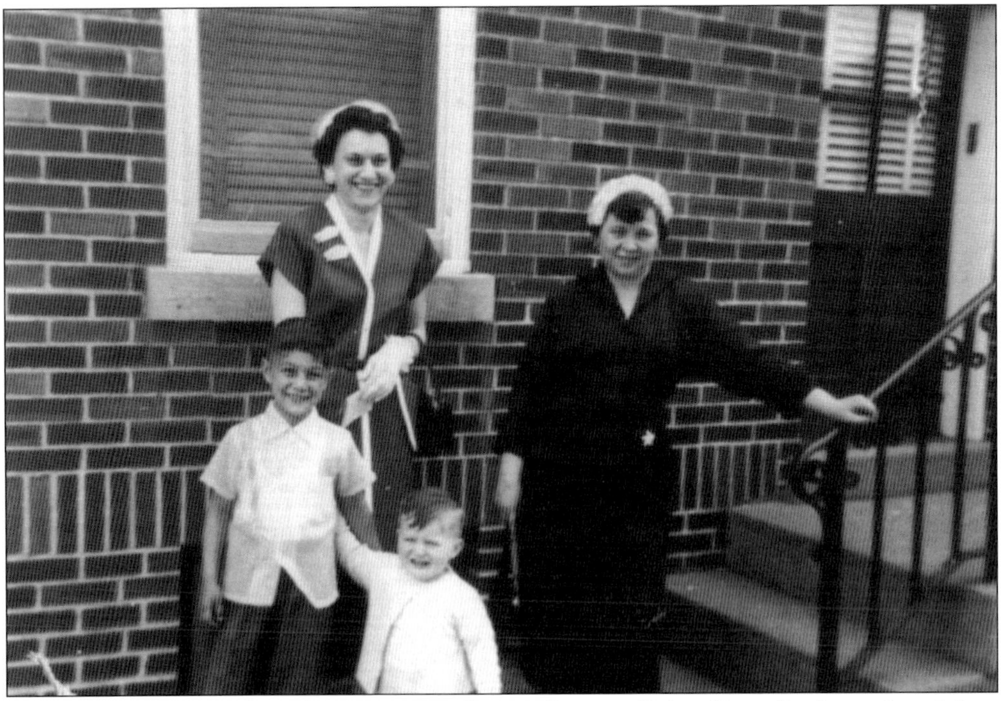

This photograph from the Fifth Avenue residence of Jerry and Mary Pitanillo shows, from left to right, (first row) Jerry Pitanillo Jr. and his cousin Thomas Kennedy; (second row) Mary Pitanillo and her niece Mary (Bottillo) Ciccarelli. Jerry Jr. later managed the family business, Troy Empty Packaging, while Thomas eventually entered medical school and became an anesthesiologist at St. Peter's Hospital. (Courtesy of Catherine Pitanillo Kuentzel.)

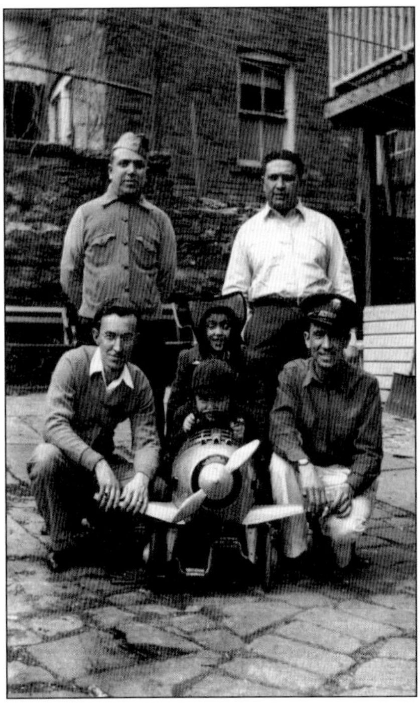

The four Visk brothers are seen here, in the back yard of their Liberty Street homestead. From left to right are (first row) Anthony, MaryAnn Tornicasa, Frank Jr. and Frank Sr.; (second row) James and Gaetano Visk. In 1937, Jimmy—the first Italian American to be elected to public office in Troy—represented the predominately Italian Eighth Ward. The brothers were known for their vaudeville revues and for creating plays and skits as fundraisers for local organizations. (Courtesy of Frank Visk.)

Pictured are attendees at the bridal shower of Donna Wince. From left to right are (first row) Sadie Luckowitz and Mary Pitanillo; (second row) Carmella Esposito, Catherine Pitanillo, Assunta Cavallo, Donna Wince, and groom-to-be Nicholas Cavallo; (third row) Antoinette Dinova and Dorothy Terrible; (fourth row) Angela Laiacona, Antoinette Esposito, Louise Stellato, Lucy Saracino, Grace Gazelone, Clara Terribile, Philomena Donato, and Maria Derrico; (fifth row) unidentified, Mary Colvin, Rose Consuelo, Theresa Marro, Anna Bruno, Rose Bevevino, and Louise Donato. (Courtesy of Catherine Pitanillo Kuentzel.)

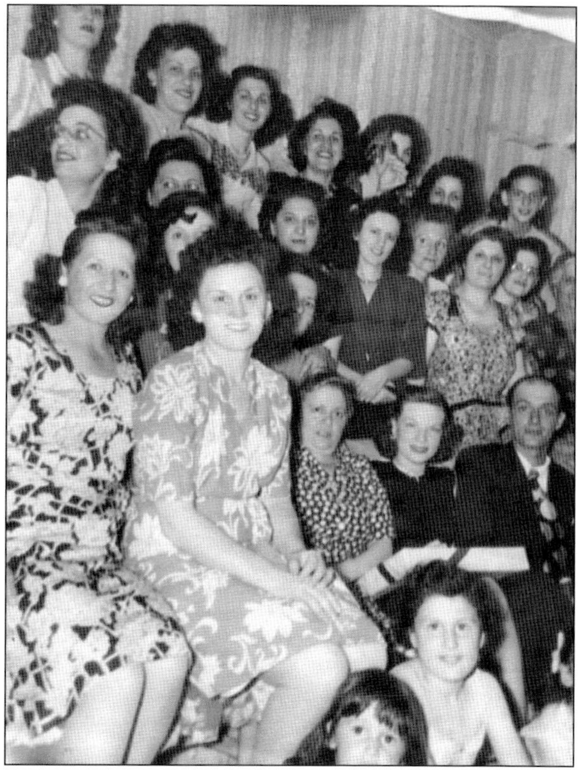

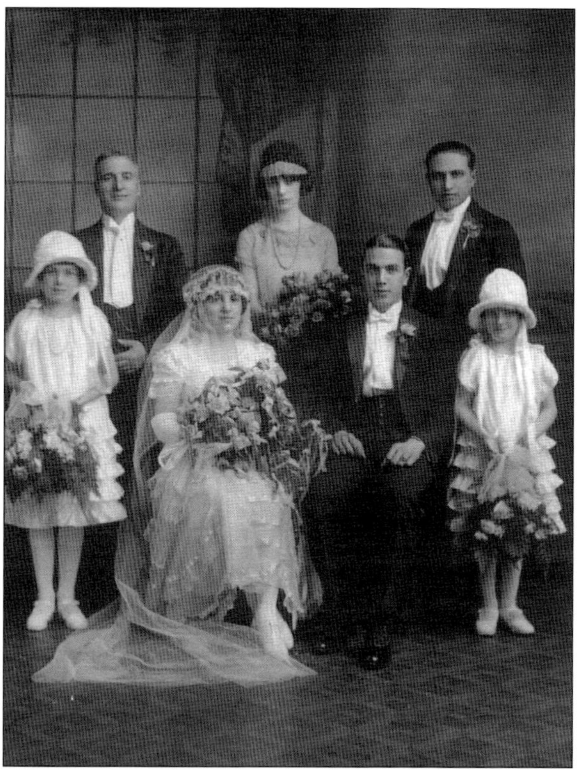

The wedding of Mary LaPosta to Gaetano "Guy" Visk took place on October 12, 1924. From left to right are (first row) Esther LaPosta, sister of the bride; Mary and Guy, the wedding couple; and an unidentified flower girl; (second row) Frank LaPosta, father of the bride; and Mary and James Visk, sister and brother of the groom. (Courtesy of Mary Ann Tornicasa Grogan.)

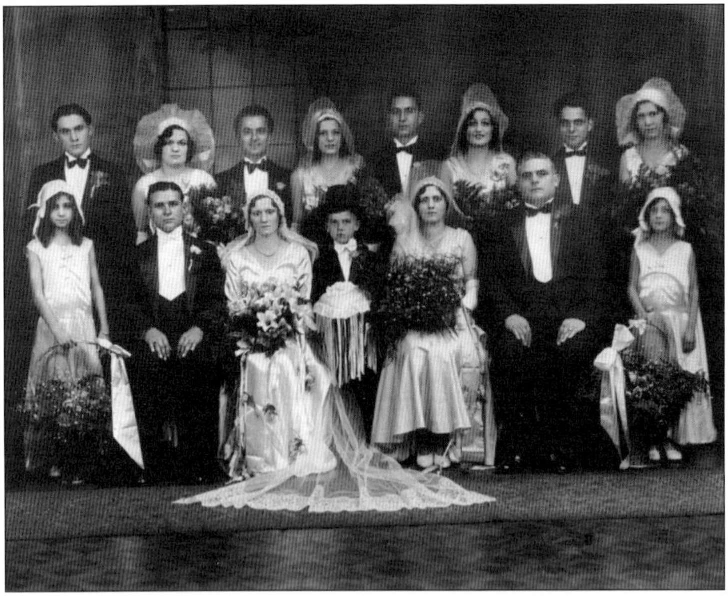

Pictured is the wedding party of Michael and Grace (Teta) Gazelone. From left to right are (first row) Mary Teta, Michael and Grace, unidentified ring bearer, Lucy (Teta) Saracino, Rocco Teta, and unidentified flower girl; (second row) Anthony Teta, Frances Bianco, unidentified usher, Sally Morano, unidentified attendant and usher, and Antoinette Terribile. (Author's collection.)

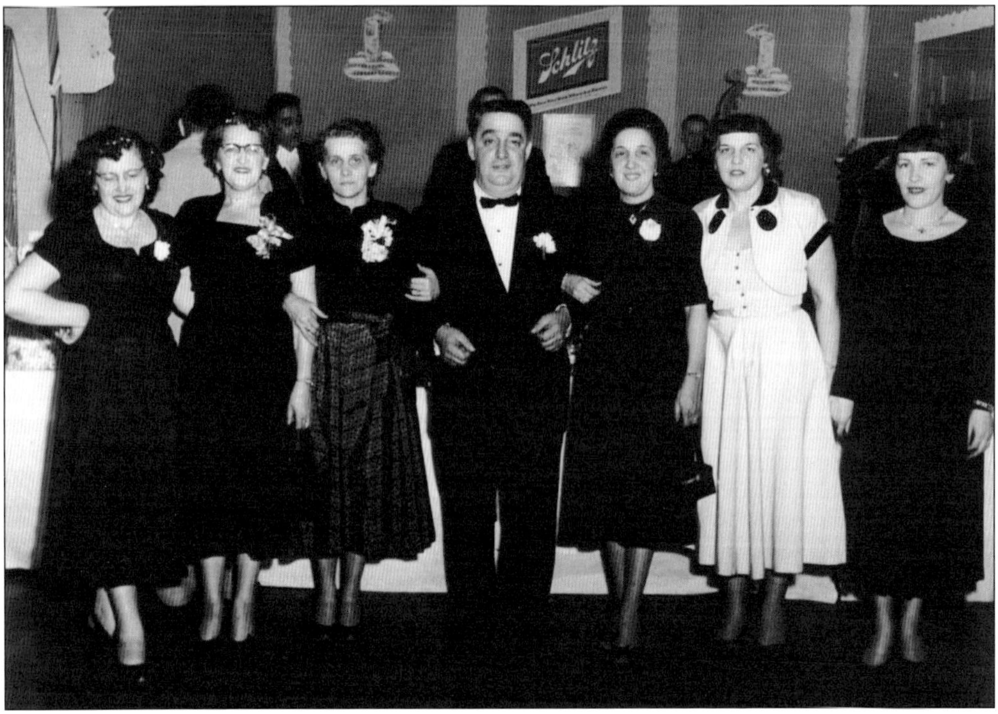

Patrick Esposito stands among his sisters at a family wedding reception. From left to right are Florence Mastan, Philomena Donato, Anna Salerno, Patrick, Madelyn White, Pauline Kapuscinski, and Mary Colvin. The Espositos were born in Port Henry, New York, a small village on Lake Champlain. All but the first born, Anna, relocated with their father Giuseppe and his second wife, Nunziata, to Little Italy's Havermans Avenue in the mid-1920s. Men went where the jobs were, and in Giuseppe's case, he moved from Cervinara, Italy, in 1903 to work as a laborer at the Witherbee-Sherman Mining near Port Henry and at Republic Steel in Troy. (Courtesy of Madelyn Kapuscinski Springer.)

Three

Beyond the Hill

The remaining 20 blocks that constitute Troy's Little Italy reach from Ferry Street in the north to Ida Street on the south and from Fourth Street east to Hill Street. Little Italy is a convenient location for those who choose to live within walking distance of the amenities of historic downtown Troy.

Shops along Fourth Street—Little Italy's "Main Street"—once provided many of the goods and services residents needed. Its blocks hosted grocers, barbers, beauty salons, druggists, taverns, dry cleaners, bakers, variety stores, meat markets, a pawnshop, a locksmith, an ice-cream parlor, and even funeral parlors. Family-owned businesses provided places where people could shop in a friendly environment, conversing with neighbors, business owners, and other customers. The LaSalle Institute was also a strong presence on the street from 1878 to 1965, and the LaSalle gymnasium is now home to the Troy Youth Association's CYO Center.

Most of the buildings on the streets of Little Italy are residences. The Italian Community Center was built at the site of the former Stanton's Brewery on Fifth Avenue. The most notable historic building on the street is the impressive Gasholder House—an architectural gem located at the corner of Fifth and Jefferson Streets. Memories of Hill Street include the huge open space between Liberty and Washington Streets, which was the site of a stoneware factory, gas works complex, retail produce market, and public playground. Along the half-mile route of Hill Street, dozens of families owned businesses that included restaurants and taverns, a store offering religious supplies, two meat markets, auto-repair shops, gas stations, a dairy, a laundry, and a funeral parlor.

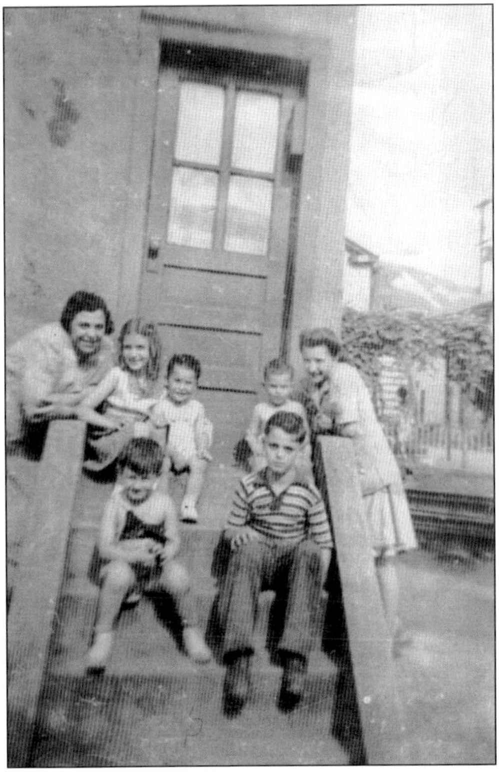

Members of the Martone family gather for a photograph on their front stoop on Fourth Street. From left to right are (first row) John DeLorenzo and Patrick Martone; (second row) Philomena Martone, Mary Pratt, Patrick Martone, John Martone, and Anna (Cioffi) Cuozzo. Charles Martone, a barber known as "Two-minute Charlie," owned a shop near the LaSalle Institute (LSI). The Christian Brothers (LSI faculty) frequently referred cadets to Charlie for a quick trim. (Courtesy of John DeLorenzo.)

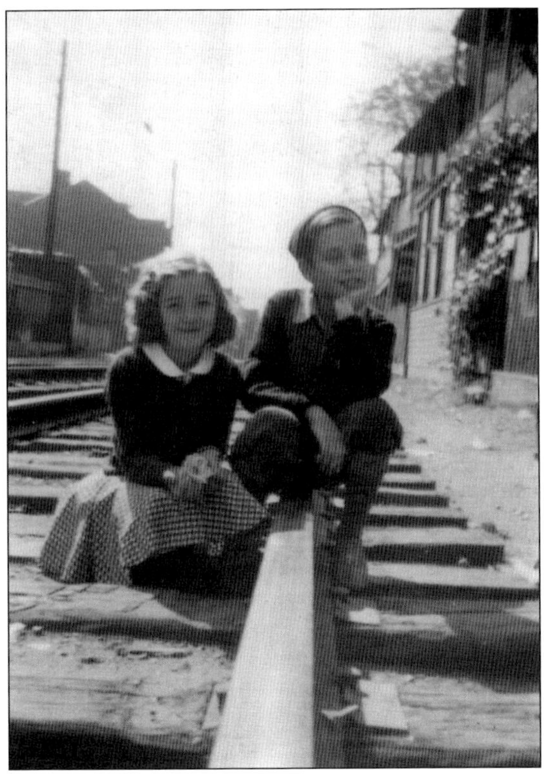

Jean Turriglio and her brother Daniel—like many neighborhood children—would often play on or near the tracks of the New York Central railroad, which crossed diagonally through the neighborhood. The Turriglios lived on Fourth Street, south of Washington Street. When train service ceased in 1958, property owners along the track bed acquired additional land to expand backyards and gardens. (Courtesy of Jean Turriglio Cavallo.)

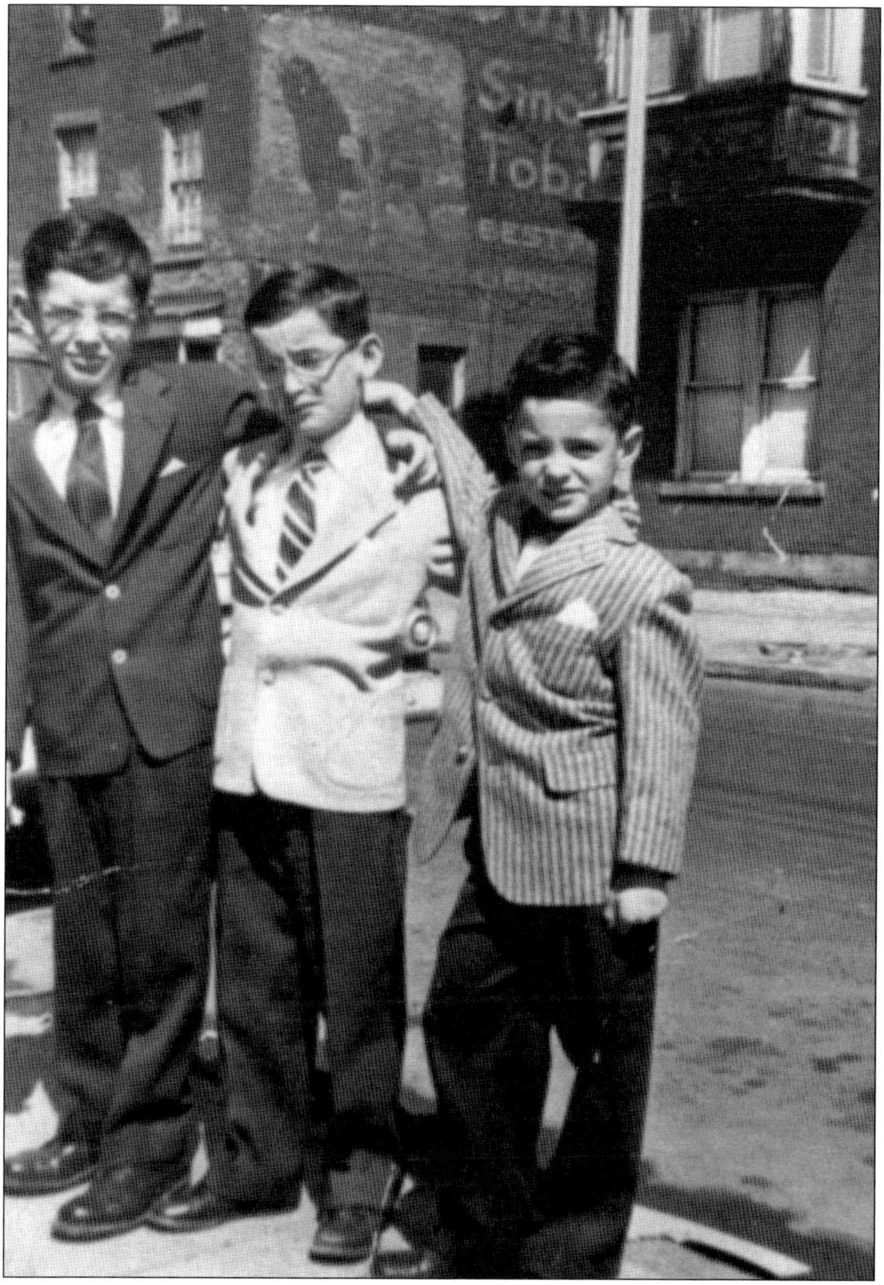

The Riley brothers, sons of Robert and Philomena (Bendetti) Riley of Fifth Avenue gather for a 1954 Easter Sunday photograph on Ferry Street, a few blocks from their residence. From left to right are Joseph ("Joe"), Michael, and Robert. They often spent free time with friends at the all-seasons playground that was the Hill Street market site. The huge lot provided a more than adequate space for softball, stickball, election eve bonfires, a staging area for parades and block parties, and marching maneuvers by the cadets at the LaSalle Institute and Troy Boys Club Drum and Bugle Corp Band. Joe Riley organized the first reunion of friends who shared great memories of the market, and each reunion draws several hundred people to the Italian Community Center. (Courtesy of Robert Riley.)

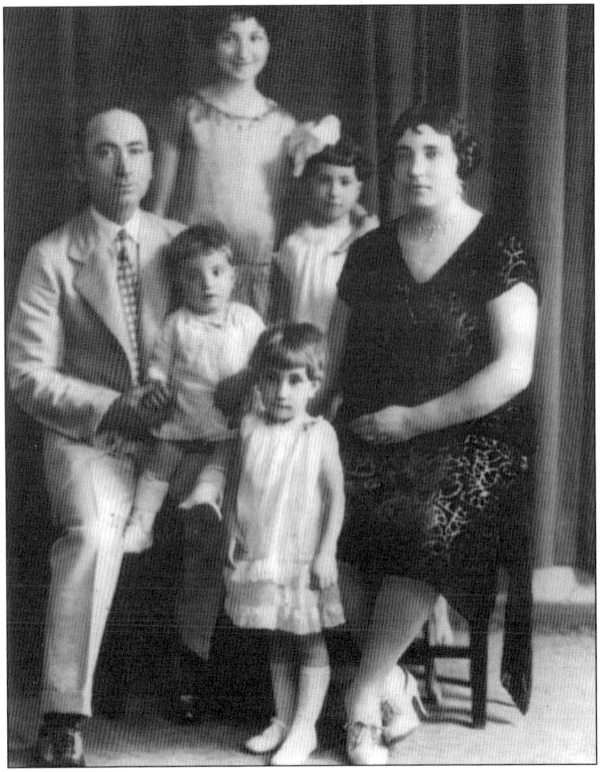

The Ciannamea family resided at 198 Fourth Street. In this 1927 family photograph are, from left to right, (first row) Carmella; (second row) Giuseppe, Nicholas, and Pasqua (Francese); (third row) Lucretia and Giustina. Sons Nicholas and Mario died in Italy, and three more daughters—Anna, Antoinette, and Nancy—were born in Troy after the photograph was taken. Pasqua worked from her home as a dressmaker, while Giuseppe was a presser. (Courtesy of Annette Rizzo Sanders.)

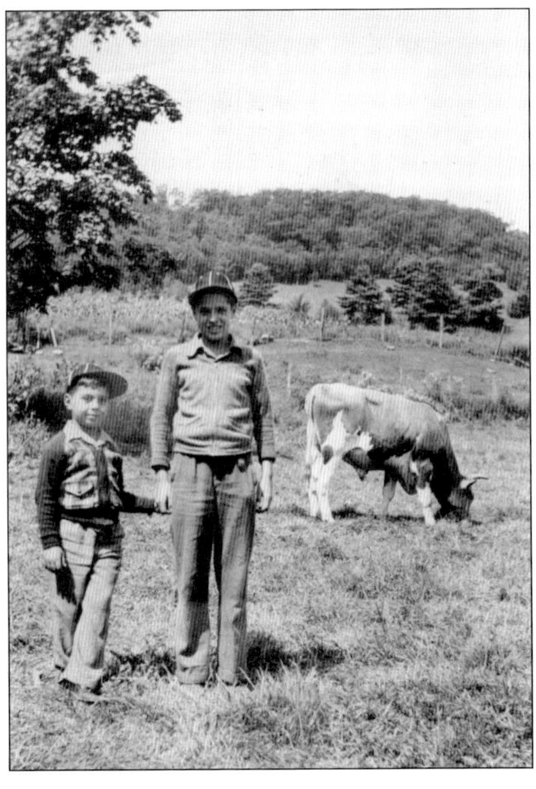

Nicholas Cristiano (left) stands alongside his cousin Gene Cuozzo at a country outing near Pittsfield. Both families owned convenience stores in Troy: Cristiano's Grocery Store on Christie Street and Cuozzo's Grocery Store on Third and Division Streets. The family's ancestral home was the village of Candela, in the Italian region of Apulia, located in the southeast area of the peninsula. (Courtesy of Nicholas Cristiano.)

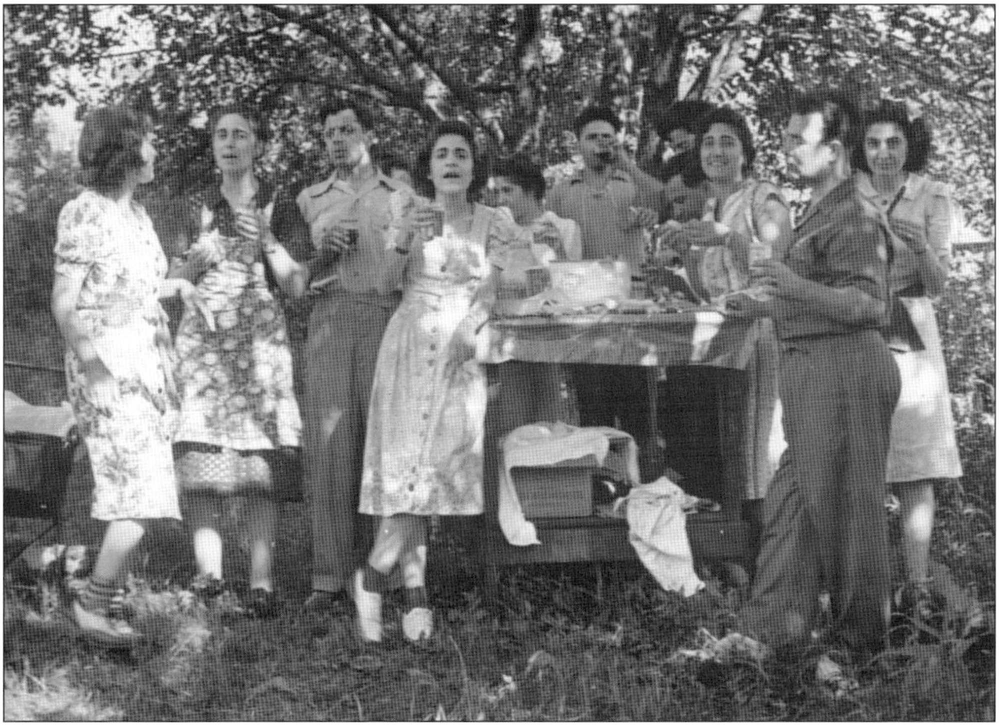

Members of the Piazza family enjoy a day of picnicking with friends at one of Rensselar County's lakeside parks. Salvatore Piazza and his wife, Beatrice, resided at 329 Fourth Street with their daughters Maria and Ann. Salvatore sold produce from his garage, located at the rear of the family residence, and delivered and picked up fruits and vegetables using a horse-drawn wagon. (Courtesy of the Piazza family.)

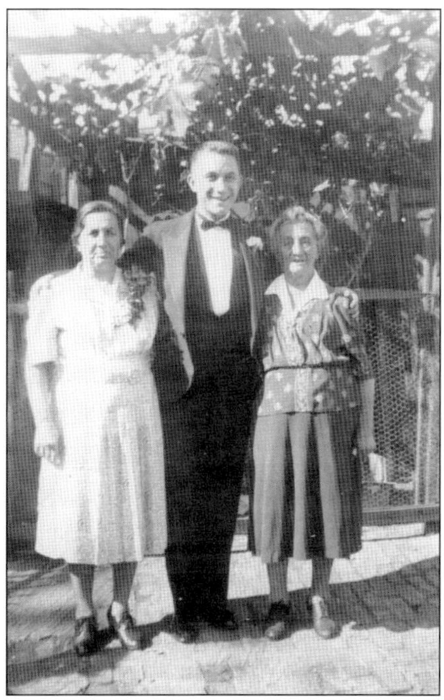

A huge grape arbor forms the backdrop for this 1944 photograph of, from left to right, Helen (Campana) Stellato, Frank Stellato, and Maria (Sylvester) Campana. The property, located on a double lot at 256 and 258 Fourth Street, contained two separate two-story residences connected by a common porch and included a piazza shared by tenants. Gennaro Campana built the complex similar to the residence he left behind in Italy. Three of his daughters married three Bruno family brothers. (Courtesy of Eleanor Szalasny.)

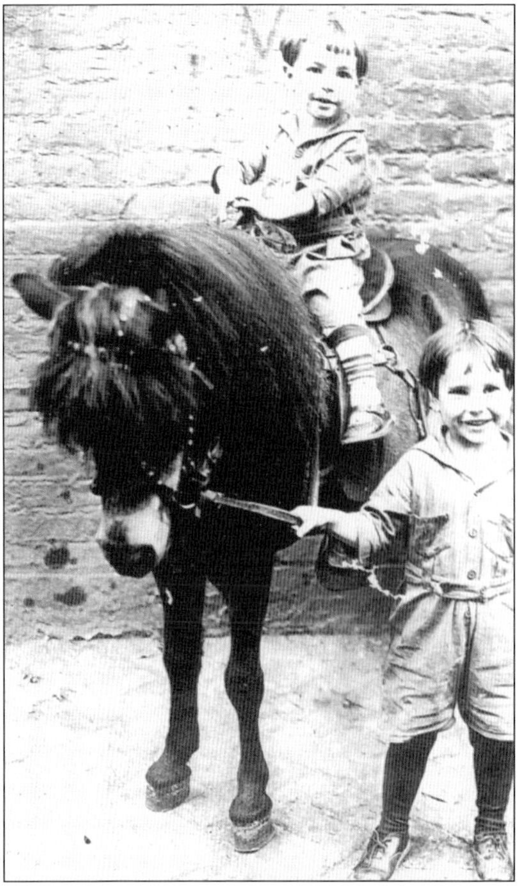

Salvatore Mosca holds the reins while his brother Joseph is astride a somewhat shaggy pony. During warmer months, it was a common to see children flocking to the pony and its master for a short ride and a photograph—all for a few coins. The boys are the sons of Carmela and Antonio Mosca, originally from Aqua Viva, Sicily. The family resided on Fourth Street with a third son, James. (Courtesy of Robert Mosca.)

This 1939 photograph shows members enjoying a summer picnic sponsored by the Frosolone Club—one of several local Italian ethnic social clubs. Frosolone, known for its scissors, is located in central Italy in the region of Molise. Frank LaPosta Visk, a writer for the *Little Italy Newsletter*, described his visits to his maternal grandparent's ancestral home in Frosolone in a series called "How Do You Say 'Roots' in Italian?" (Courtesy of Judy Gerger Brearton.)

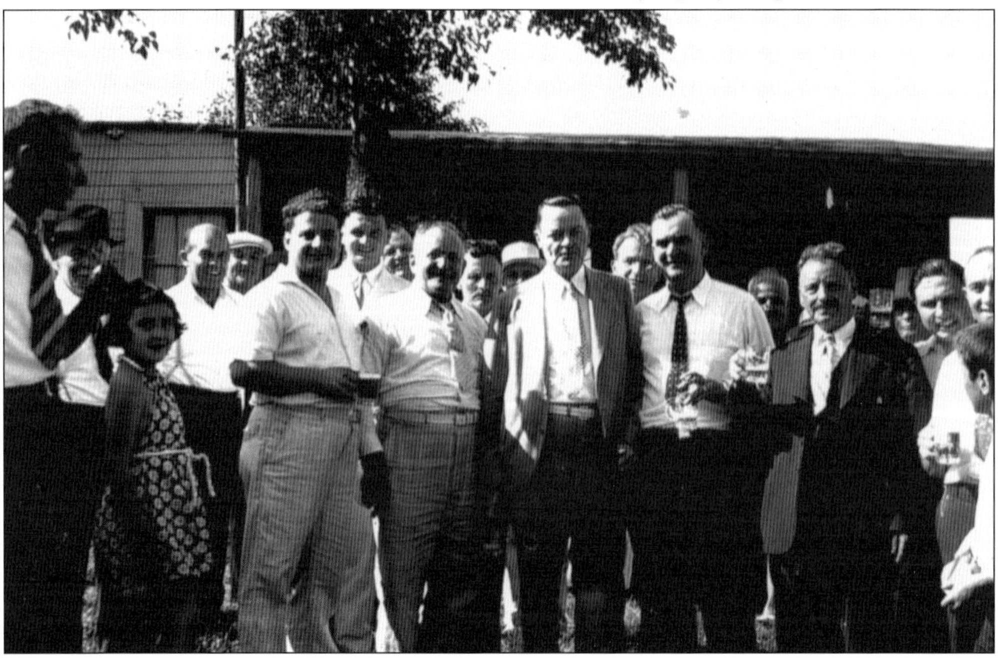

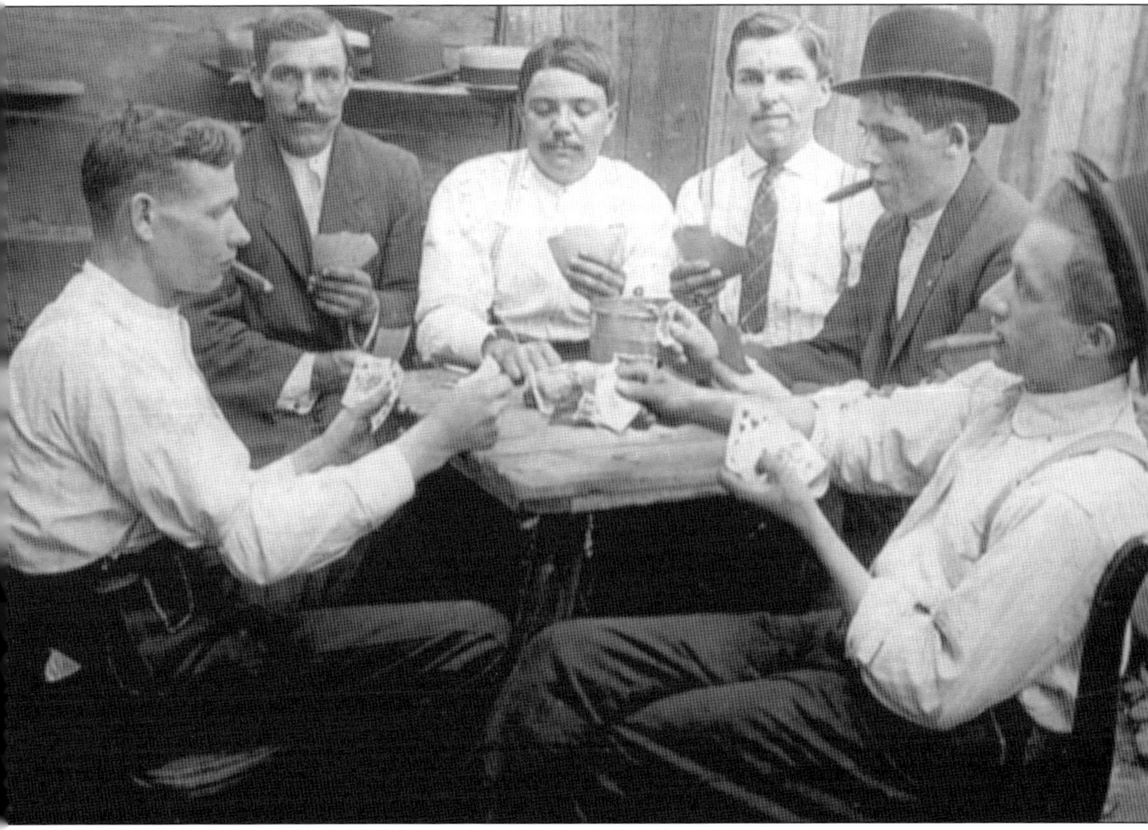

John J. Gerger (right front) smokes a cigar with friends during an afternoon at cards in the backyard of his home at 1037 Fifth Avenue. Many Italian immigrants enjoyed playing Briscola, a traditional Italian card game that often featured secret signals and code words that partners used to direct the game. Gerger was proprietor of John's, a popular neighborhood tavern that was first located in the lower level of his residence on "short Fifth" before relocating to a site at Hill and Ida Streets. John collected and preserved photographs and letters from community members serving in World War II, which were exhibited at the tavern for many years. The Gerger family later donated the collection to the Rensselaer County Historical Society. (Courtesy of Judy Gerger Brearton.)

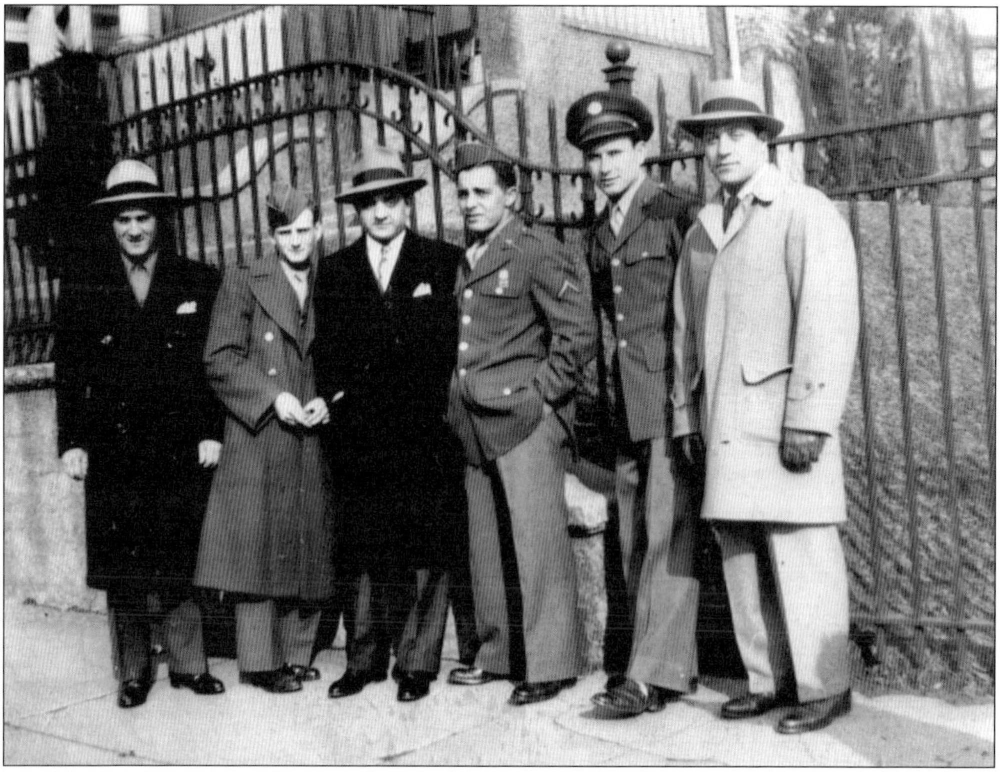

Neighborhood members who served in World War II are reunited with friends during a furlough. From left to right are Dominick Potenza, Michael Ciarlone, Bernie Bove, Michael Clemente, Vincent Ciarlone, and Nicholas DeGeorge. Over 1,000 residents of the three wards of Little Italy served in World War II. (Courtesy of Robert Riley.)

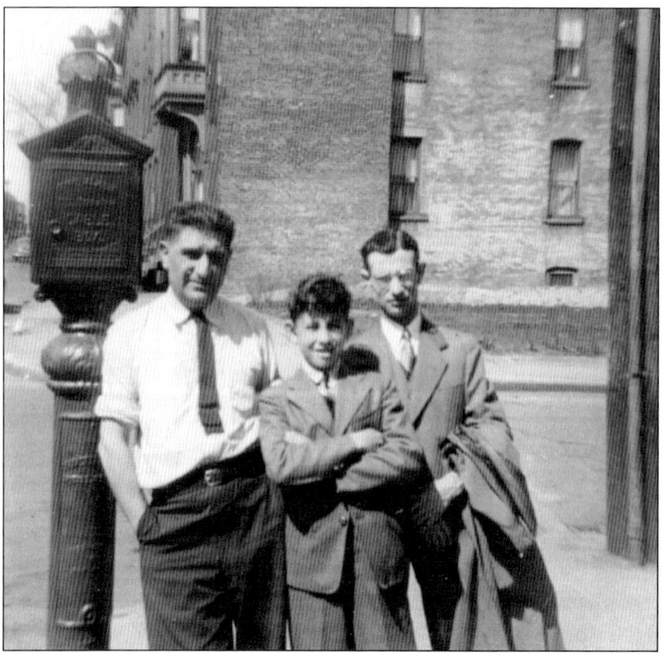

From left to right are Michael Cuozzo Sr., Jerry Cristiano, and Jerry's father, Gateano Cristiano, standing alongside Cuozzo's Grocery Store at the corner of Third and Division Streets. Michael and Gaetano were first cousins. Jerry Cristiano, a former Merchant Marine and retired secondary school teacher, is now a deacon at St. Anthony of Padua Shrine Church. His father owned Guy's Leather Repair Shop, located at 46 State Street. (Courtesy of Nicholas Cristiano.)

The children of Anthony and Josephine Ciarlone pose for a photograph near their residence at 105 Ferry Street in 1942. From left to right are Madelyn, Ralph, Ginger, Anthony, and Francis. Their father owned Dinny's Hat Repair, working from a shop in the lower level of the family home. The business originally started in the 1920s by Dominick and Anthony Ciarlone. (Courtesy of Anthony Ciarlone.)

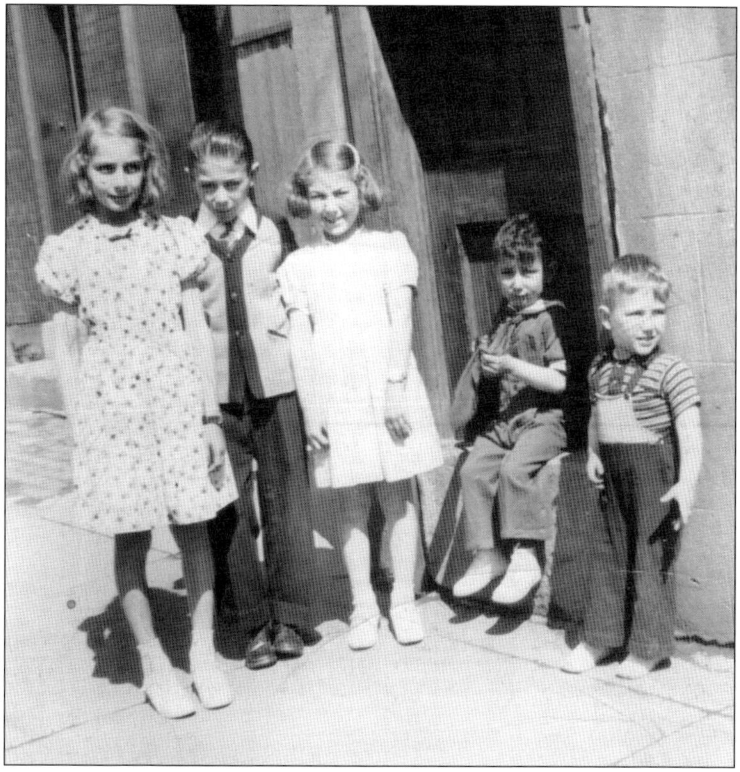

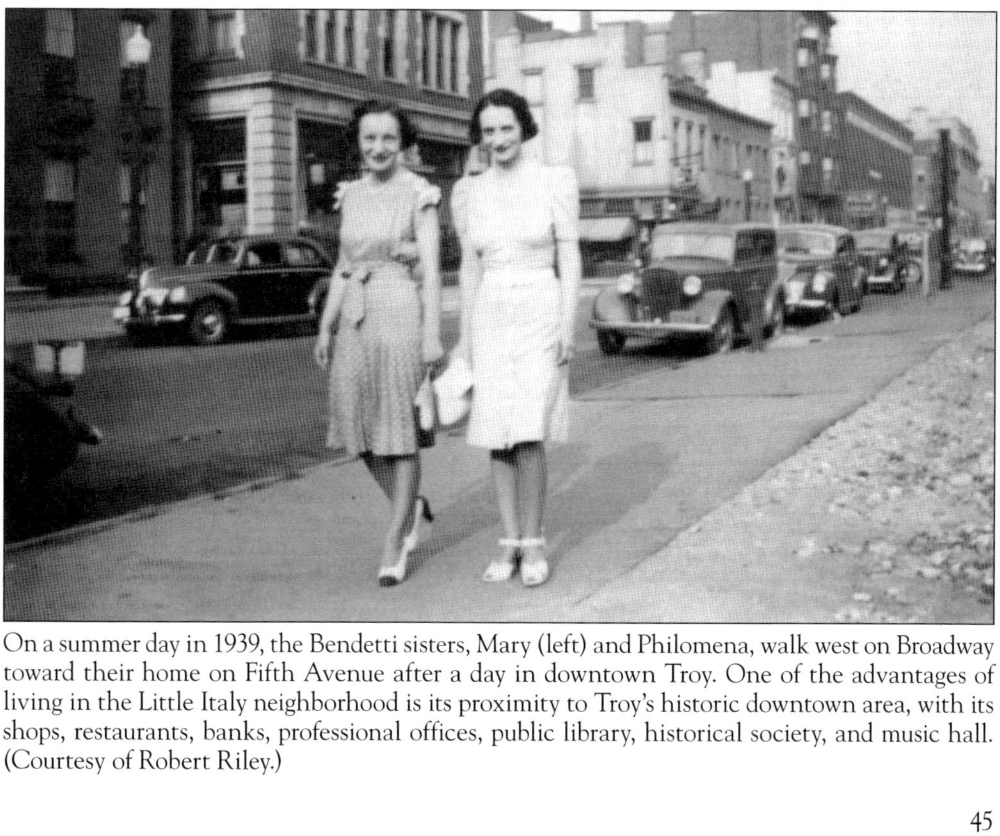

On a summer day in 1939, the Bendetti sisters, Mary (left) and Philomena, walk west on Broadway toward their home on Fifth Avenue after a day in downtown Troy. One of the advantages of living in the Little Italy neighborhood is its proximity to Troy's historic downtown area, with its shops, restaurants, banks, professional offices, public library, historical society, and music hall. (Courtesy of Robert Riley.)

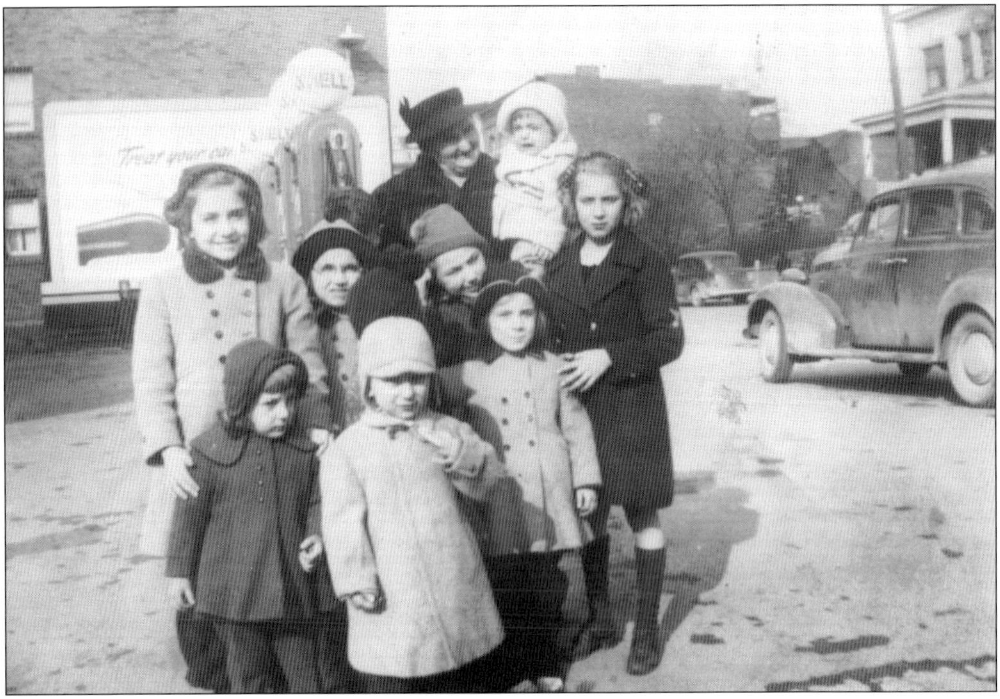

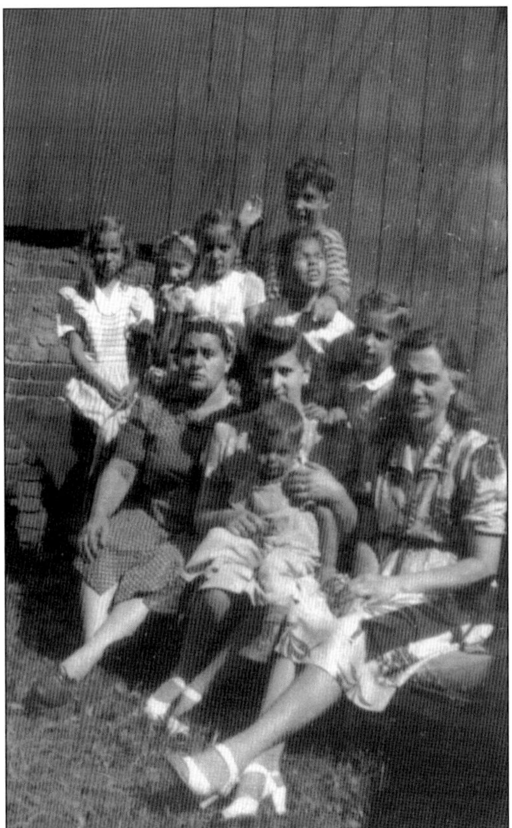

The former Shell Gas Station, once located at the corner of Ferry Street and Fifth Avenue, is the setting for a photograph of Raffela Ciarlone and her grandchildren. From left to right are (first row) Marie Ciarlone, Anthony Ciarlone, and Doris Polito; (second row) Frances Ann, Phyllis, Joan, and Madelyn Ciarlone; (third row) Raffela Ciarlone and Phyllis Polito. (Courtesy of the Ciarlone family.)

Members of the Casale-Gross families are in the backyard of their residence at 167 Fourth Street. From left to right are (first row) Nicholas Casale and Angela Gross; (second row) Madeline (Gross) Pisaniello and sister Lucy (Gross) Casale. The cluster of children at the back include Lucy's daughters Marie, Amelia ("Millie"), and Josephine and Angela's daughters Lucy and Rose and son Joseph. (Courtesy of Marie Casale Santora.)

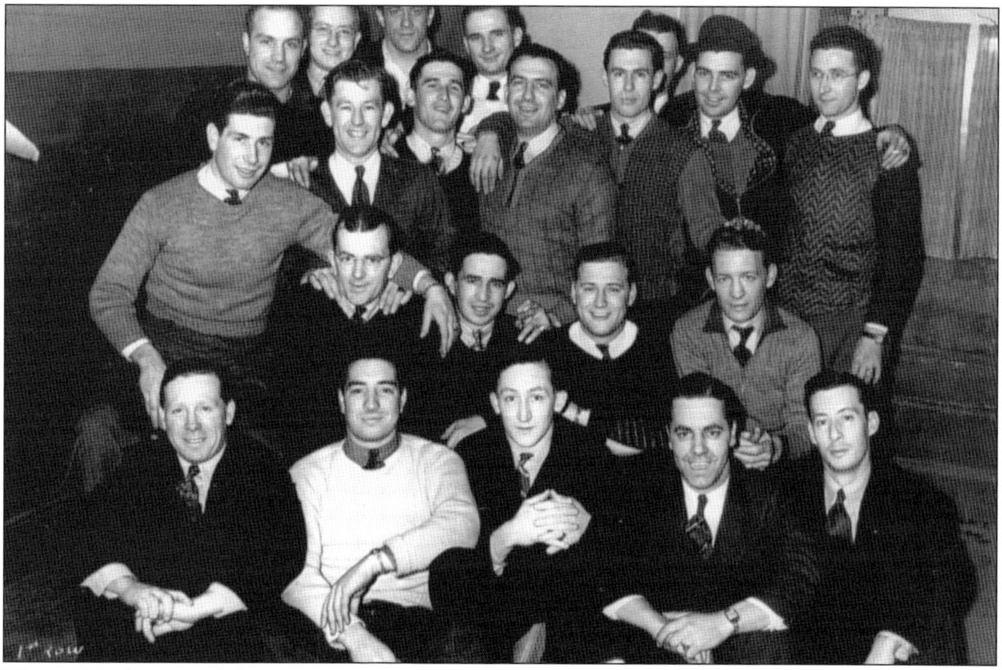

This 1937 photograph brings together members of the Cardinal Club. From left to right are (first row) James Grady, Michael Gully, John Fox, Nicholas Padalino, and Bill Cavanaugh; (second row) B. Miorin, Edward Lillibridge, B. Dolan, Bert Grady, and Michael Mahr; (third row) Thomas Butler, D. Dolan, Edward Ruff, John Osterhout, D. McDermott, and J. Cunningham; (fourth row) Philip Colarusso, John Gerger, Deek Pillsworth, Joseph Ryan, and W. O'Brien. (Courtesy of Judy Gerger Brearton.)

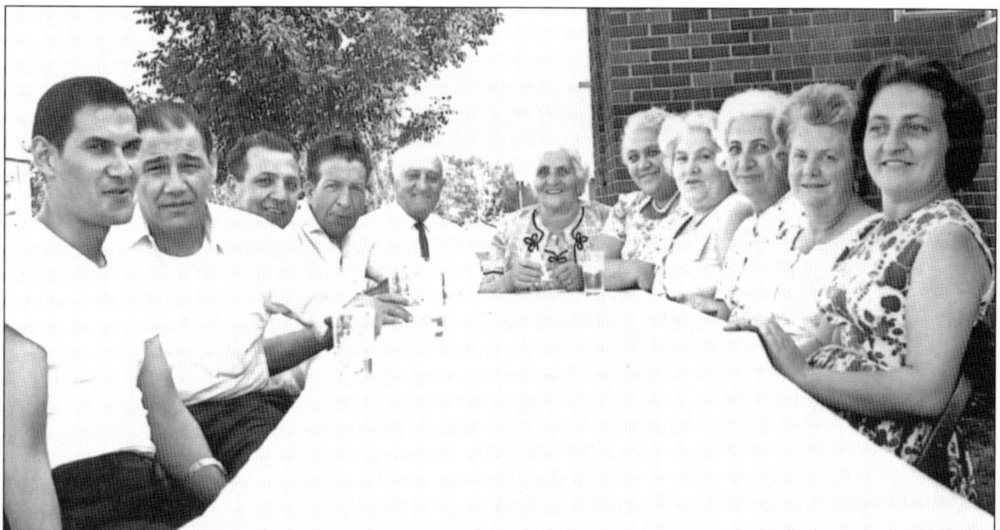

Women of the Pignuola family gather with their husbands and their mother, Filomena Pignuola, for a reunion on Sherman Avenue. From left to right are Corrado DeGenero, Ralph Renna, Jerry Casile, Salvatore Mamone, Louis Tangredi, Filomena, Josephine Tangredi, Mary Mamone, Rose Casile, Antoinette Renna, and Jennie DeGenero. (Courtesy of Angela Ciccarelli Renna.)

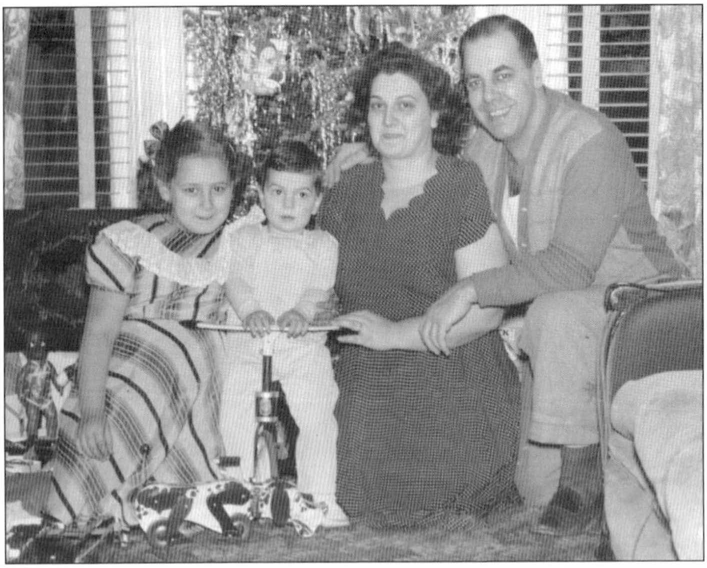

The Padalino family, of 211 Fourth Street, gathers at the Christmas tree for this 1951 family photograph. From left to right are Marianne, Joseph, Jiuanne ("Jennie"), and Nicholas ("Nick"). Nick will be remembered by many locals as Troy's patrolman on duty, spending years directing traffic at the site of the city's busiest downtown junction: River and Fulton Streets. (Courtesy of Marianne Padalino.)

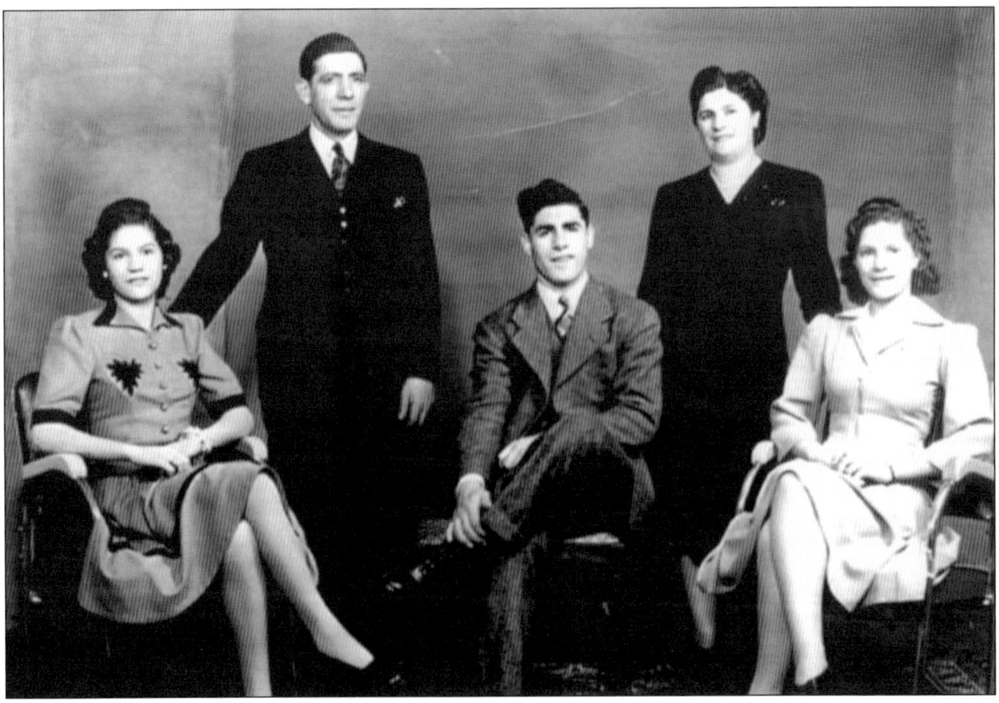

In this 1942 family photograph, John and Josephine Rea, of 105 Hill Street, are joined by their children, seated from left to right, Catherine, John, and Josephine. John, a corporal in the US Army, was killed in action on June 9, 1943, at the age of 20. The neighborhood veterans' post, Ciccarelli-Rea-Agars-Bevevino, bears his name. Shortly after hearing of her brother's death, Josephine enlisted in the Women's Air Corp. (Courtesy of Josephine Rea Ostwald.)

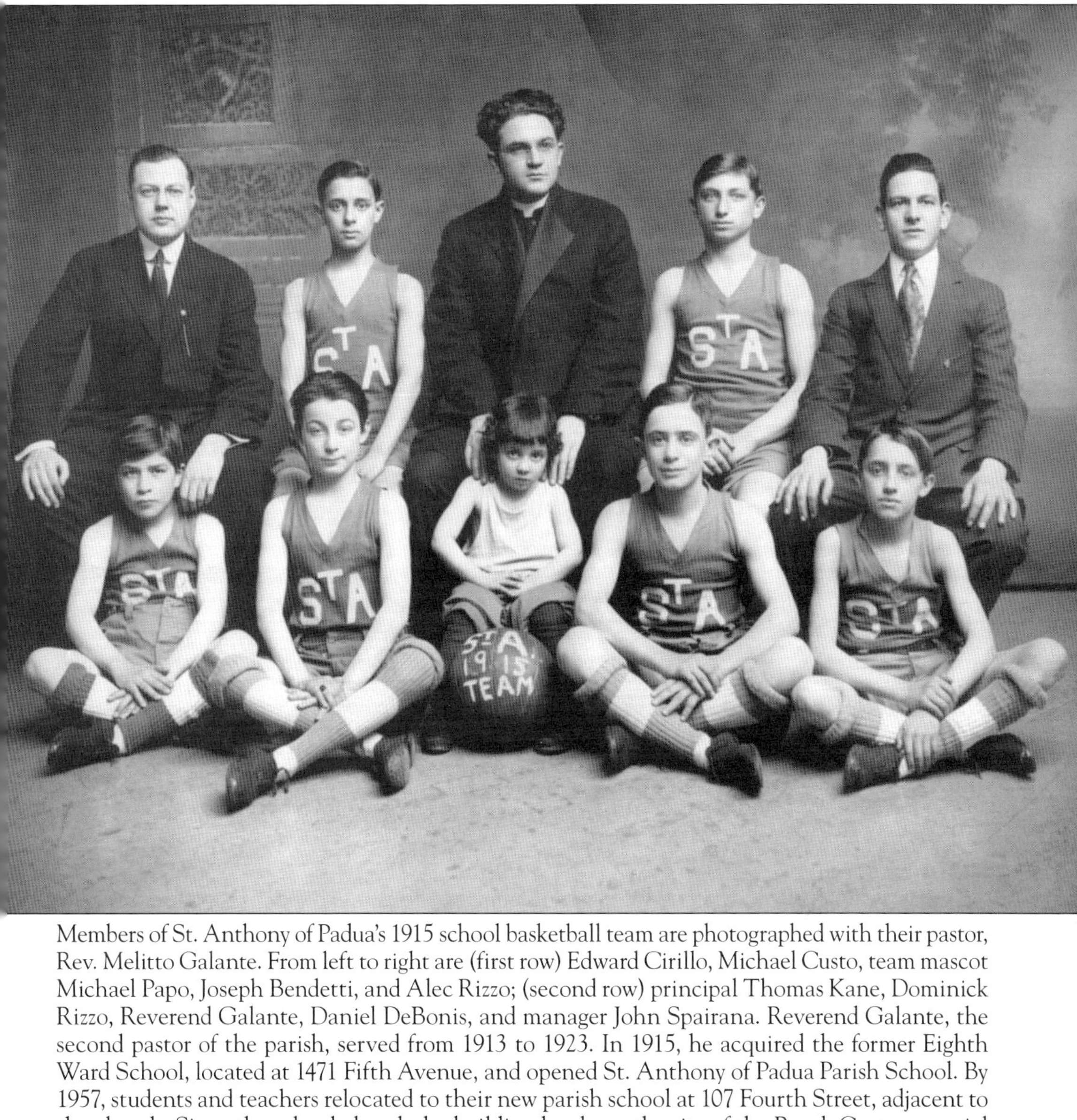

Members of St. Anthony of Padua's 1915 school basketball team are photographed with their pastor, Rev. Melitto Galante. From left to right are (first row) Edward Cirillo, Michael Custo, team mascot Michael Papo, Joseph Bendetti, and Alec Rizzo; (second row) principal Thomas Kane, Dominick Rizzo, Reverend Galante, Daniel DeBonis, and manager John Spairana. Reverend Galante, the second pastor of the parish, served from 1913 to 1923. In 1915, he acquired the former Eighth Ward School, located at 1471 Fifth Avenue, and opened St. Anthony of Padua Parish School. By 1957, students and teachers relocated to their new parish school at 107 Fourth Street, adjacent to the church. Since the school closed, the building has been the site of the Roark Center, a social service center sponsored by Catholic Charities. (Courtesy of Robert Riley.)

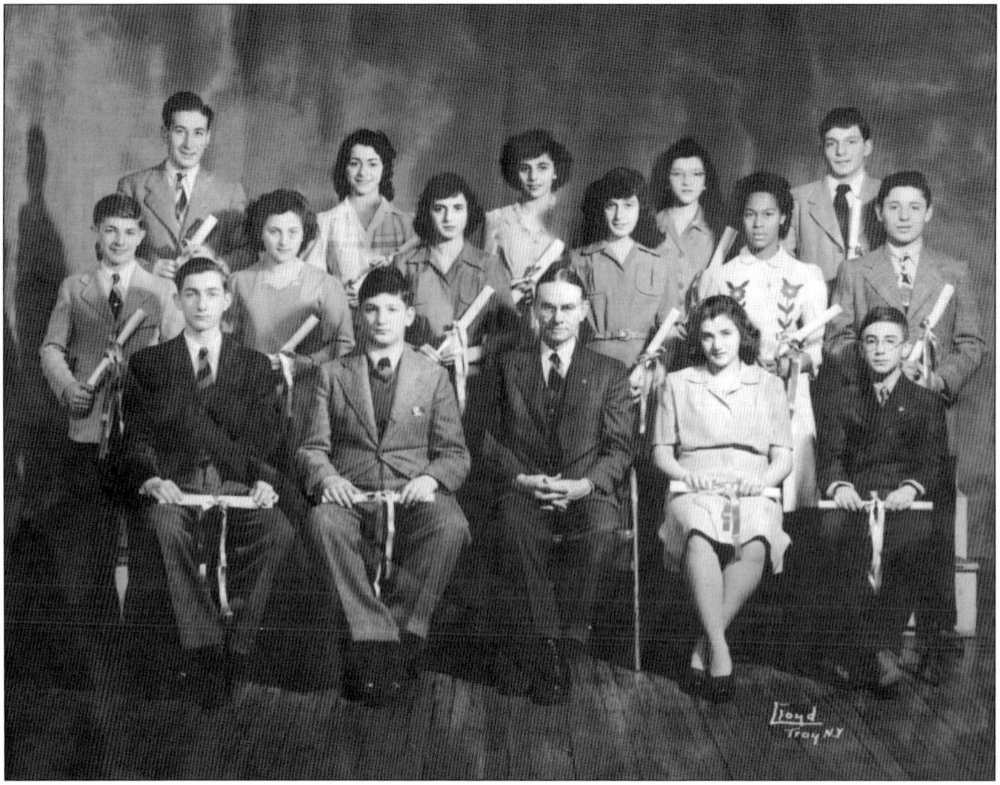

Public School 10 was a short walk away for the majority of its students. Pictured is longtime principal Michael Kling, seated among 15 graduates. From left to right are (first row) Robert Lanni, Michael Silverman, Mr. Kling, Phyllis Dembro, and Vincent Piertano; (second row) Joseph Pasenello, Dorothy Marchese, Eleanor Melite, Josephine Galle, Sharlot LaRoda, and Michael Pascarella; (third row) Lawrence Koening, Marion Bevevino, Mary Verdile, Philomena Colabresse, and Daniel Pirella. (Courtesy of Dawn Liberty Merola.)

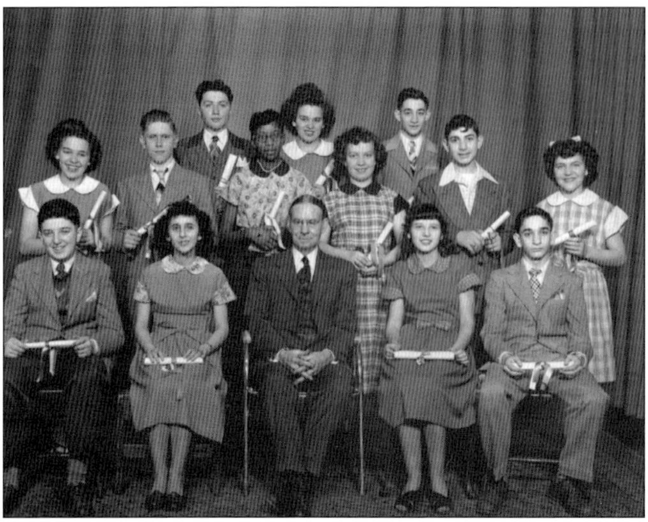

Eighth graders from the School 10 class of 1948 pose with the school's principal for this graduation photograph. From left to right are (first row) Morton Meyers, Ann Verdile, principal Michael Kling, Ada Silverman, and Alan Butler; (second row) Josephine Renna, John Smith, Rita Stinney, Mary Dillenbach, James Gulli, and Dolores Pasinella; (third row) Dominick Colucci, Anna Renna, and Joseph Manogian. (Courtesy of Anna Renna Riley.)

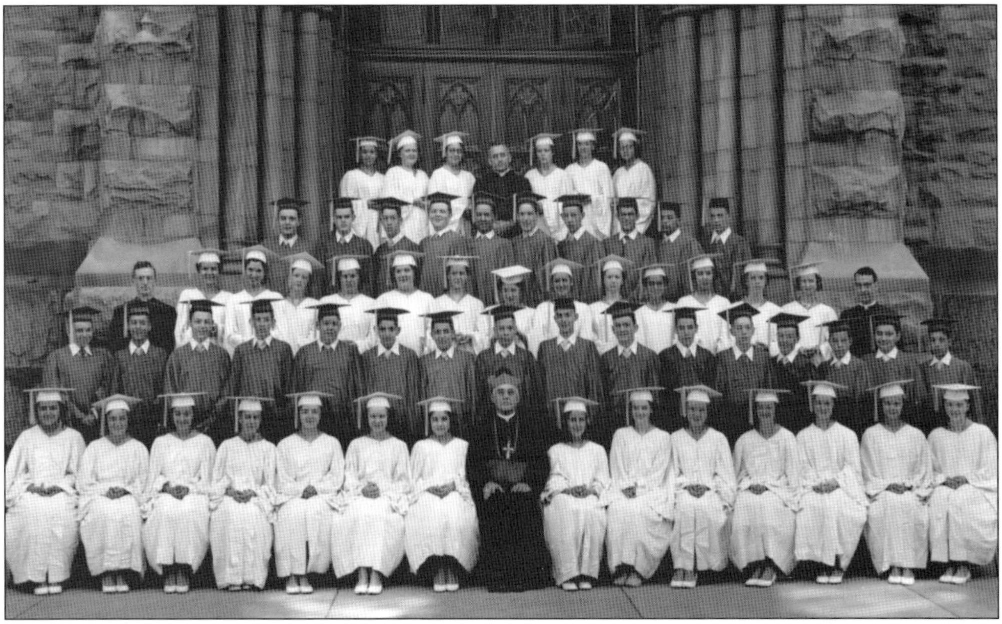

The 1954 graduating class of St. Mary's Parish School gathers with Bishop William A. Scully, DD (pastor of St. Mary's Parish, 1946–1954) on the steps of St. Mary's Church, located at 190 Third Street. Assistant pastors Rev. Edward Ryan and Rev. James Vaughn are at the far left and right of the third row, respectively, and Rev. Edward O'Malley is at center in the fifth row. The school closed in 1975, after providing 125 years of service to the parish community. (Author's collection.)

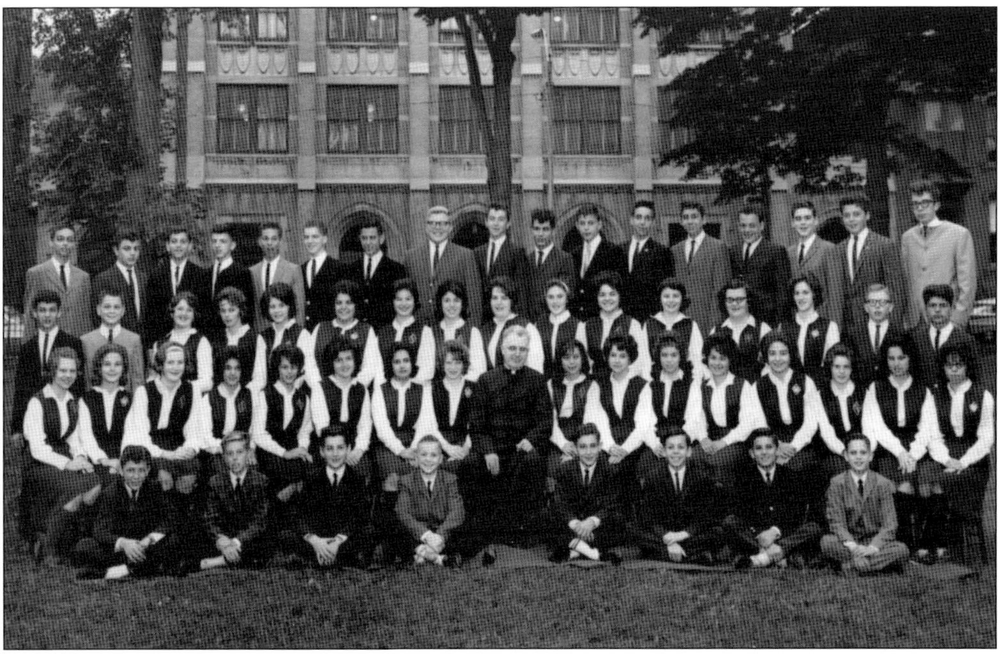

Troy's Washington Park was often the setting for St. Mary's School class photographs. Here, Rev. Daniel P. Markham (pastor of St. Mary's Parish, 1954–1970) joins the 1964 graduating class. The Daughters of Charity organized the first parish school for girls in 1850. The cornerstone for the school building in the background was laid in 1916. (Courtesy of Dawn Liberty Merola.)

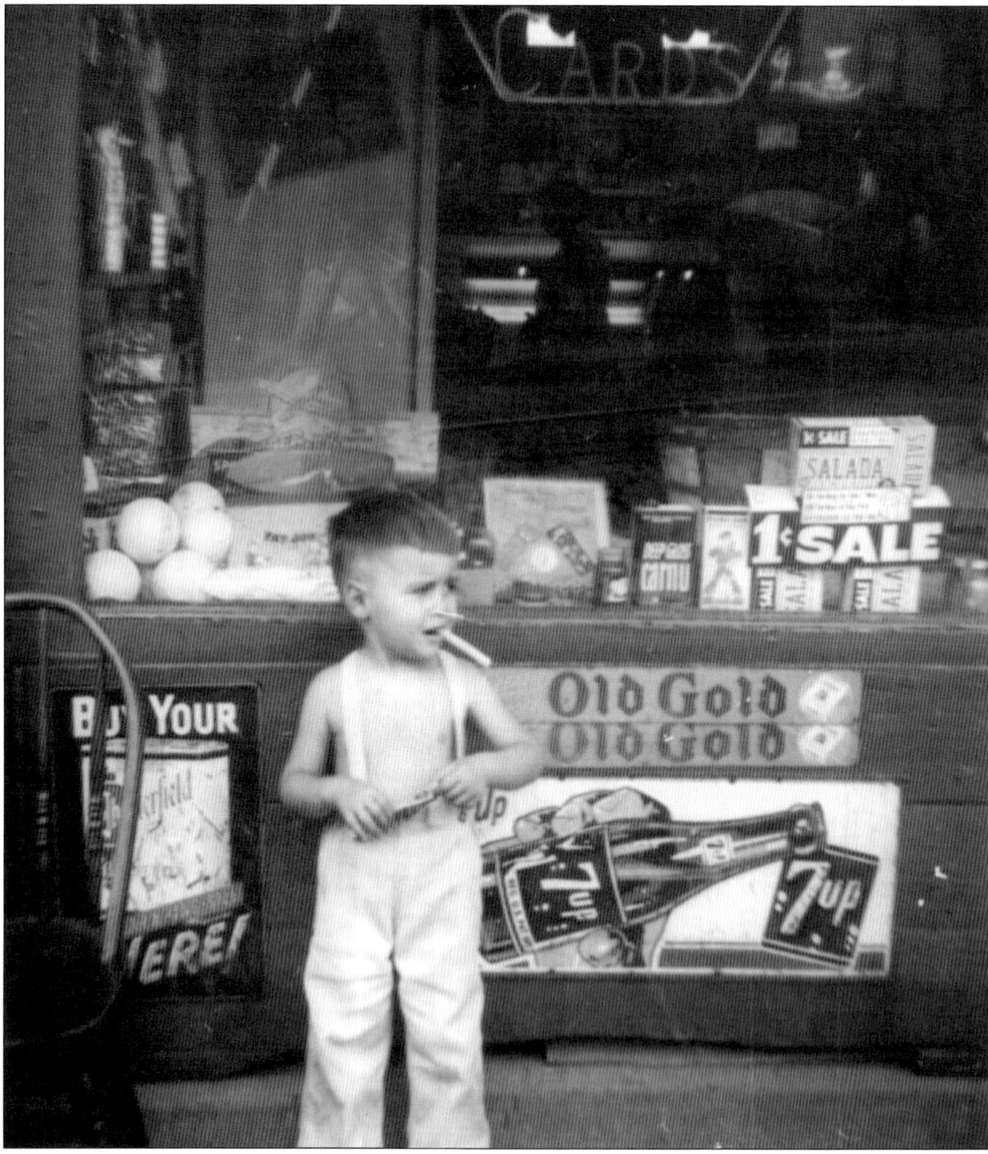

Four-year-old Rocco DeFazio, with a candy cigarette dangling from his mouth, stands in front of the 264 Fourth Street Italian import store owned by his parents, Josephine and Anthony DeFazio. Inspired by his parents' lifelong dedication to the community, Rocco would eventually form the Friends of Little Italy in 2002 and assume a leadership role in neighborhood association activities, including the organization of two New York State Neighborhood Conferences, founding the Troy Neighborhood Action Council, and helping to establish the first peer court in Troy. He was honored by his alma mater, Catholic Central High School, with the prestigious Crusader Award in 2014, named the Troy Youth Associations' person of the year in 2010, and shared in the honor bestowed on his family by the Rensselaer County Historical Society in 2005 for their service to the community. (Courtesy of Rocco DeFazio.)

Summertime is picnic time. Rensselaer County residents are fortunate to have a number of lakes with adjoining picnic areas located a few miles from their homes. Enjoying the day are, from left to right, Louise (Stellato) Szalasny, Philomena (Bruno) Campana, Anna (Bruno) Milanese, and Dorothy Terribile. (Courtesy of Eleanor Szalasny)

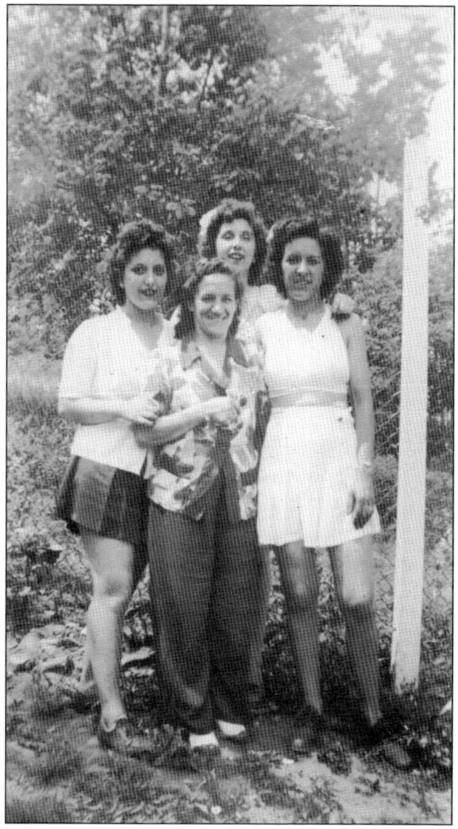

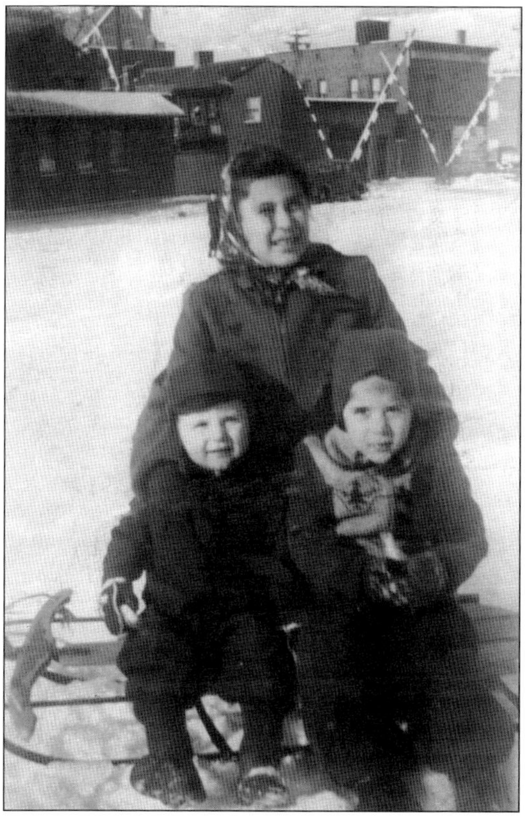

Margaret Williams watches over her younger brother and sister, Billy and Florence, as they take a break from sleighing on their Firefly sled in this photograph from winter, 1947. St. Joseph's Street, alongside the Williams home, made a fine hill for sledding. These three, along with their sister Judy, are the children of Edward and Angela (Fera) Williams. (Courtesy of Florence Williams.)

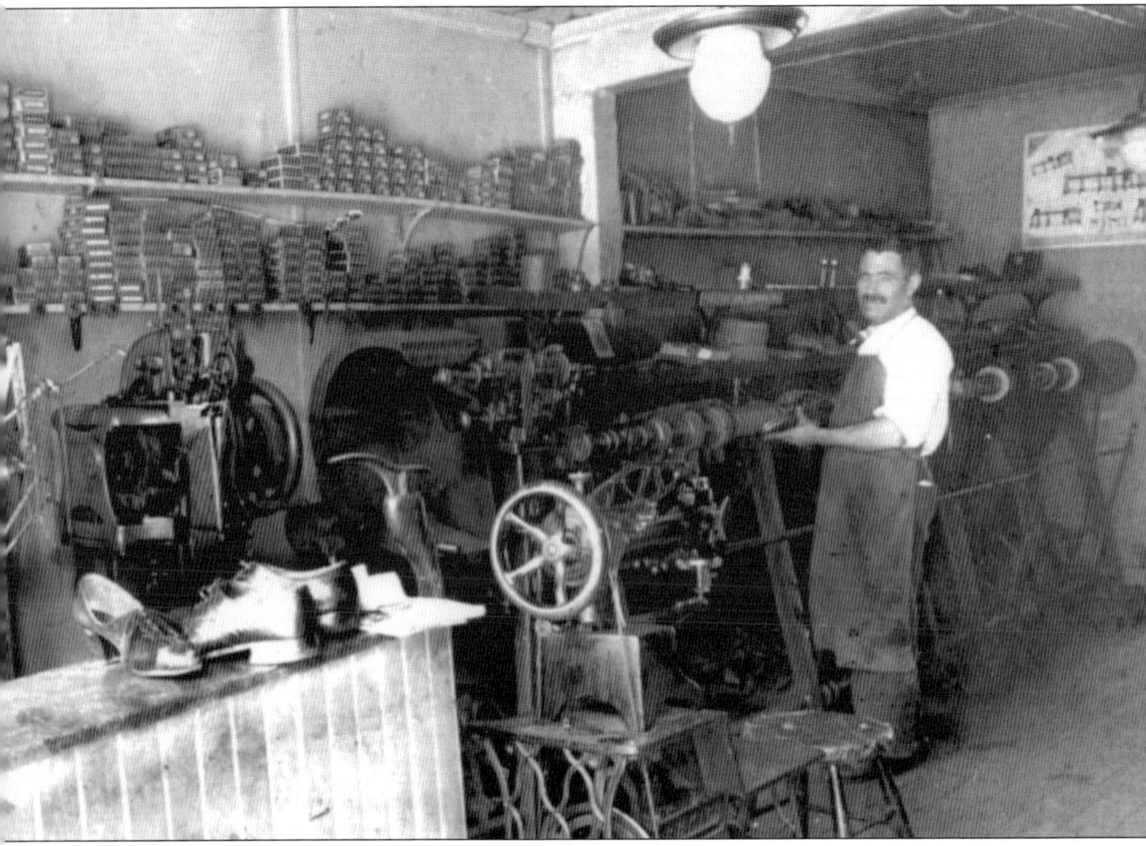

In 1920, Benevenuto "Ben" Lomaestro and his wife Elizabeth, known as "Bettina," were among the earliest Italian immigrants to open businesses in Little Italy. Ben's shoe repair shop shared the first floor of a modest two-story frame building at 408 Washington Street with Bettina's confectionery. The Lomaestro family lived on the second floor. Bakers, barbers, tailors, fruit peddlers, tavern owners, dry cleaners, and others lived in and worked from their own buildings. Ben and Bettina's son Jerry continued to operate the shoe repair shop at the same location well into the 1990s. Both father and son used much of the machinery seen here for decades. Youngsters were fascinated by the bench machines, sewing machines, and hand tools used by the Lomaestros. (Courtesy of Bonnie Lomaestro Walsh.)

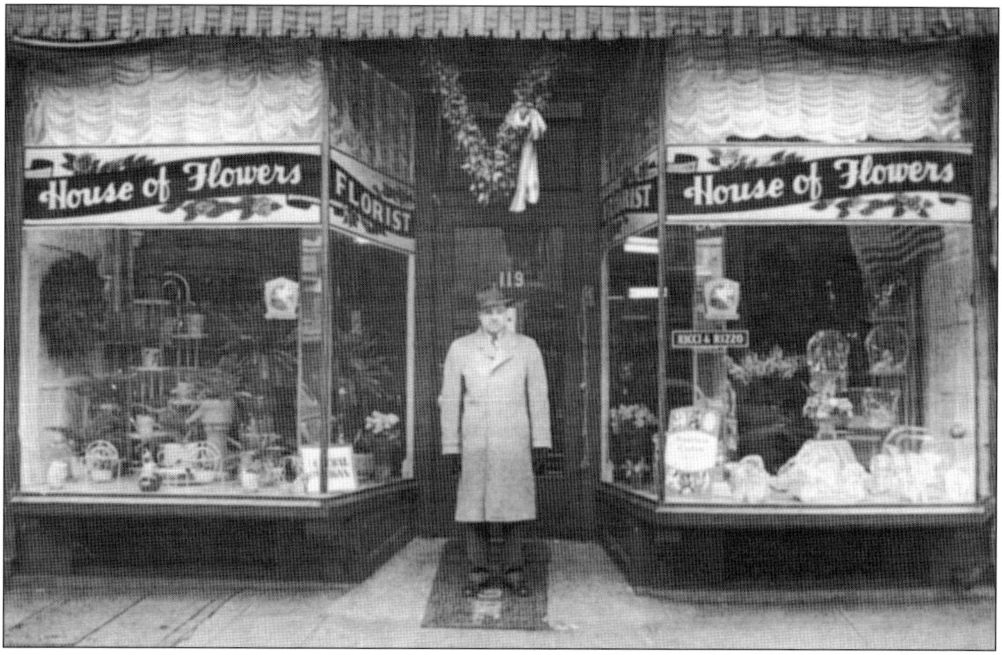

Louis Rizzo stands at the front door of the House of Flowers, located at 119 Fourth Street. He established the company with his friend and business partner, John Ricci, in 1939. The shop was three blocks north of the Rizzo homestead. His wife, Lucrezia (Ciannamea), was owner of Lucretia's Bridal Shop, situated at 106 Fourth Street. (Courtesy of Annette Rizzo Sanders.)

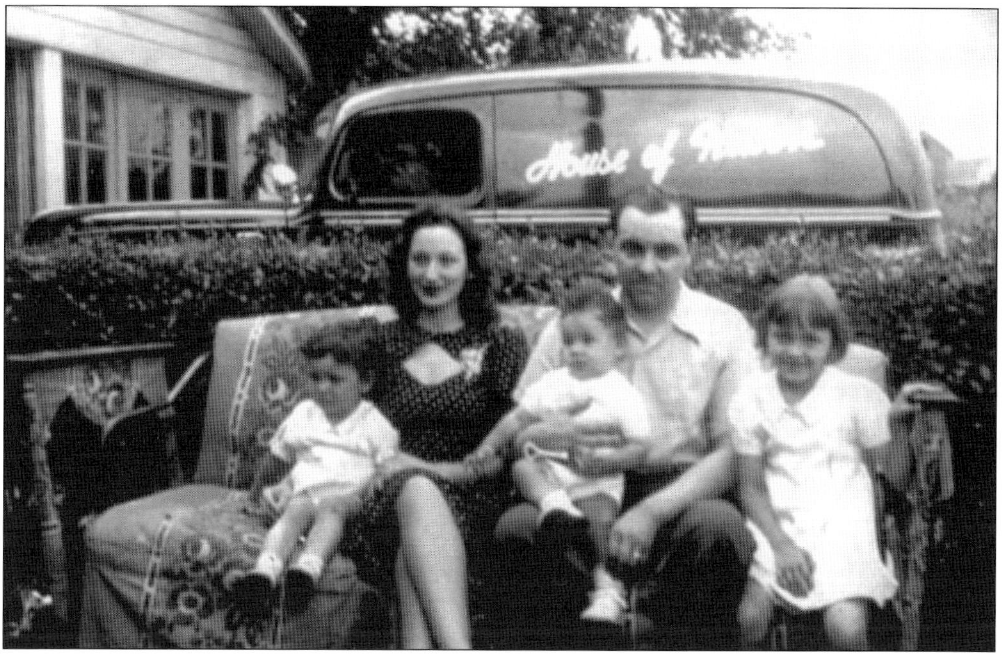

Lucretia and Louis Rizzo are seen here with their three children during a visit to the home of a grandparent. The children are, from left to right, Michael, Joseph, and Annette. Long active in the Republican Party, Louis was a committeeman from the First Ward for many years and served on the Troy City Council. (Courtesy of Annette Rizzo Sanders.)

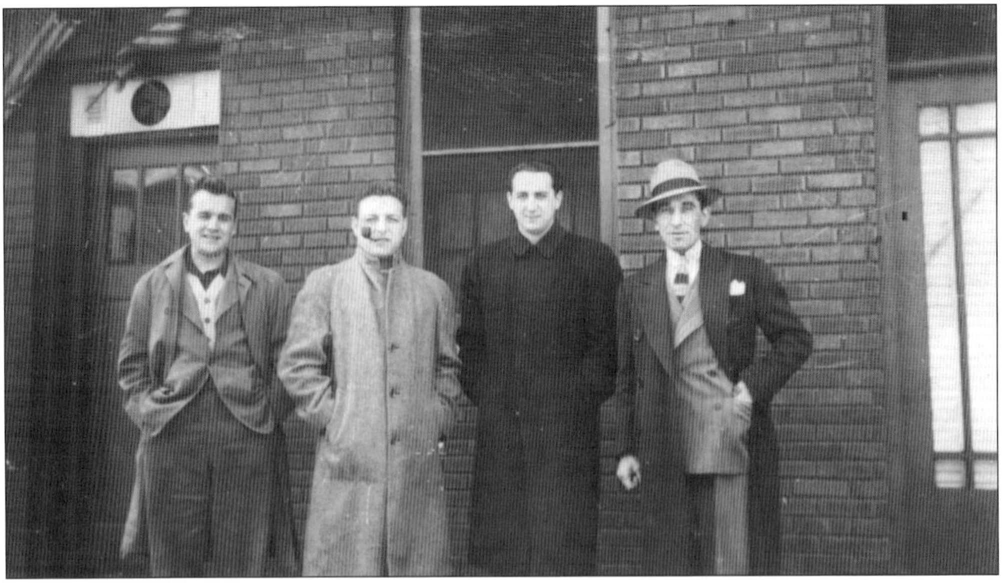

Gennaro Riggione was the owner of Jerry's Tavern, located at 55 Hill Street, which became a social center for the area by providing a neighborhood restaurant and tavern as well as a reception space for bridal showers, banquets, and other family gatherings. Seen standing in front of the tavern are, from left to right, regulars Louis Moscatello, Nicholas Riggione, Dr. Richard Testo, and John Dagostino. (Courtesy of Marie Casale Santora.)

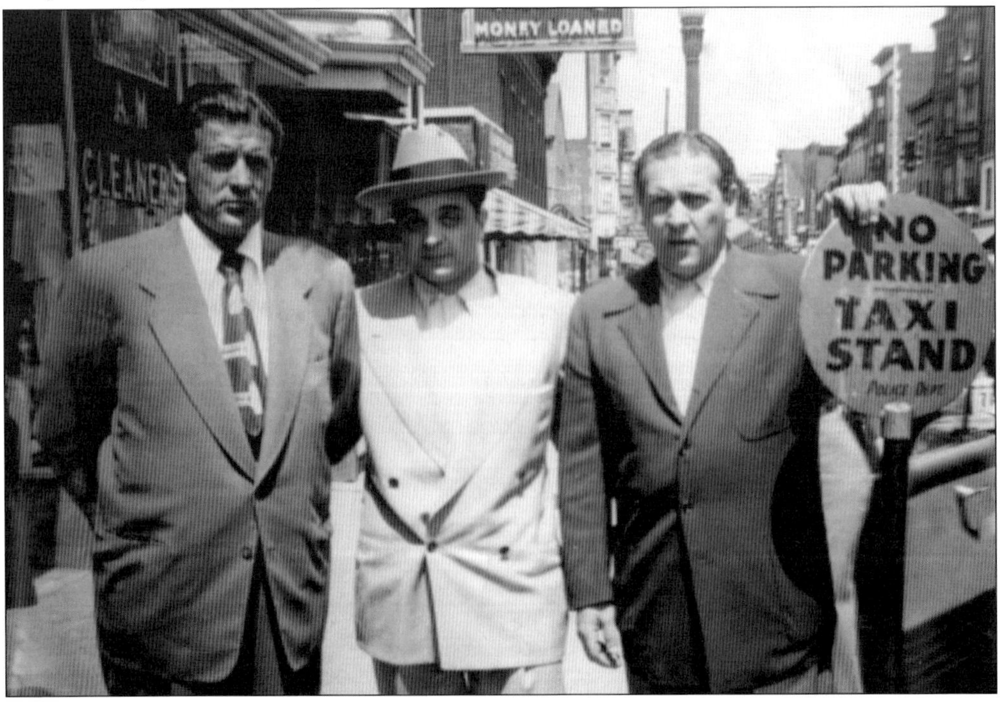

This photograph was taken in front of Frank Rossetti's taxi stand at 165 Fourth Street. From left to right are Anthony Gross, Anthony Bove, and Joseph Gross. In the background, looking north toward Ferry Street, is the beginning of Troy's business district. There were over 60 mom-and-pop shops between Ferry and Ida Streets by the late 1960s. (Courtesy of Marie Casale Santora.)

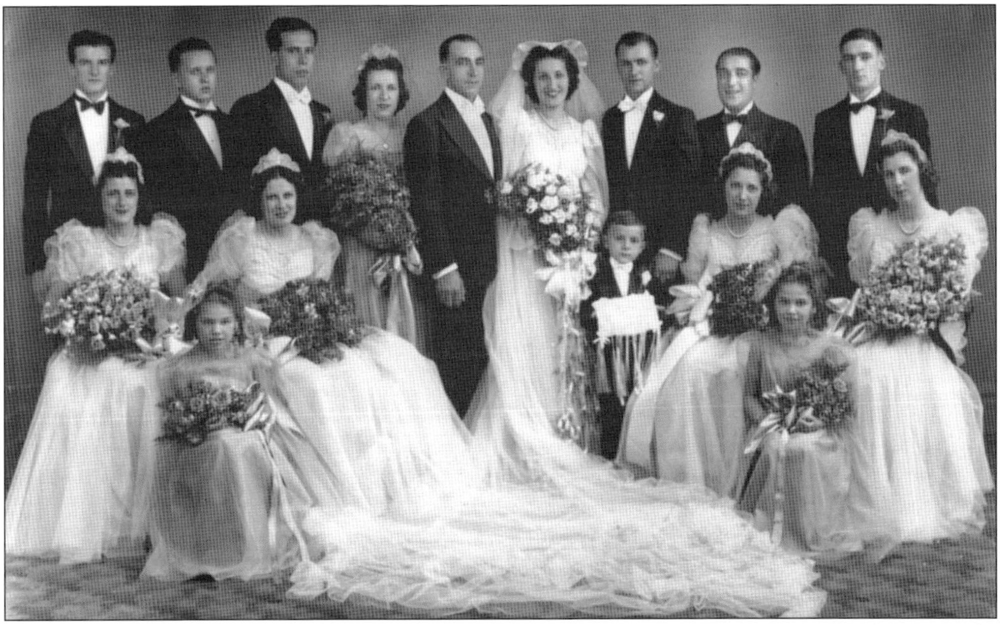

Pictured here is the wedding party of John and Theresa (Marro) Mayba. From left to right are (first row) twin flower girls Josephine and Anna Renna; (second row) Catherine Mango, Margaret Mamone, an unidentified ring bearer, Louise Stellato, and Anna Bruno; (third row) two unidentified ushers, Francis Mamone, Dorothy Terribile, Francis Marro, Theresa, John, and two unidentified ushers. (Author's collection.)

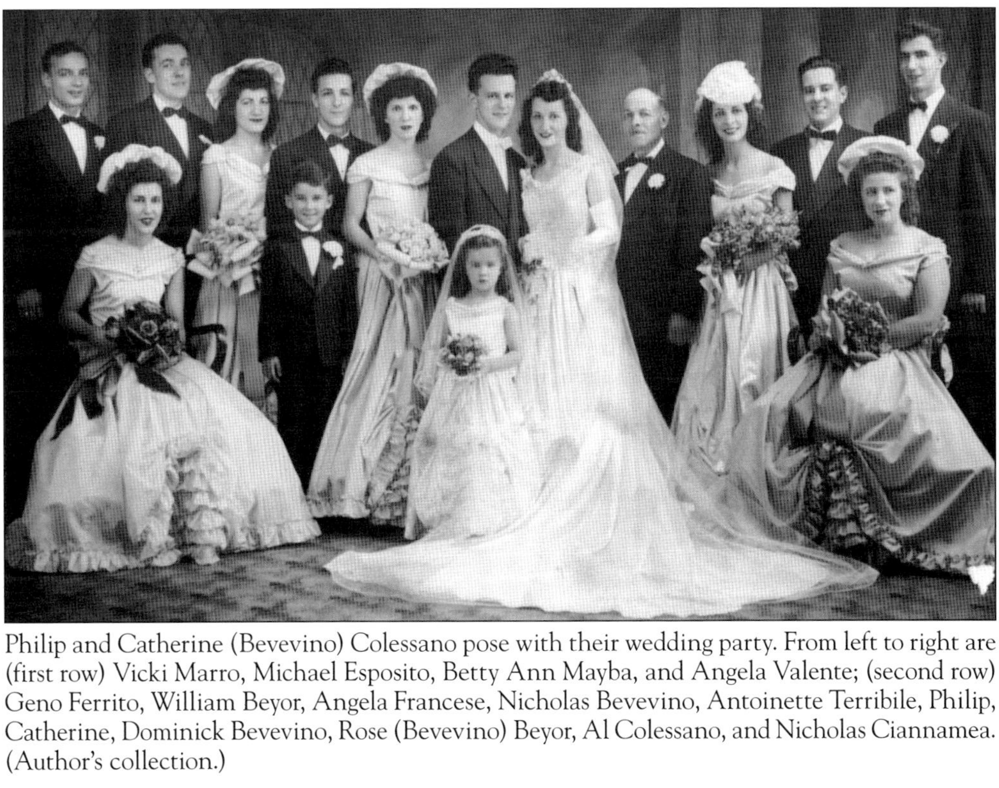

Philip and Catherine (Bevevino) Colessano pose with their wedding party. From left to right are (first row) Vicki Marro, Michael Esposito, Betty Ann Mayba, and Angela Valente; (second row) Geno Ferrito, William Beyor, Angela Francese, Nicholas Bevevino, Antoinette Terribile, Philip, Catherine, Dominick Bevevino, Rose (Bevevino) Beyor, Al Colessano, and Nicholas Ciannamea. (Author's collection.)

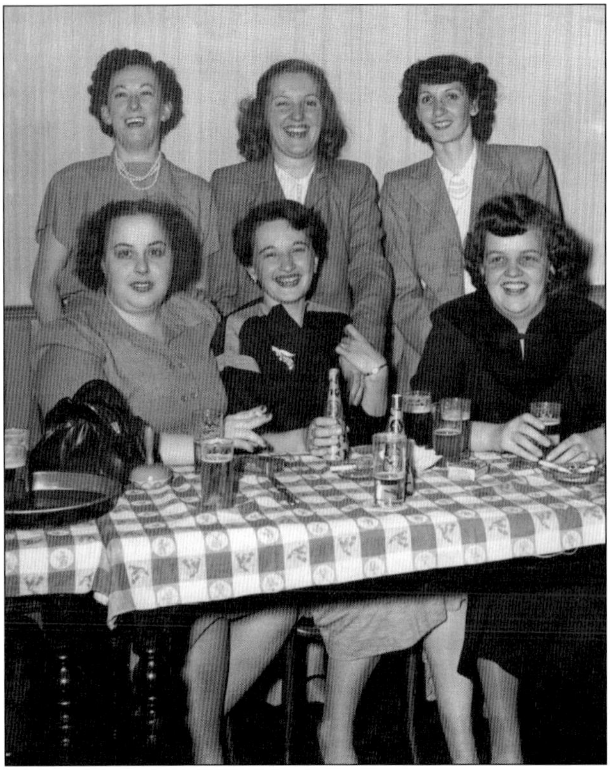

Friends and coworkers gather to celebrate at the bridal shower of Anna Cioffi, who married Michael Cuozzo. From left to right are (first row) Mary Martone, Cioffi, and Mae Rogers; (second row) unidentified, Frances Greene, and Betty (Turriglio) DeBonis. (Courtesy of John DeLorenzo.)

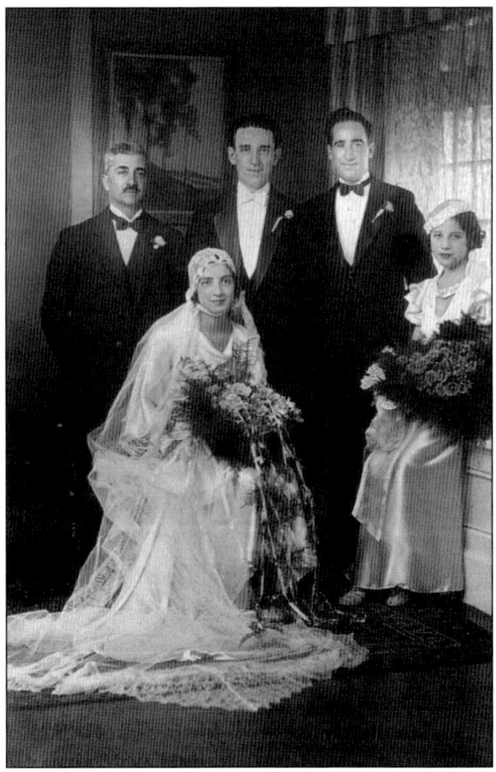

Celia (DeMaria) and James Church were married in 1933 at St. Anthony of Padua Shrine Church. From left to right are Giuseppe "Don Pepe" DeMaria, Celia, James, Herbert Lauffler, and Mary Lanzillo. James and Herbert worked for the *Troy Record* newspaper. Celia was employed for many years at Troy Surgical Pharmacy. Celia and Jim were the parents of Ann, James Jr., and Marion. (Courtesy of Marion Church Field.)

The members of the wedding party of Nicholas Casale and Lucia Gross gather for a group photograph following their 1935 ceremony at St. Anthony of Padua Shrine Church. From left to right are (first row) Theresa Gross, Lucia, Mary Gross, and Grace Pisaniello; (second row) Nicholas, Anthony Gross, and Frank D'Agostino. The two youngsters are nieces of the bride. (Courtesy of Marie Casale Santora.)

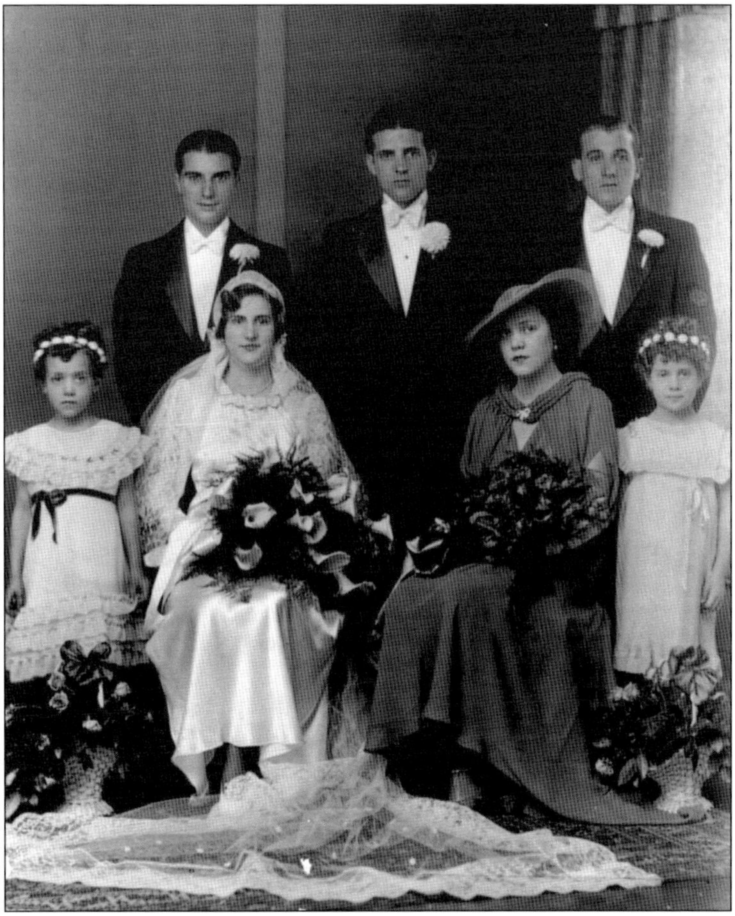

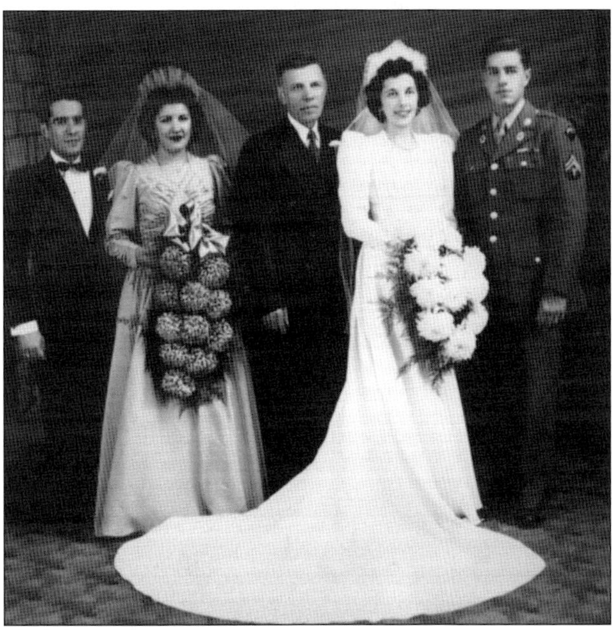

A true story of two heroes unfolds in the 1943 wedding photograph of Frances Derico and Ida Street's Samuel Chiappone. From left to right are Charles Chiappone, Grace (Gill) Pignatelli, Santos Derico, Frances, and Samuel. In December 1944, Cpl. Sam Chiappone would be seriously wounded in a battle at Hurtgen Forest on the German-Belgian border—carrying the scars of war until his death. Less than two years later, in August 1946, his brother Charlie would die along with his 10-year-old nephew Robert Fazioli, whom Charlie was attempting to save after he collapsed at the bottom of a cistern. (Courtesy of Samuel Chiappone.)

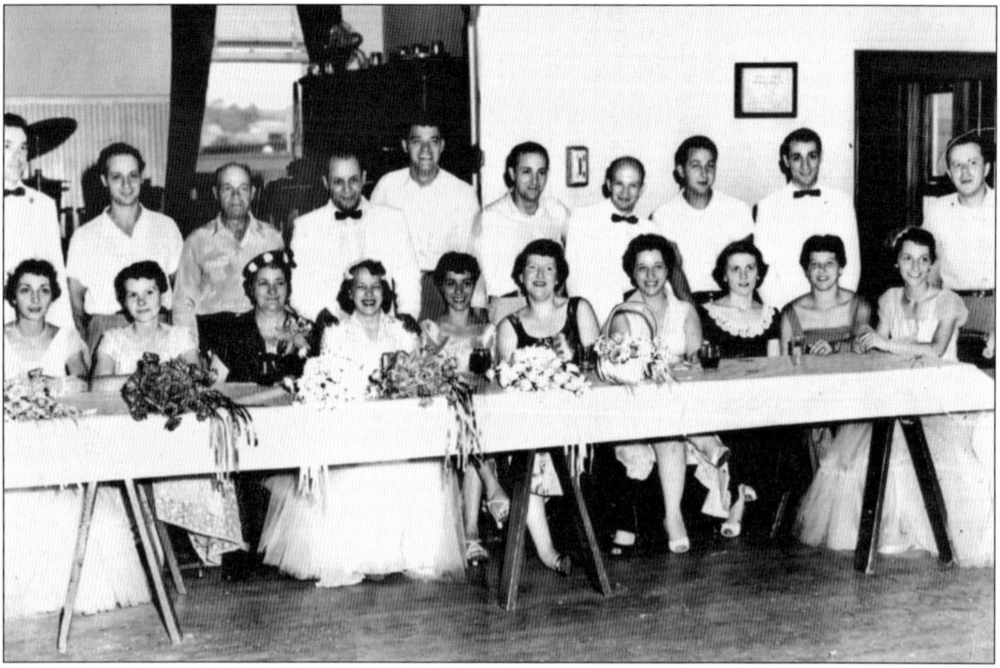

Dominick and Elizabeth Bevevino are photographed with their family at the wedding reception of their son Joseph to Claudia Conlin. From left to right are (first row) Rose Beyor, Millie Bevevino, Elizabeth, Claudia Bevevino, Marion Liberty, Doris Bevevino, Mary Maloney, Mary and Joan Bevevino, and Catherine Colessano; (second row) William Beyor, James, Dominick Sr. and Joseph Bevevino, Robert Liberty, Nicholas Bevevino, Philip Maloney, Dominick and Francis Bevevino, and Philip Colessano. The Ciccarelli-Rea-Agars-Bevevino Veterans Post bears the name of the eldest Bevevino son, Bruno—a master sergeant and veteran of both World War II and the Korean War—who was reported missing in action in Korea. (Courtesy of Mary Bevevino Maloney.)

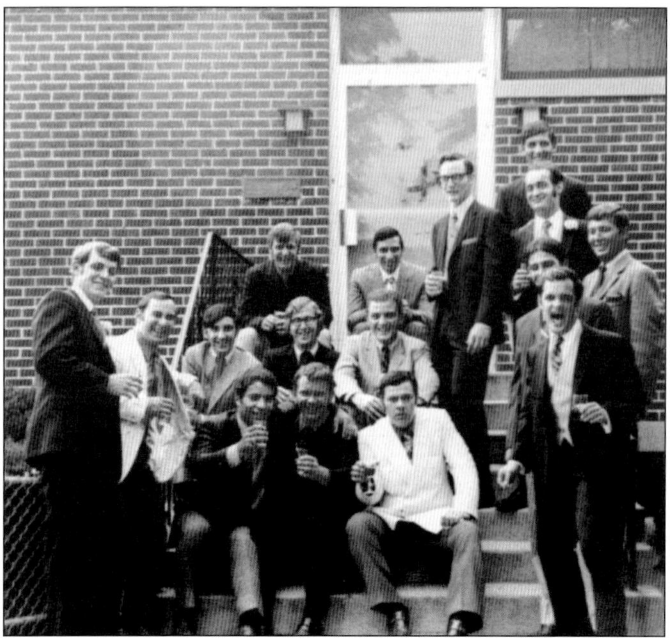

The entrance to Germania Hall is the setting for a drink toasting Robert "Rabbit" Riley on his 1970 marriage to Dody Mattoon. From left to right are (first row) John Tedesco, James Gully, Nicholas Bocketti, Joseph Berlino, James DePaul, and Joseph Riley; (second row) Thomas Riley, Daniel DeBonis, Richard Gilholley, Paul Moran, and Anthony Tedesco; (third row) Paul Montarello, Patrick Armao, Michael Riley, and James Fisher; (fourth row) Steve Debboli. (Courtesy of Robert Riley.)

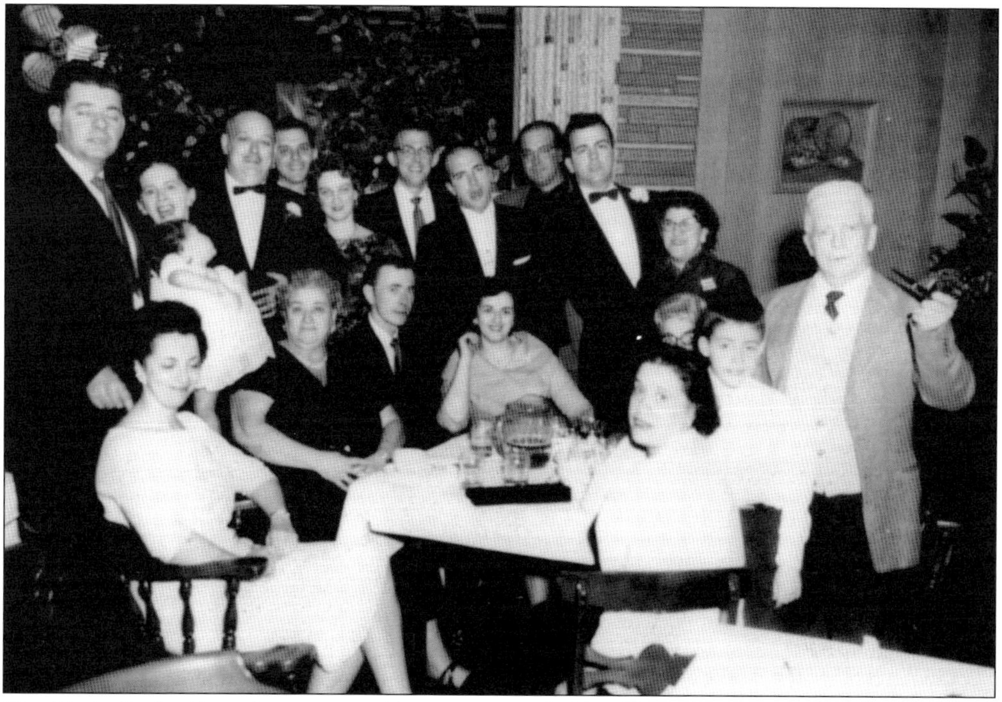

The Piscitella family gathers at a wedding reception held at Troy's Sunset Inn in 1962. From left to right are (first row) Anna, David Pagano, and family patriarch Sebastiano Piscitella; (second row) Rose, Angeline, Jack and Patricia Pickett, and Joan; (third row) Thomas and Mary Pagano (with daughter Donna) and Dominick, Louis, Edna, Francis, James, Joseph, Thomas, and Palomina "Babe" Piscitella. (Courtesy of Angela Piscitella Gavin.)

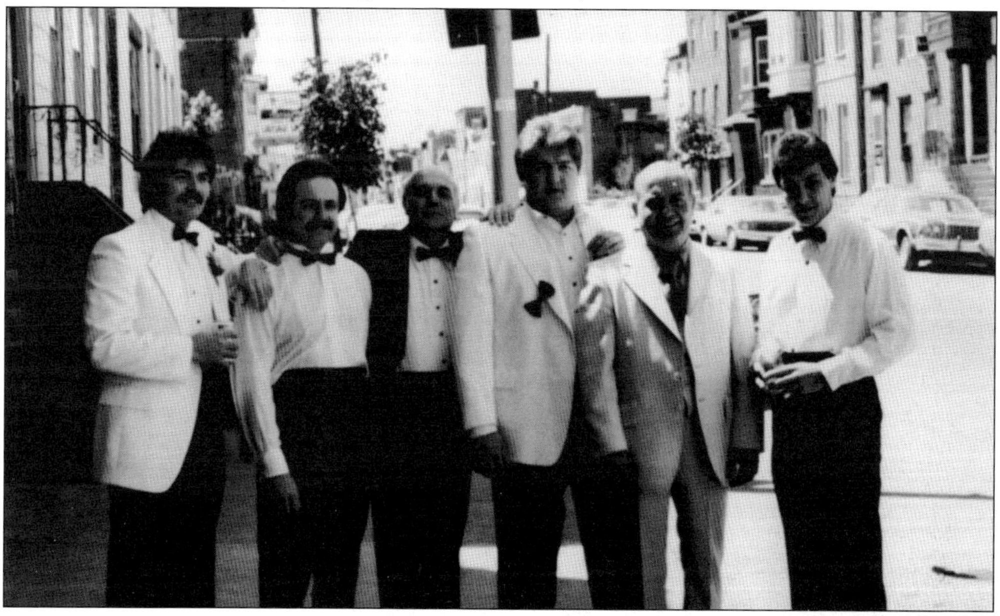

Fourth Street is the backdrop for this photograph, taken after the 1982 wedding of Joseph Cavallo and Laura Clark. From left to right are brothers Anthony and Joseph Cavallo, dad Joseph, Carmen Casale, uncle Vincent Cavallo, and Vincent Pelozzi. (Courtesy of Jean Turriglio Cavallo.)

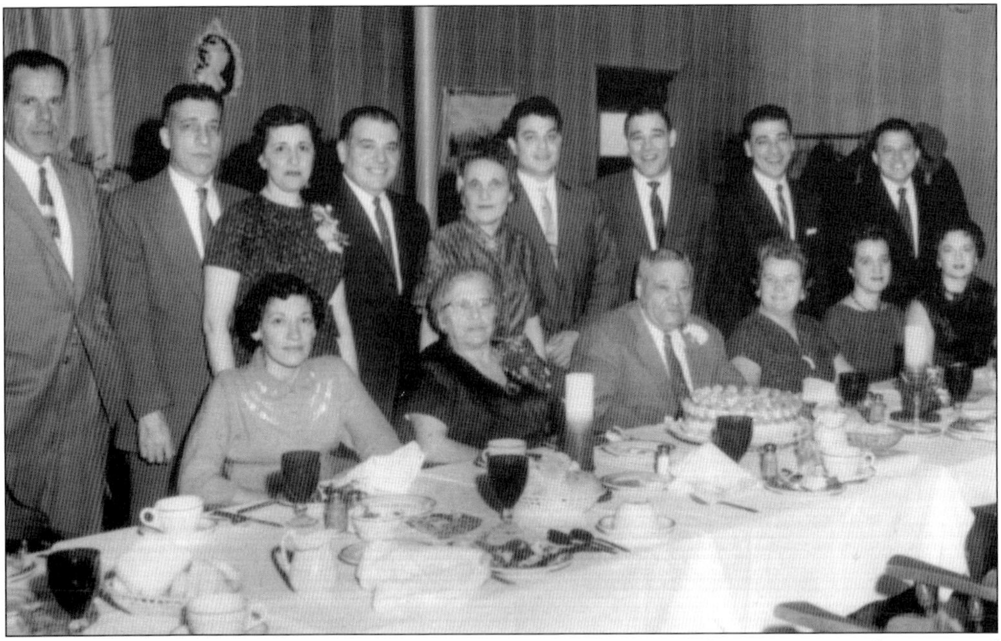

The Renna family celebrated the golden wedding anniversary of their parents, Adrianna and Angelo, at Troy's Sunset Inn, a popular restaurant and tavern that was owned by Rudy Ciccoti for many years. From left to right are (first row) Josephine Hemion and Adrianna, Angelo, Antoinette, Mary, and Charlene Renna; (second row) Frank Hemion and Anthony, Catherine, Frank, Mary, Patrick, Ralph, John, and Charles Renna. (Courtesy of Anna Renna Riley.)

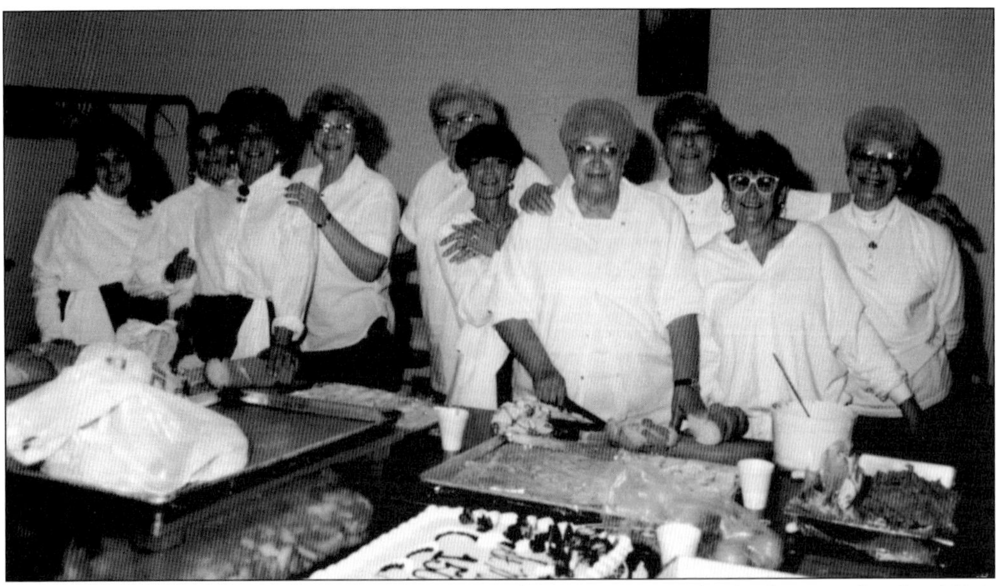

Members of the Coli-Germano family assist in the preparation of refreshments for the 150th anniversary celebration of St. Mary's Church. From left to right are Cathy (Petrofoski) Ziter, Susan (Tedesco) Valenti, Karen (Tedesco) Campana, Carmella (Germano) Petrofoski, Virginia (Germano) Gagnon, Cathy Margo, Lucy (Germano) Coli, Ann (Germano) Pascale, Antoinette Pascarella, and Felicia (Germano) Tedesco. (Courtesy of St. Mary's Church Archives.)

Four

Community Partners

Successful community development requires collaboration, and efforts to revitalize Little Italy owe much to the support of a number of neighborhood organizations.

The Italian Community Center, located at 1450 Fifth Avenue, was established in 1935 in response to the needs of large numbers of Italian immigrants. It is an important contributor to the Van Rensselaer Manor and has a distinguished history of charitable contributions to local institutions. Events such as Festa Italiana and the Empty Bowl project, first proposed by the Friends of Little Italy and area potters, bring thousands to the neighborhood. Wedding receptions, family gatherings, reunions, sports banquets, and dinner theater productions are frequent events at the ICC. Both the ICC and the CYO assist Troy Little Italy in sponsoring the Drop in Center, a summer recreation program.

The Troy Youth Association's CYO Center, organized in 1952, is located at 237 Fourth Street, in the former LaSalle Institute gymnasium. Its mission is to foster and develop the cultural, moral, and physical wellbeing of youth and adults—nurturing and aiding in the development of character. Since 1973, its director has been Raymond Piscitelli. The nonprofit association sponsors supervised activities for youngsters, including after-school child care programs, a popular summer day camp, recreational and educational programs for teens and adults, and an expanded basketball league consisting of 220 teams from throughout the Capital District.

Joseph House & Shelter, established in 1982 by Sr. Rita Shaw and Sr. Maria Cokely—members of the Sisters of St. Joseph of Carondolet—maintains two facilities in the neighborhood. The site at 74 Ferry Street is a temporary shelter, offering homeless members of the community a safe place to rest, nutritious meals, medical care, and access to personal items and laundry facilities. Meanwhile, the Hill Street Inn, located at 200 Fourth Street, accommodates 20 chronically homeless and disabled individuals. Residents and staff also volunteer for Earth Day neighborhood activities, the Stickball Tournament, and the annual Christmas in Little Italy event.

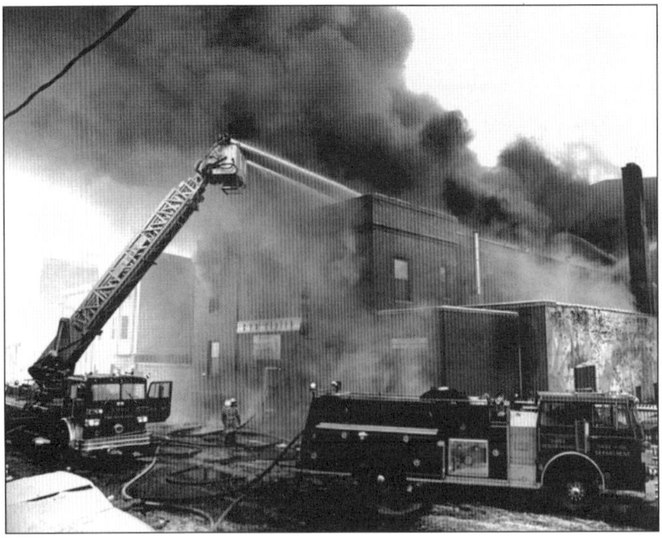

On a frigid morning in December 1985, a disastrous fire did major damage to the Troy Youth Associations CYO Center, located at 237 Fourth Street. Five firefighters were injured in the blaze when a section of the roof collapsed. All of the building's gym and kitchen equipment was ruined. Just weeks after an engineer reported on the stability of the structure, a successful campaign was started to rebuild the center. (Courtesy of CYO Center Archives.)

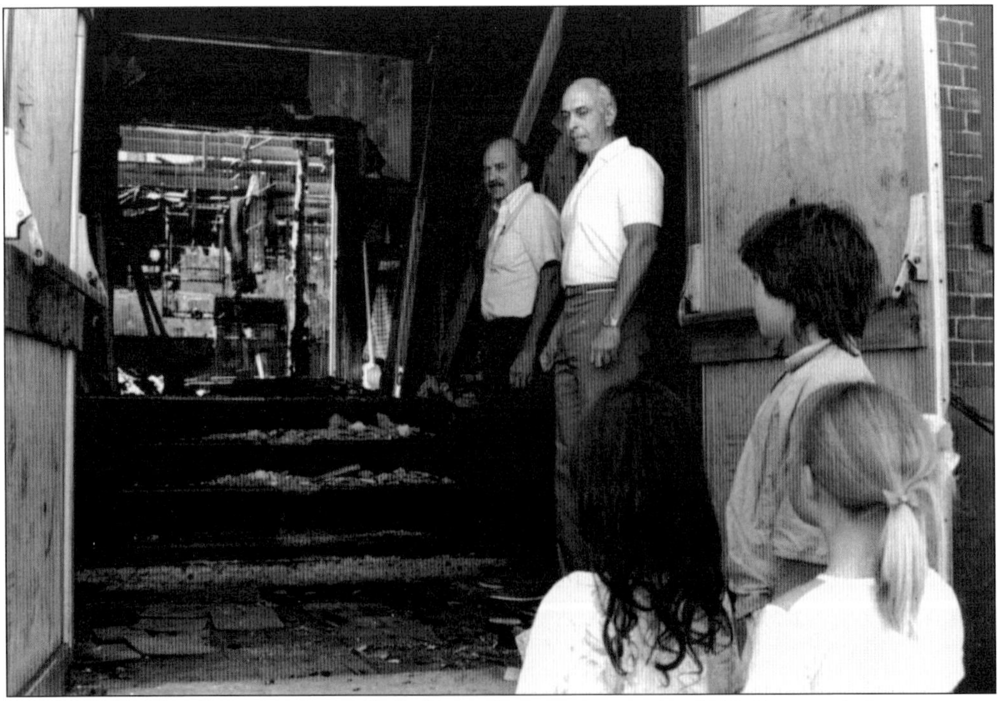

A local contractor joins Ray Piscitelli (right) at the entrance to the CYO Center while youngsters observe the charred interior of the building. Churches in the area came to the rescue: St. Mary's provided space for after school programs and an office, St. John's Episcopal provided a gym program, St. Basil's provided space for basketball programs, and St. Ann's allowed the use of their hall to continue bingo. The CYO Center was rebuilt and remains a strong presence in the community. (Courtesy of CYO Center Archives.)

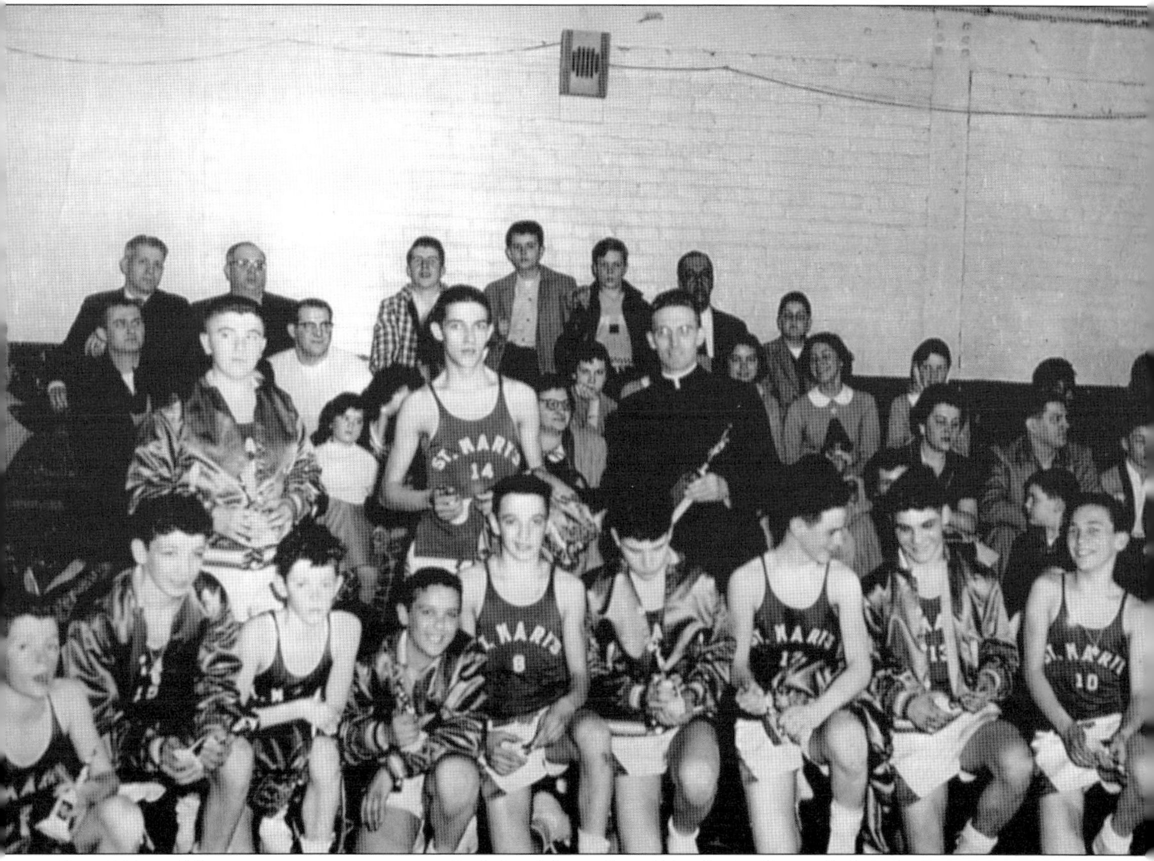

Rev. Edward Ryan, assistant pastor at St. Mary's Parish and basketball coach, holds a tournament trophy awarded to the team in 1958. From left to right are (first row) Frank Kehn, Jerry Barry, William Kehn, Fred Gabriel, Anthony Santora, Rocco DeBonis, John Marchese, Terry Valente, and Angelo Renna; (second row) Dominick Pasinella, Joseph Mahoney, and Reverend Ryan. Several men sitting in the back of the bleachers have been identified as well; from left to right are unidentified, Nick Marchese, Pete Gully, three unidentified boys, Nicholas Padalino, and Joseph Padalino. Patrick Case, wearing glasses, is seated directly below Pete Gully. The center's basketball leagues total some 2,100 youth and adults during the program period. CYO programs are made up of children in grades five and six in "biddy teams," and children in grades seven and eight in "junior teams." (Courtesy of Rev. Edward Ryan.)

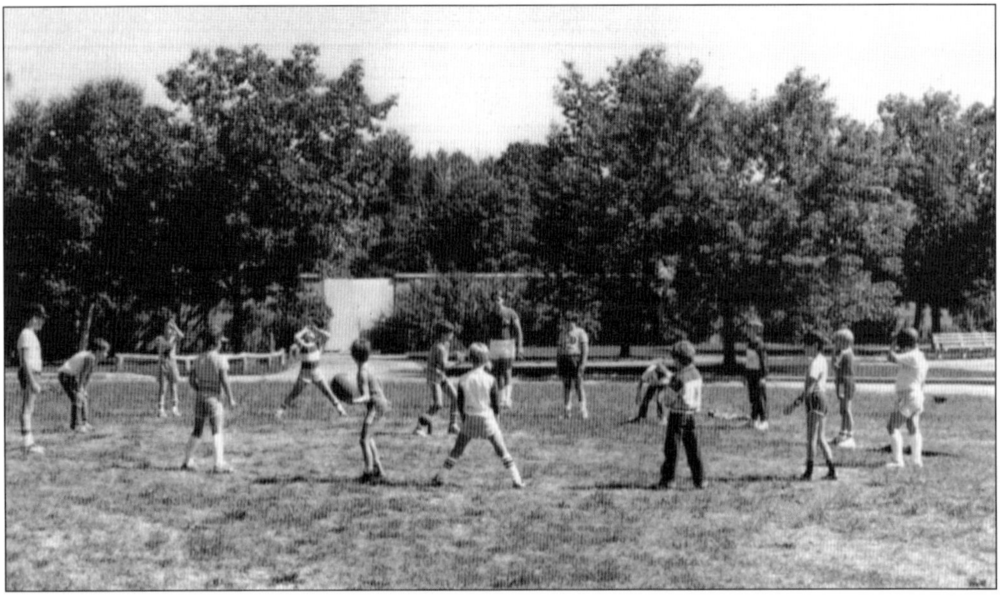

At the summer day camp program, children enjoy outdoor recreation, arts and crafts, and the occasional side trip to an amusement park or local lake. The CYO Center offers affordable fees for low-income families, and the after-school child care program includes tutorial aid and use of the gym, game room, and computer lab. A special tiny tot area is also available for the youngest of those who use the center. All programs are supervised by adults. (Courtesy of CYO Center Archives.)

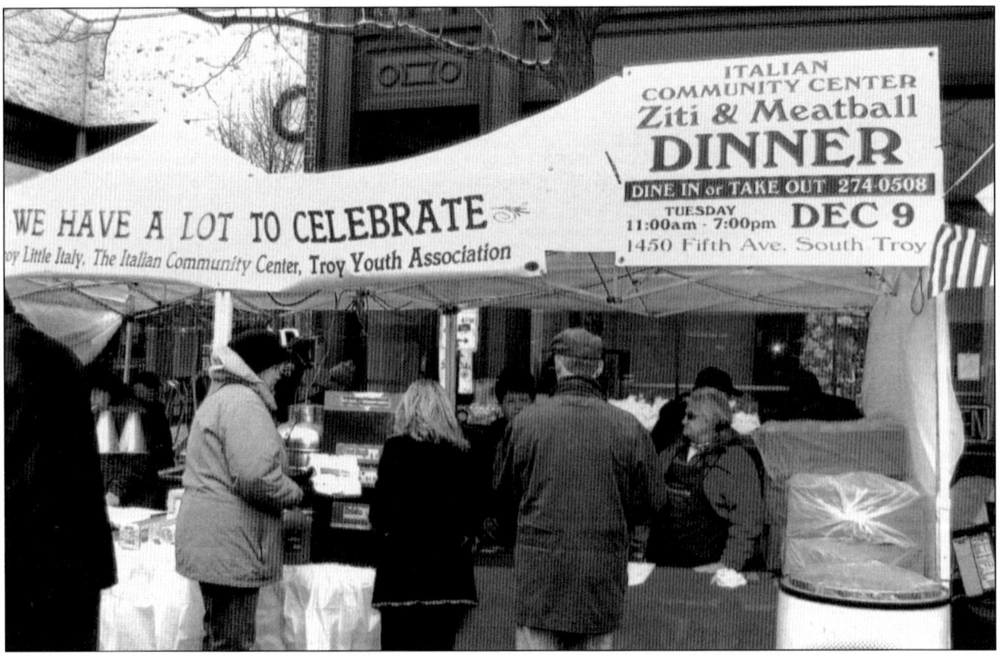

Volunteers from the Italian Community Center, the CYO Center, and Troy Little Italy staff an information booth at the annual Victorian Stroll—considered the start of the holiday season. The stroll was first proposed by former Little Italy resident Geri (Campese) DeSeve and Sandra Gull in 1978. (Courtesy of Marion Field.)

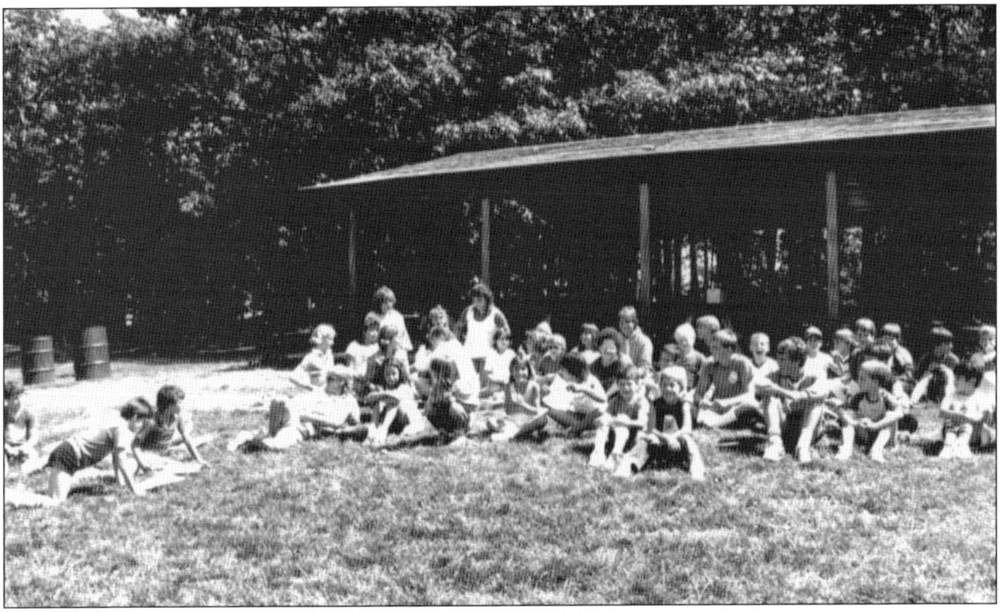

The CYO is a youth centered organization. It offers Red Cross certified swimming programs, a drug awareness program for teenagers, and the Challenger program for youth with disabilities. Its facility is often available to the community for public meetings, including pre-election candidate forums. The CYO sponsors a weekly bingo fundraiser. (Courtesy of CYO Center Archives.)

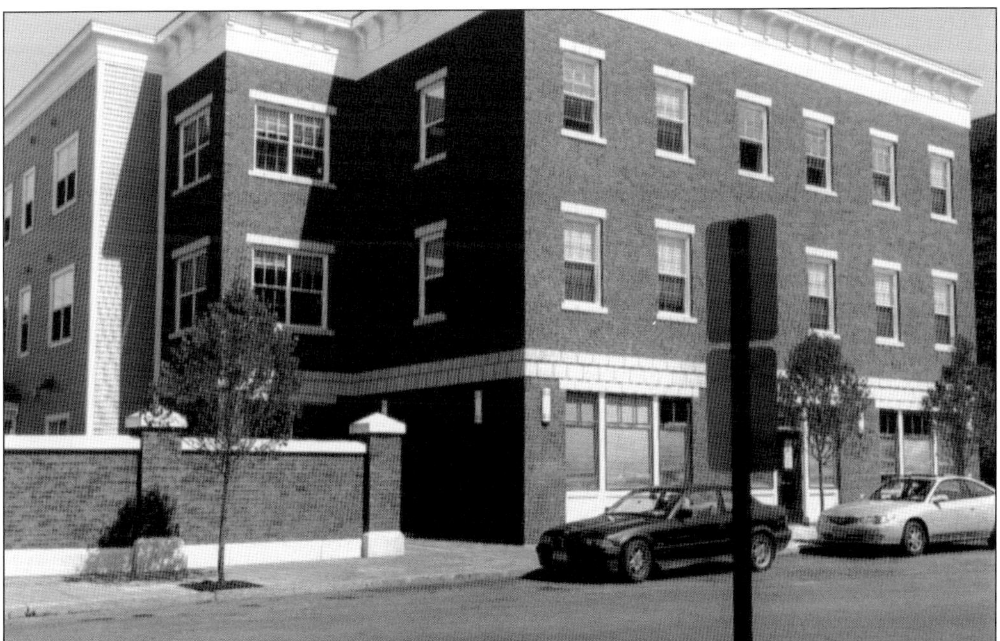

Joseph's House & Shelter (JH&S) is a community-based not-for-profit organized in 1982 to address the increasing number of homeless in the community by providing shelter, support, and guidance to individuals, young people, and families. Pictured is the Hill Street Inn at 204 Fourth Street, which accommodates 20 chronically homeless and disabled individuals. A second facility, located at 74 Ferry Street, is available as a temporary shelter. (Courtesy of Marion Field.)

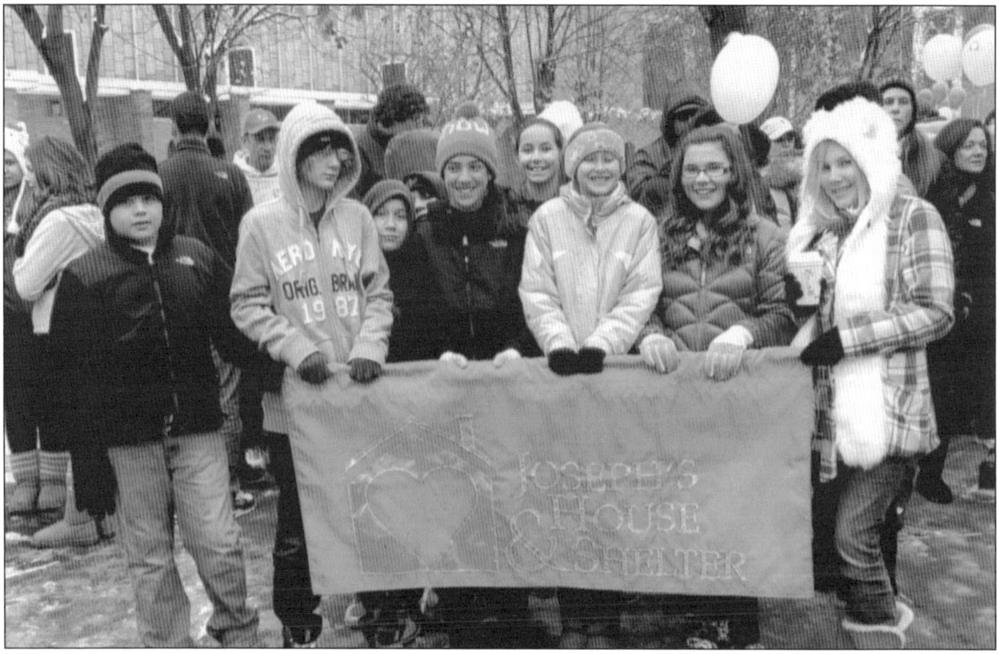

Young supporters of Joseph's House & Shelter gather to begin the annual Winter Walk for the Homeless with their traditional walk through the streets of downtown Troy. The walk, which is now planned to begin and end at Little Italy's outdoor MarketPlace on Hill Street, is a major fundraiser for the shelter. (Courtesy of Joseph's House & Shelter.)

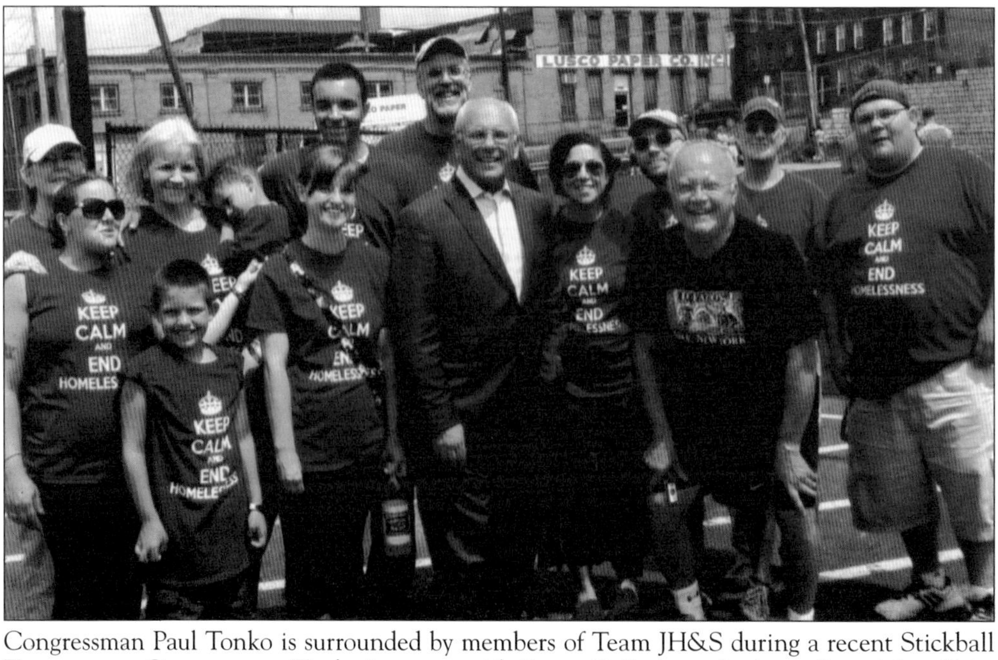

Congressman Paul Tonko is surrounded by members of Team JH&S during a recent Stickball Tournament. Congressman Tonko is center, with Rocco DeFazio to the immediate right of him in the foreground. In the crowd behind him are Agnes Zink and Kevin O'Connor, executive director of Joseph's House & Shelter. (Courtesy of Joseph's House & Shelter.)

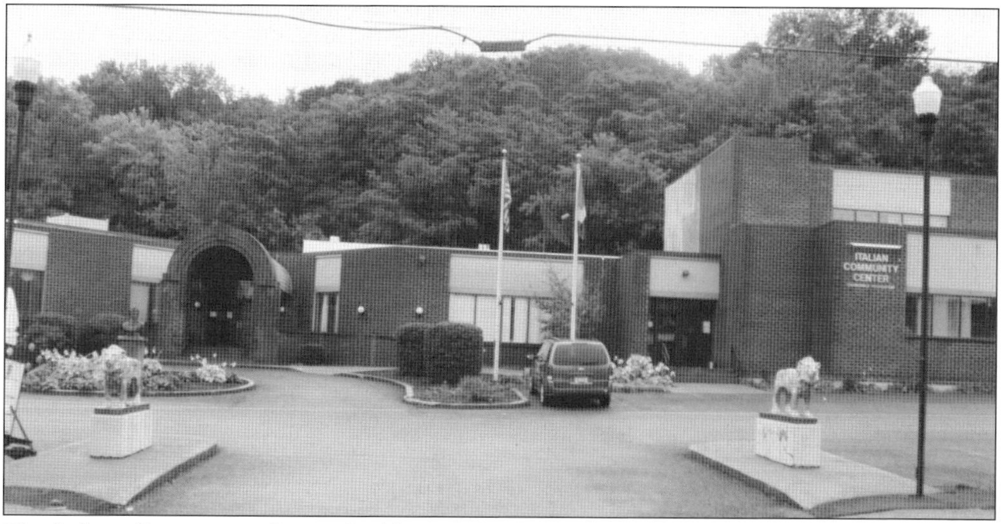

The Italian Community Center building was a joint project by Troy architect Vincent Lepara and contractor Louis Bianchi. The new center was built in 1983 on the site of the former John Stanton Brewery at 1450 Fifth Avenue. It serves the needs of its members, but also is the site of a variety of events, including weddings, banquets, community meetings, and dinner theater productions. (Courtesy of the Italian Community Center.)

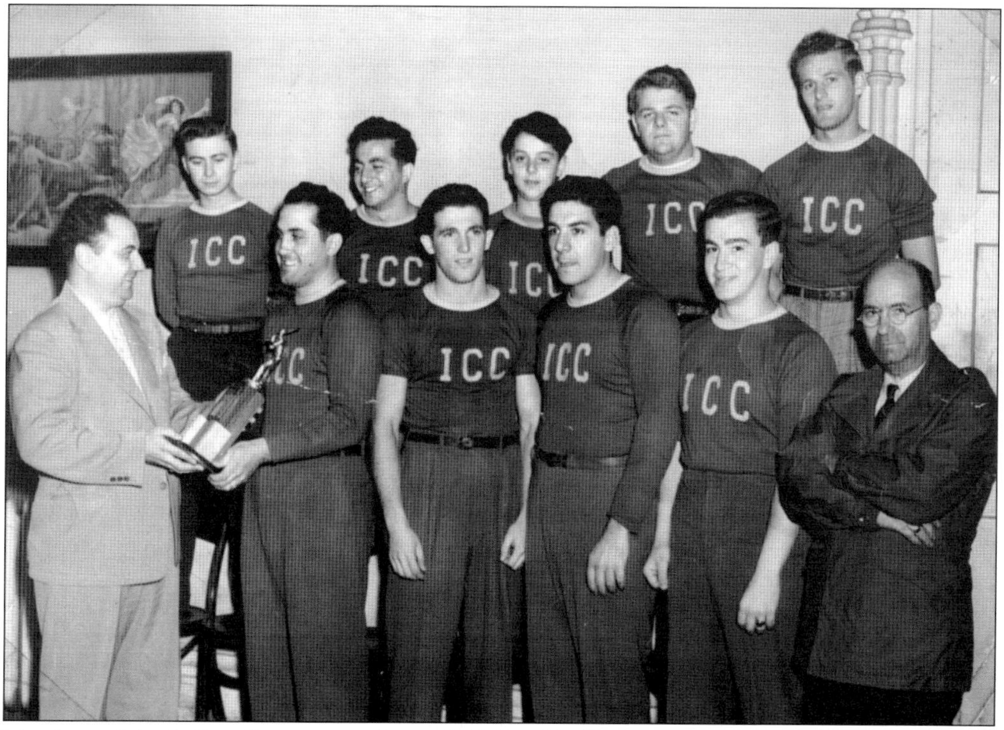

Members of the Italian Community Center's 1948 softball team receive a trophy from the center's president, Eugene Bizzarro. From left to right are (first row) Bizzarro, Lozette Marchese, Charles Abrunza, Anthony Lanzillo, Marco Zucaro, and Anthony Cioffi; (second row) William Pascarell, Charles Marchese, Patrick "Buster" Martone, Charles Testo, and Louis Cioffi. (Courtesy of John DeLorenzo.)

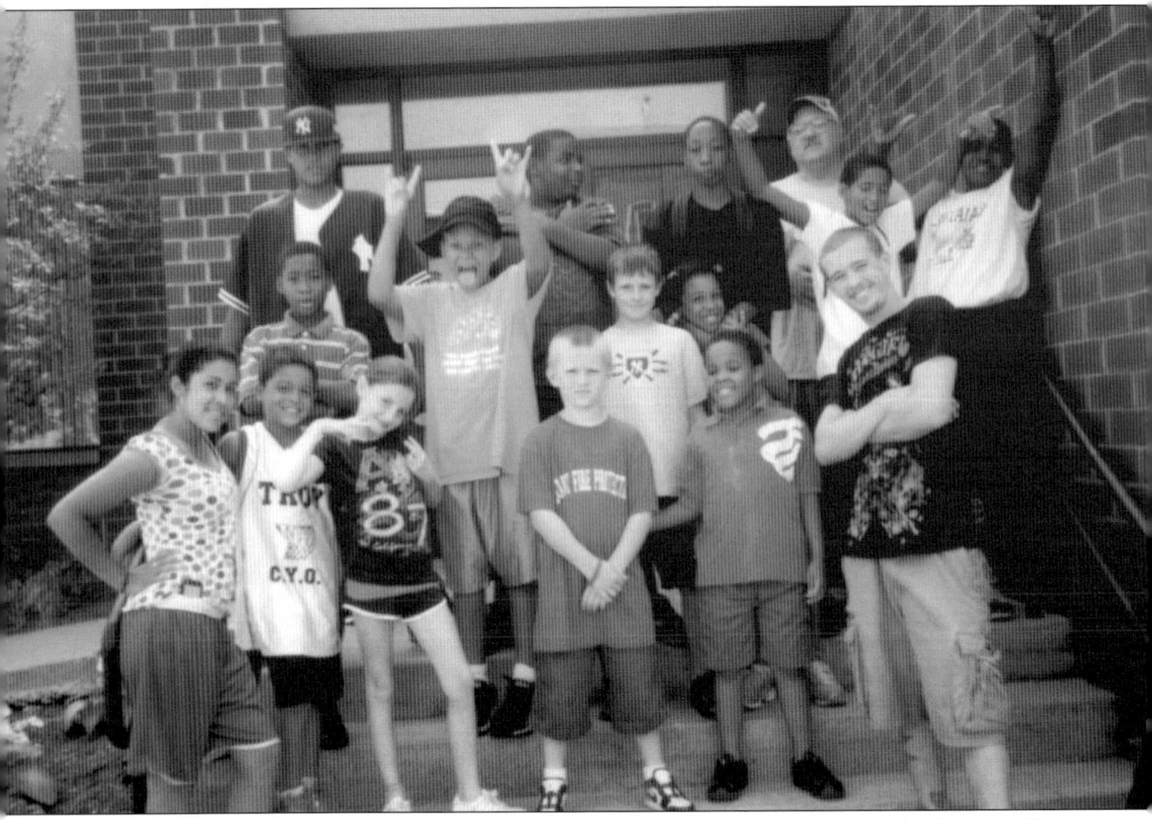

Area youngsters participating in the summer recreation program known as the Drop in Center leave the ICC after playing bocce. The program is cosponsored by Troy Little Italy and several community partners, including the Italian Community Center, the Troy Youth Association's CYO Center, Troy's Community Police unit, and the Rensselaer County Sheriff's Department. Youngsters between the ages of 12 and 16 participate in organized play at baseball, stickball, basketball, and bocce at the Hill Street MarketPlace, ICC, and CYO Center. Arrangements are also made for day trips to local lakes and the Tri City ValleyCats baseball stadium. Each youngster is provided with snacks and a free lunch. The summer recreation program runs from mid-July to mid-August, 9:30 a.m. to 4:00 p.m., Monday through Friday. (Courtesy of Marion Field.)

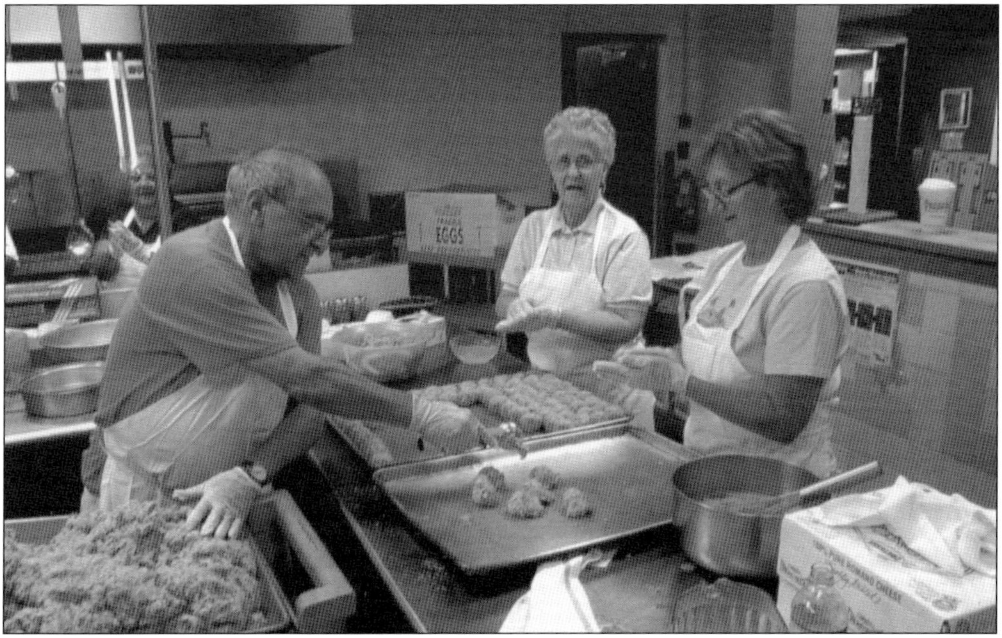

Kitchen staffs are an important and necessary part of the operation of the Italian Community Center. From left to right are Jean Sestito, Michael Dinova, Rita Taddeo, and Ann Stafford. Since St. Mary's Church closed, the ICC and former parishioners continue to operate the weekly soup kitchen and the Election Eve spaghetti/ziti supper initially sponsored by the church. (Courtesy of the Italian Community Center.)

Each year, members of the Italian Community Center dressed in the uniform of the Carabinieri—the national military police of Italy—and form a color guard to precede their Flag Day parade float and the drum and bugle corps sponsored by the center. From left to right are Martino Tedesco, Dominick Mamone, Vincent Mamone, Paul Zelenke, and Nicholas Casale. (Courtesy of the Italian Community Center.)

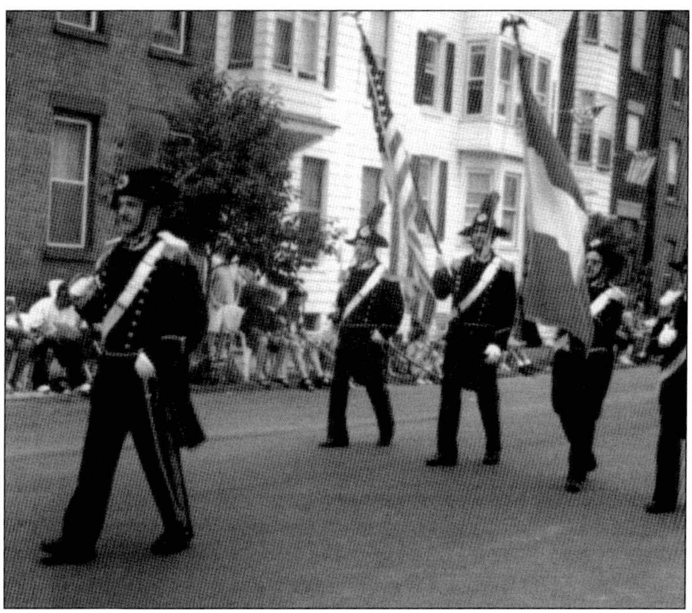

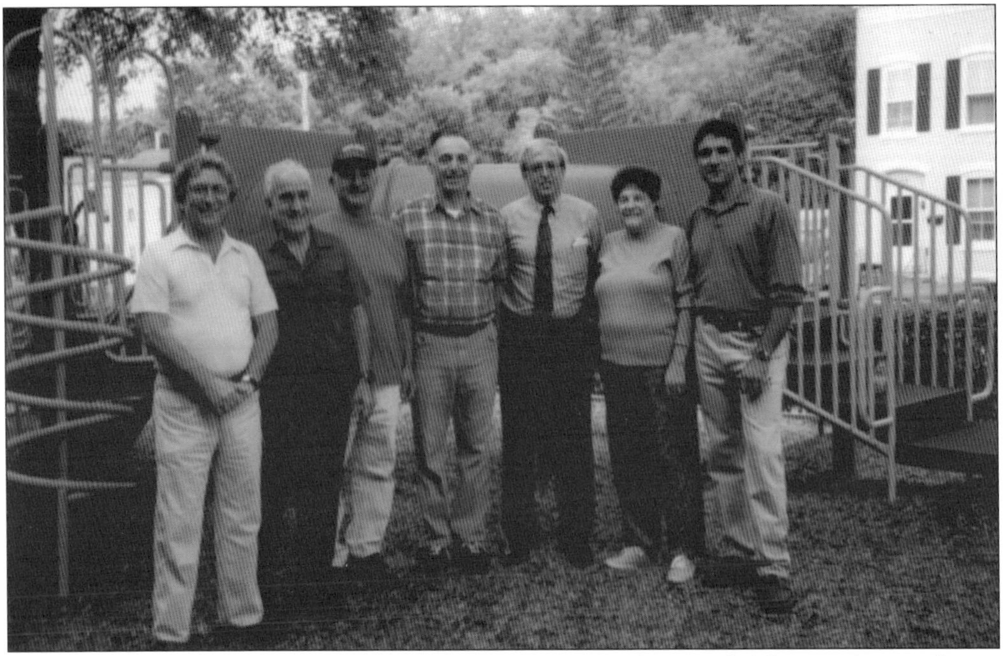

Members of the Italian Community Center gather for a group photograph following the installation of playground equipment that they donated to Unity House Sunshine Day Care Center. From left to right are Rocco Sorriento, Louis Pisaniello, Dominick Bevevino, Joseph Taddeo, Joseph Mazzariello, Catherine (Rea) Esposito, and Vincent Mamone. (Courtesy of the Italian Community Center.)

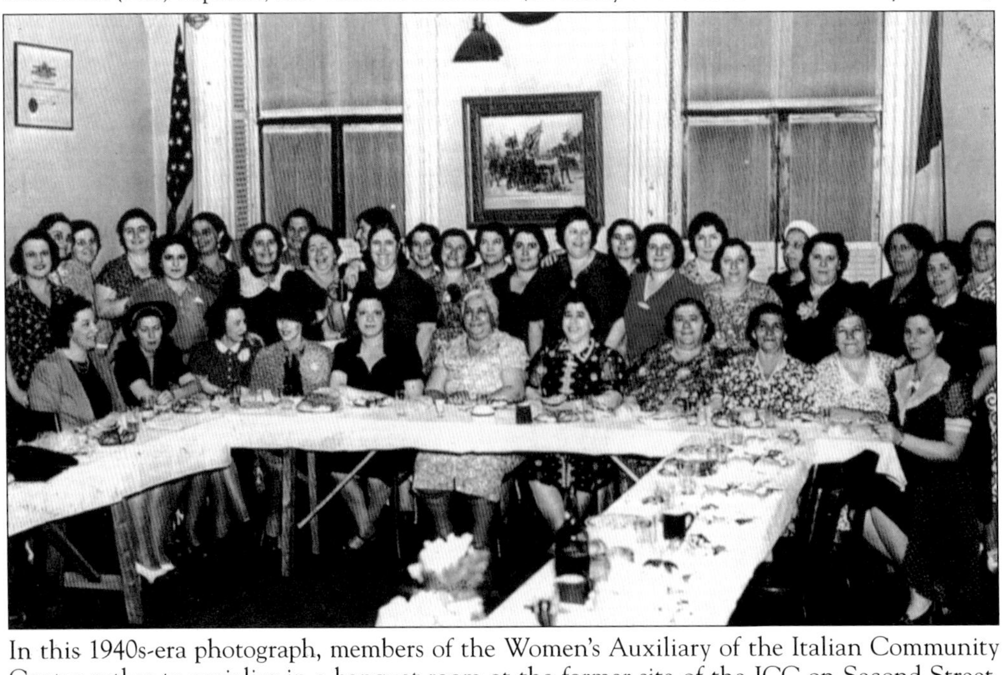

In this 1940s-era photograph, members of the Women's Auxiliary of the Italian Community Center gather to socialize in a banquet room at the former site of the ICC on Second Street. The motto of the auxiliary is a simple prayer: "Lord help us in all the work we do, Lord help us to be sincere and true to our club, ourselves and our community." (Courtesy of the Italian Community Center.)

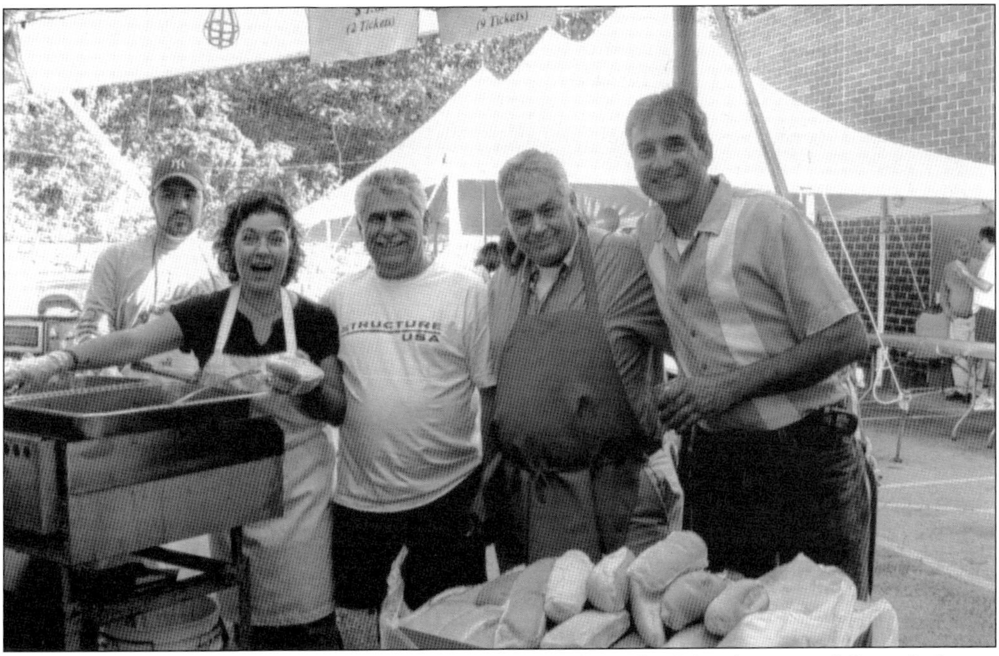

Members of the Italian Community Center prepare ethnic food for the annual Festa Italiana. From left to right are Peter Testa, his parents Debra and Peter Testa, Dominic Carridi, and Vincent Mamone. The first Italian *festa* in Troy was held in 1906. (Courtesy of Marion Field.)

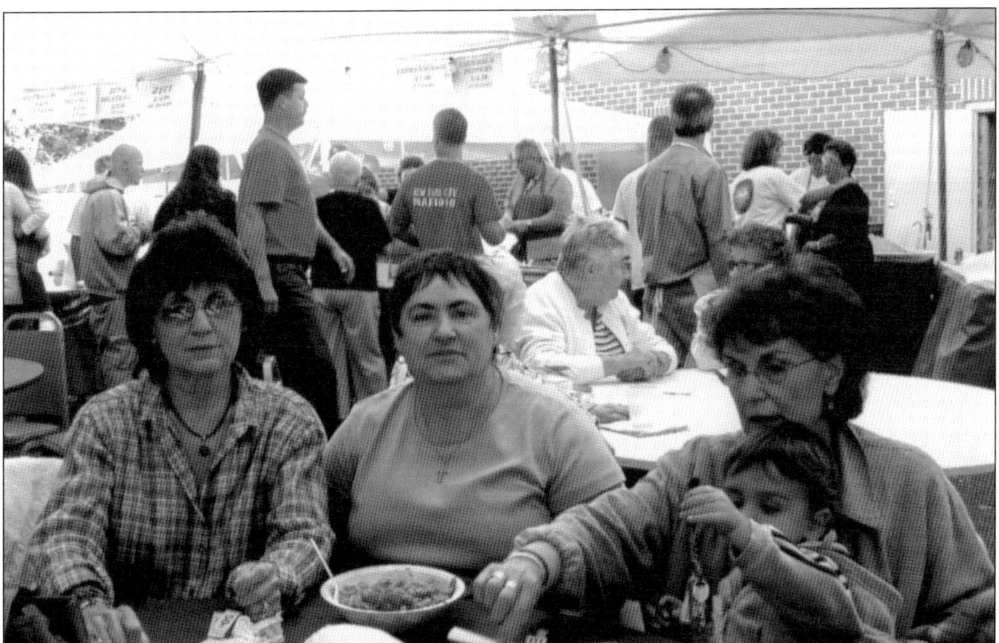

Hundreds of people enjoy an evening at the Festa Italiana, which features Italian food, desserts, beverages, music, games of chance, games and rides for children, raffles, and Italian souvenirs. From left to right are Geraldine (Pitanillo) Montello, Nancy (Teta) Ishkanian, Catherine (Pitanillo) Kuentzel, and her grandson Genero Pitanillo. (Courtesy of Marion Field.)

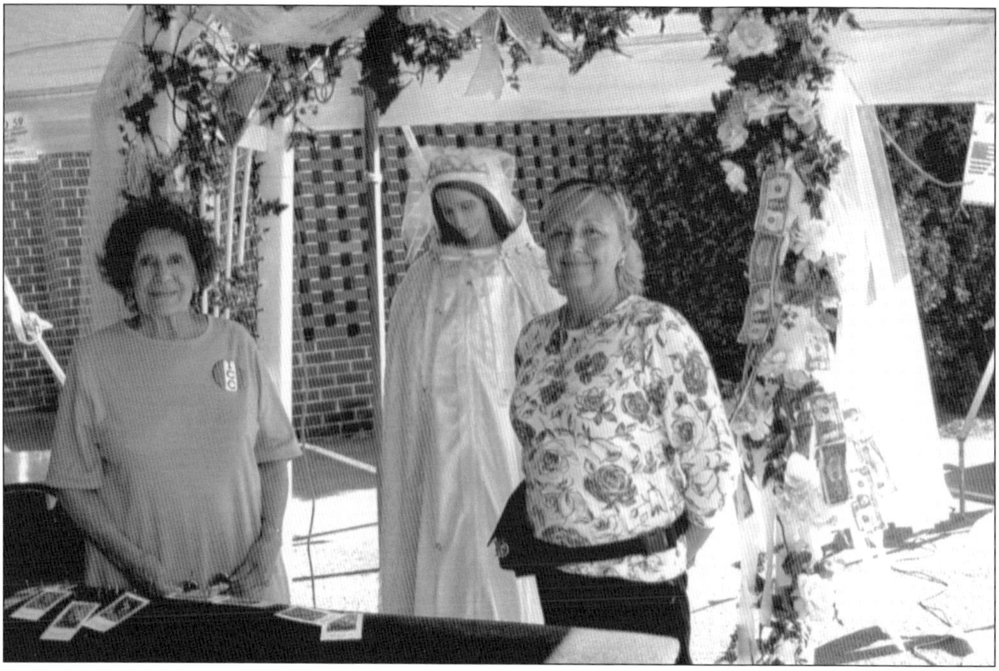

Italian Community Center members Josephine (Rea) Ostwald (left) and Annette (Rizzo) Sanders greet Festa goers at the entrance to the annual event. In the background is a statue of the Virgin Mary, carried through the streets of Little Italy. Many Italian enclaves in American cities observe the tradition of honoring a particular saint, such as San Gennaro, Our Lady of Mount Carmel, St. Rocco, and Saints Cosmos and Damian. (Courtesy of the Italian Community Center.)

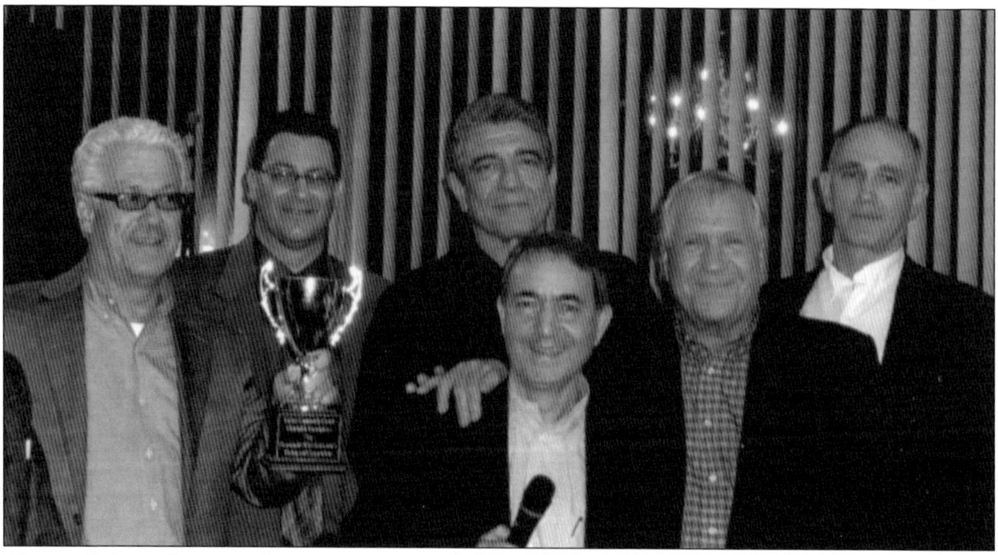

The tradition of winemaking is encouraged through the Italian Community Center's Annual Homemade Wine Enthusiast's Tasting and Competition. From left to right are (first row) Dominick Russomanno and Robert Caprara; (second row) Peter Hanley (with trophy), Michael Cazzato, Steve Ercole, and Jeff Anderson. Prominent area chefs, food and wine critics, and homebrewing experts judge the formal competition, and the event also includes seminars on winemaking techniques. (Courtesy of Vincent Mamone.)

Five

Our Great Good Place

The centerpiece of Little Italy's revitalization is the former site of the outdoor public market on Hill Street. In his 1989 book, *The Great Good Place*, author and sociologist Ray Oldenburg recalls "those happy gathering places a community may contain where unrelated people relate. Much to the detriment of our lives, these great good places are vanishing from the urban American landscape." Residents of Troy's Little Italy have vivid, happy memories of the market and easily agree that it qualifies as a "great good place."

There are several stories that can be told of the 1.2-acre plot of land between Liberty, Hill, and Washington Streets and Fifth Avenue. Its earliest use was as a stoneware factory, from 1813 to 1837. From 1848 to 1899, it was the location of the Troy Gas Light Company. The company sold the property to the city of Troy in July 1899 after they relocated their complex. In 1918, the city opened the Troy Public Retail Market, which continued until the 1950s. In November 1975, when the city sold the property to the Troy News Company, the lot was surrounded by a chain-link fence, topped with barbed wire, which protected the company's parked trucks.

In 2002, the city reclaimed ownership of the site through the encouragement and planning efforts of the Friends of Little Italy. Once again, the space is a public place where people of all ages gather to enjoy an informal public life in the center of one of Troy's oldest and most historic neighborhoods.

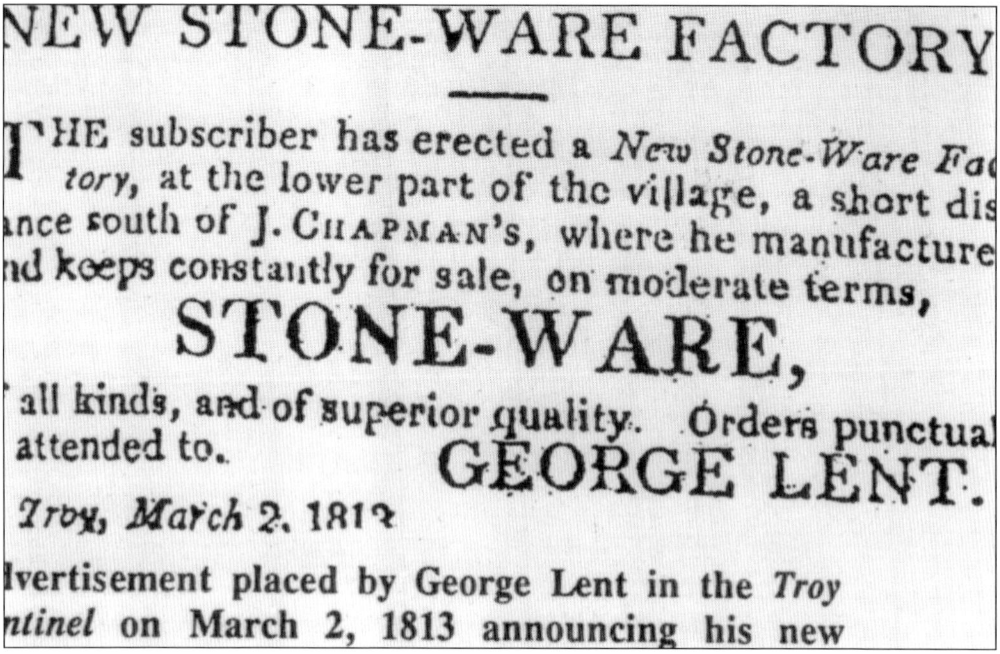

NEW STONE-WARE FACTORY

THE subscriber has erected a *New Stone-Ware Fa*
tory, at the lower part of the village, a short dis
ance south of J. CHAPMAN's, where he manufacture
nd keeps constantly for sale, on moderate terms,

STONE-WARE,

all kinds, and of superior quality. Orders punctua
attended to.

GEORGE LENT.

Troy, March 2. 181

lvertisement placed by George Lent in the *Troy*
ntinel on March 2, 1813 announcing his new

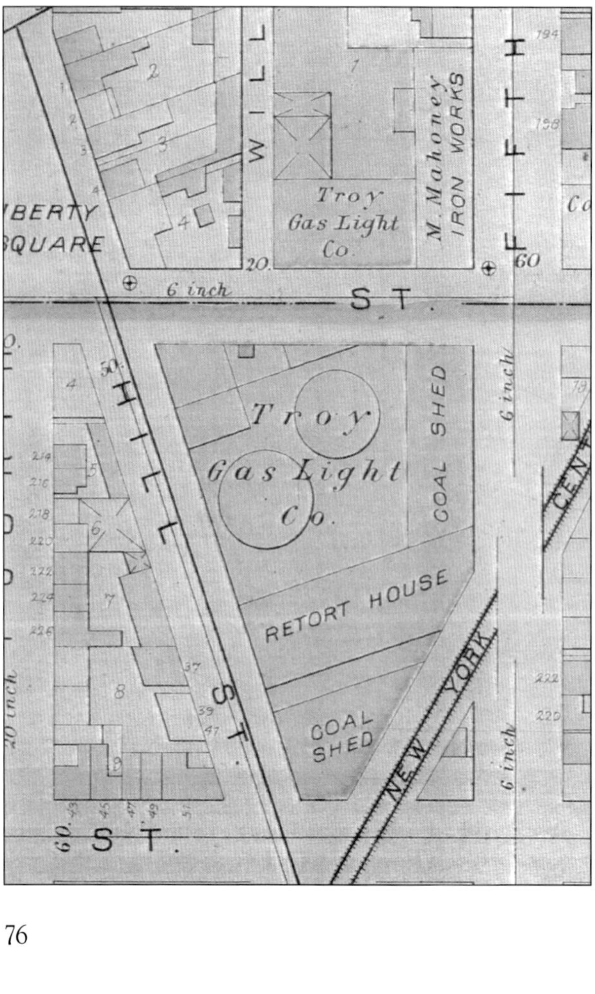

Local potter George Lent advertised a new factory in the *Troy Centennial* on March 2, 1813. The stoneware factory operated from 1813 to 1837, when a major Mount Ida landslide took the lives of several people and destroyed the pottery works. (Courtesy of the Troy Public Library.)

The *City Atlas of Troy* shows the layout of the Troy Gas Light Company facility located on Hill Street from 1848 to 1899. The act to incorporate the company was passed by the New York State Legislature on February 16, 1848. The capital stock was $100,000. Of this, $11,000 was taken by the citizens of Troy, and the remainder was claimed by the citizens of Philadelphia. (Courtesy of Rensselaer County Historical Society.)

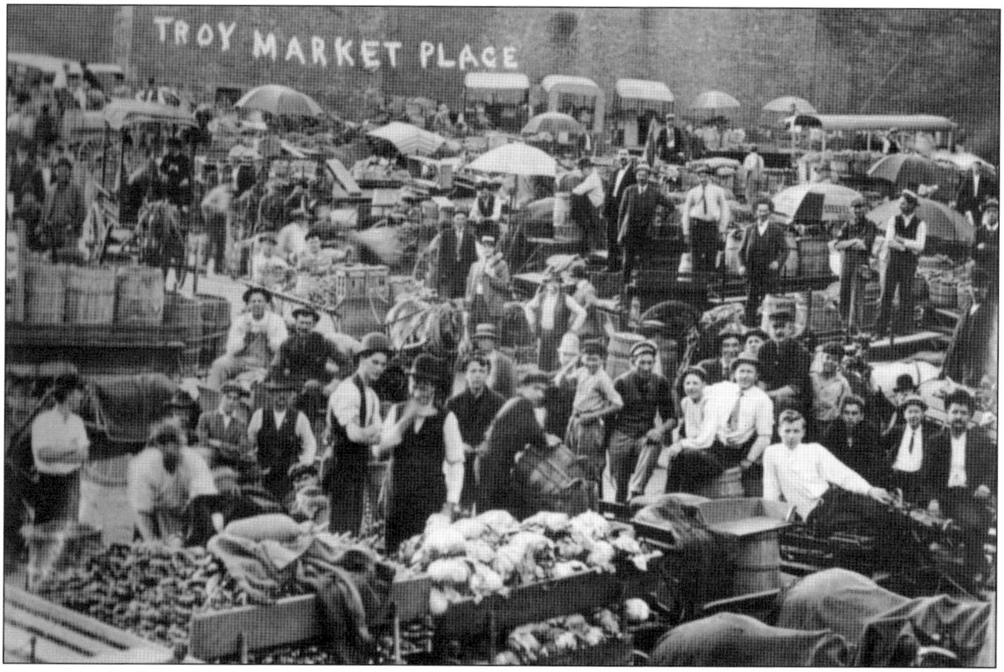

Between 1905 and 1920, several successful produce establishments opened along the west side of Hill Street, from Liberty to Washington Streets. Women of the city expressed a great interest in the establishment of a retail farmers' market in the huge vacant lot across the street from the wholesale produce businesses. On July 5, 1918, the Troy Public Retail Market opened with 150 stalls of produce from area farmers. (Courtesy of Rensselaer County Historical Society.)

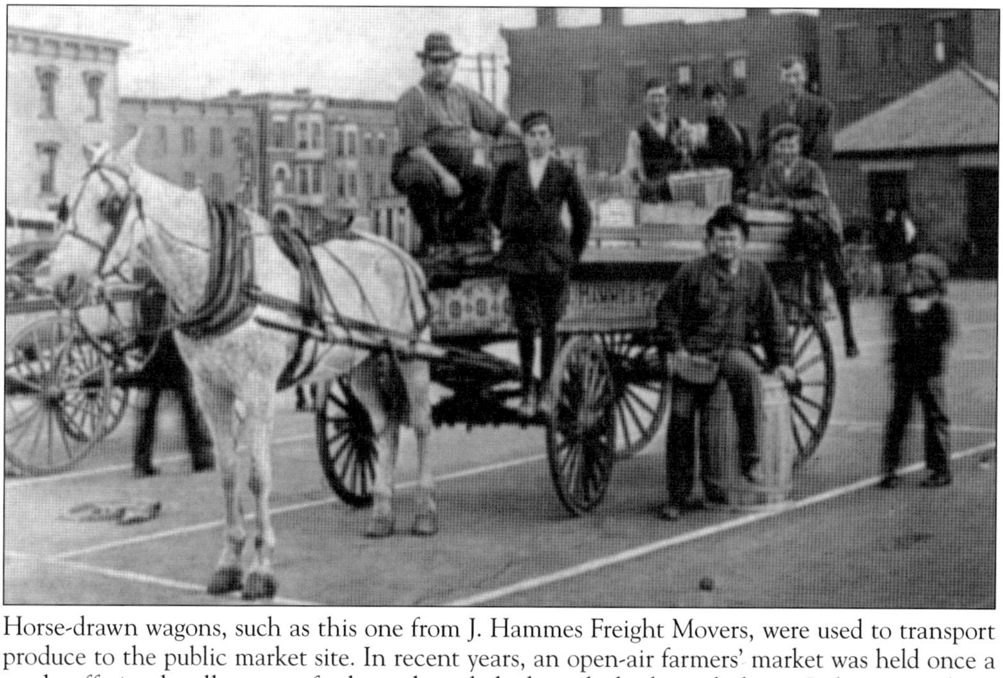

Horse-drawn wagons, such as this one from J. Hammes Freight Movers, were used to transport produce to the public market site. In recent years, an open-air farmers' market was held once a week, offering locally grown fresh produce, baked goods, herbs and plants, Italian specialties, cheese, gourmet spreads, and handcrafted arts. (Courtesy of Donald Gardner.)

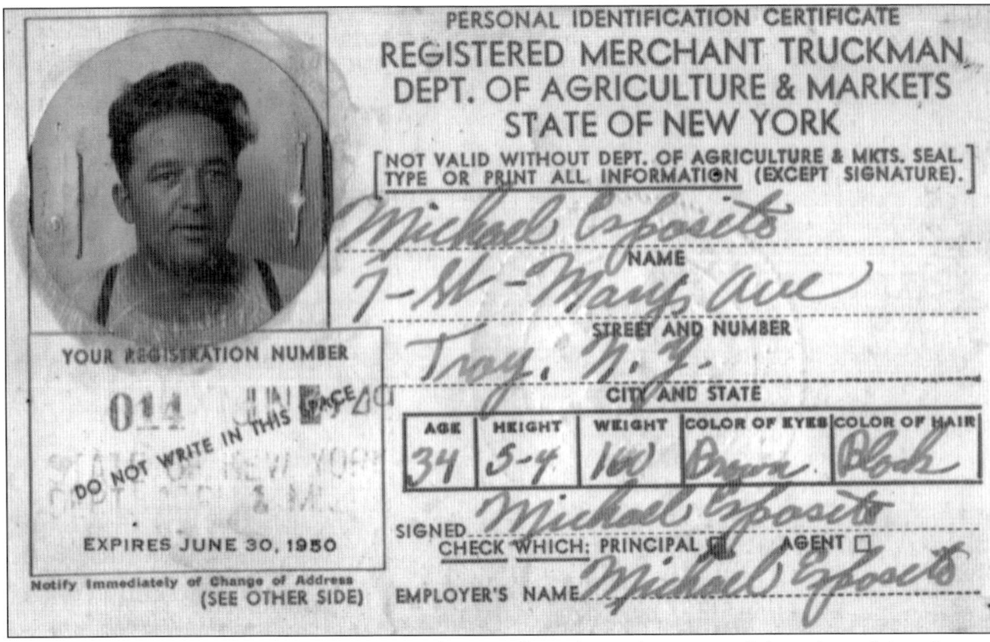
PERSONAL IDENTIFICATION CERTIFICATE
REGISTERED MERCHANT TRUCKMAN
DEPT. OF AGRICULTURE & MARKETS
STATE OF NEW YORK
[NOT VALID WITHOUT DEPT. OF AGRICULTURE & MKTS. SEAL.
TYPE OR PRINT ALL INFORMATION (EXCEPT SIGNATURE).]

Michael Esposito
NAME
7-St-Marys Ave
STREET AND NUMBER
Troy, N.Y.
CITY AND STATE

AGE	HEIGHT	WEIGHT	COLOR OF EYES	COLOR OF HAIR
34	5-4	160	Brown	Black

SIGNED Michael Esposito
CHECK WHICH: PRINCIPAL ☒ AGENT ☐
EMPLOYER'S NAME Michael Esposito

YOUR REGISTRATION NUMBER
014
DO NOT WRITE IN THIS SPACE
EXPIRES JUNE 30, 1950
Notify Immediately of Change of Address
(SEE OTHER SIDE)

The New York State Department of Agriculture and Markets administered the sale and distribution of produce. They issued this license to the author's father, Michael. From the 1920s through the 1950s, over a dozen neighborhood men made their living peddling fruits and vegetables from their trucks. (Author's collection.)

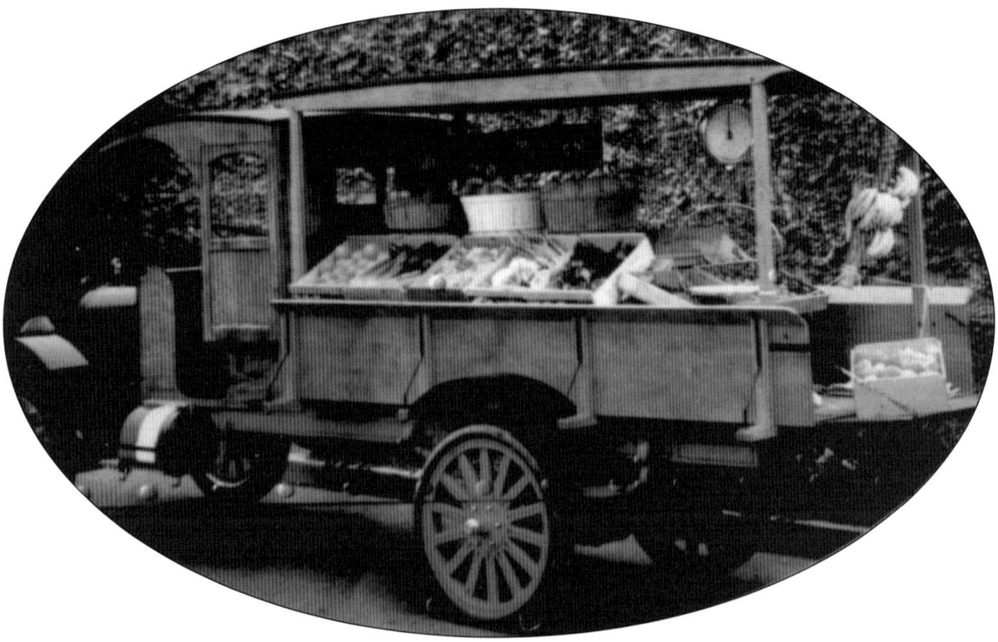

Neighbors had access to fresh produce, thanks to peddlers such as John Farron of C&S Produce, who started working in the business at the age of 10 in the old public market on Hill Street. In 1967, Farron bought into a partnership established over 60 years ago by Ray Cipperley and Joe Sacala at 37 Hill Street. He retired in 2010. His white panel truck, stenciled with a reproduction of the original truck, is a reminder of the peddler tradition. (Courtesy of John Farron.)

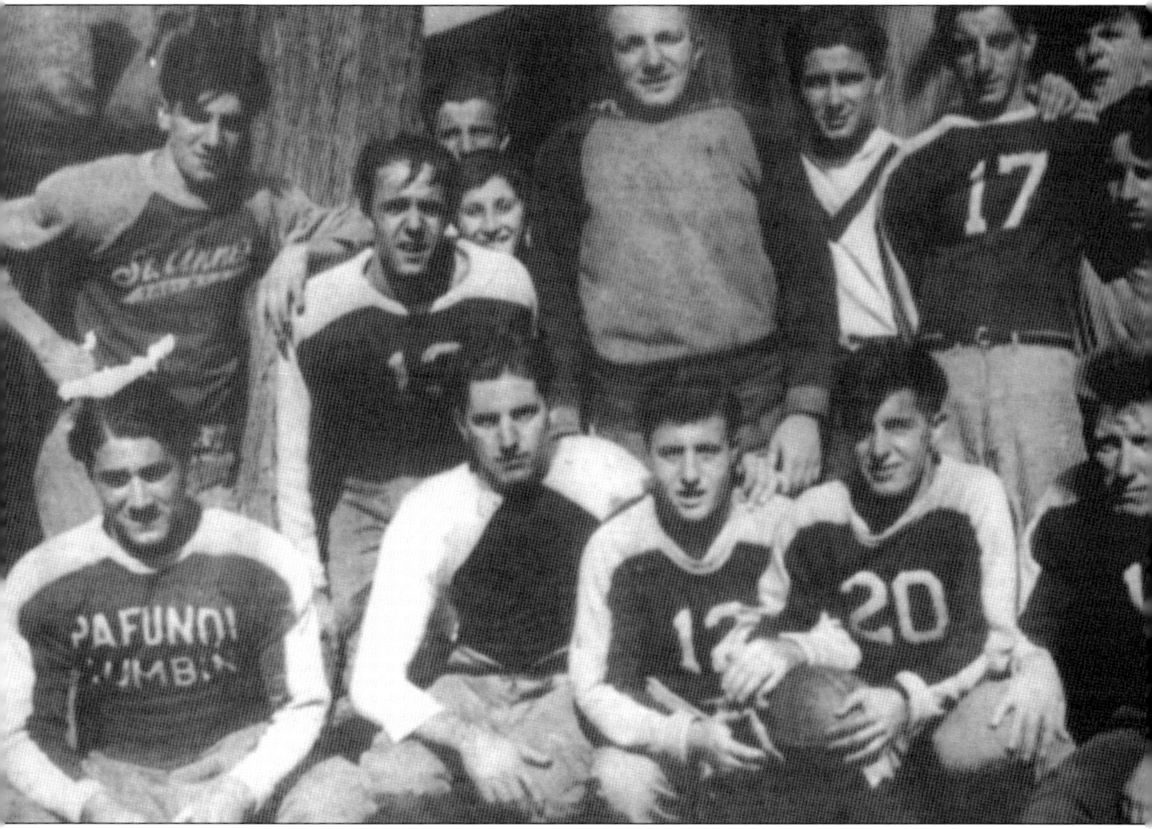

A group of neighborhood athletes, known as the Fifth Avenue Ramblers, gather for this 1936 team photograph. From left to right are (first row) Dominick Potenza, Martin Cardenuto, Joseph Debboli, Michael Clemente, and unidentified; (second row) Albert Deeb, T. Cocco, unidentified, Francis Villa, Vincent Ciarlone, Joseph Mariano, Daniel Cocco, and Francis Cardenuto. Nicholas Mariano can be seen at the very back, alongside the tree. Residents fondly remember the market as their year-round playground. Its huge space was an open invitation to youngsters to play, meet friends, and hang out and a perfect place for bicycle riding and handball. (Courtesy of Robert Riley.)

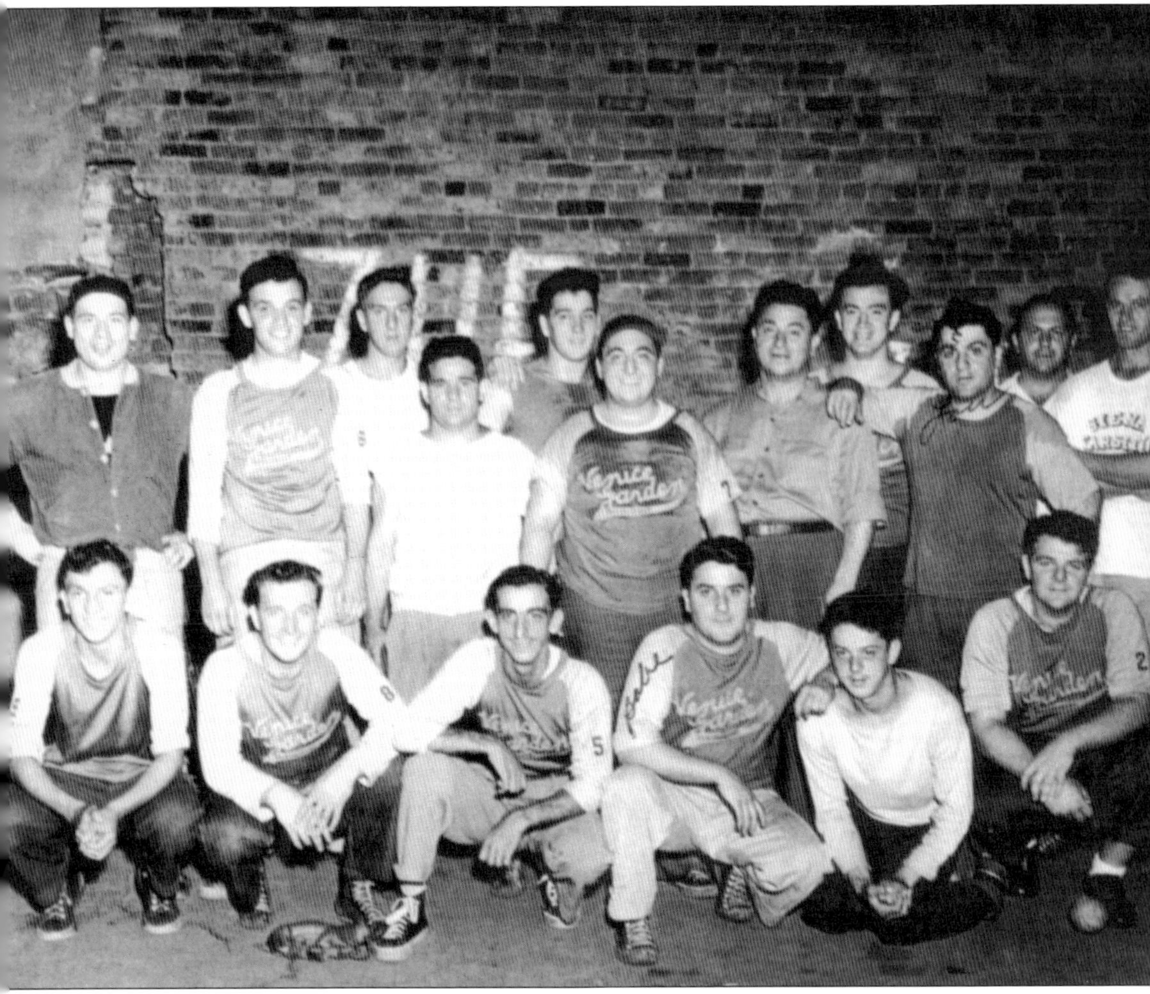

Rocco Valenti's Venice Garden tavern, located at 123 Ferry Street, was one of many local businesses that sponsored the softball teams that played regularly in the old public market site. From left to right are (first row) O'Neil Valente, unidentified, Joseph "Buff" Mariano, Anthony "Babe" DeLucia, Patrick "Buster" Martone, and Charles Testo; (second row) unidentified, Lawrence Moscatello, Louis Lanzillo, John Cardenuto, Anthony "Butch" Bucciero, Frank "Gigi" Marchese, Rocco Valenti, Marco Zucaro, Louis DeLucia, unidentified, and Louis Cioffi. Most of the ball players were from the neighborhood. Hundreds of people would attend the games. A popular treat at the games was Italian ice, which sold for 5¢ a cup. (Courtesy of Anthony DeLucia.)

An unidentified peddler prepares to start his workday. Many neighborhood youngsters who played in the old market place on Hill Street, or on any of the streets in Little Italy, saw people at work on a daily basis, such as peddlers, laborers, tradesmen, small business owners, tailors, shoe repairmen, bakers, and more. (Author's collection.)

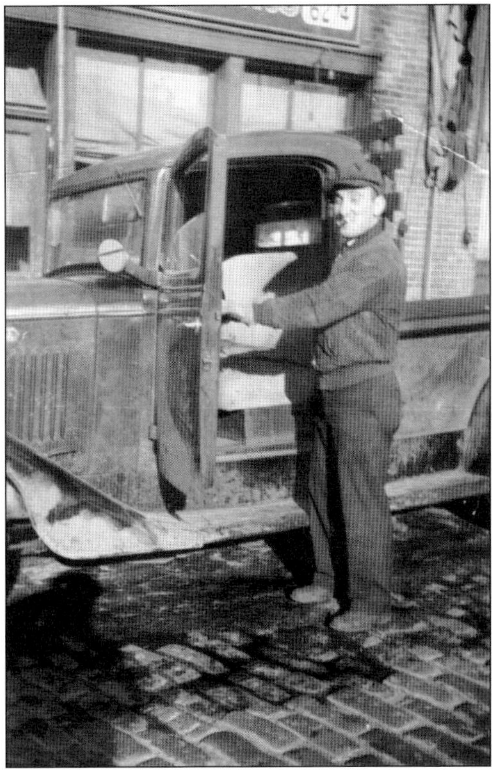

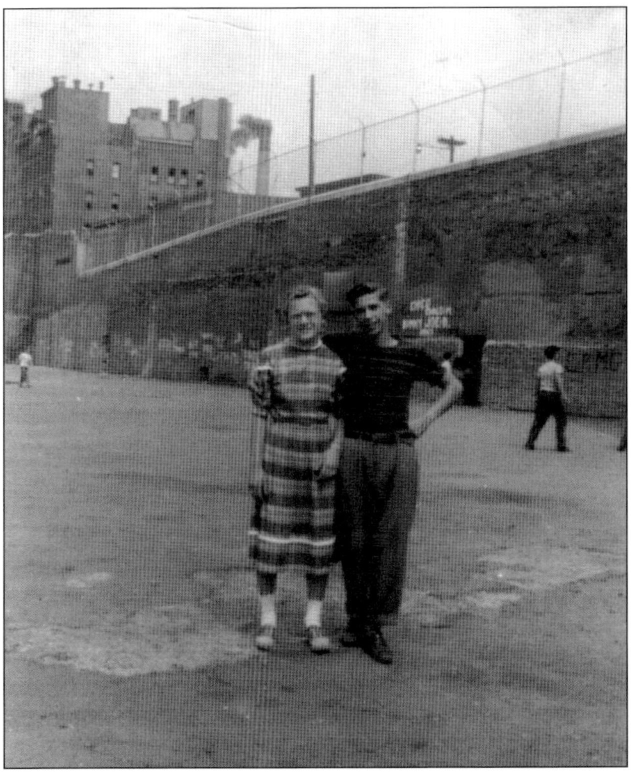

Standing in the center of the former Hill Street public market is Mary (Valente) Bevevino and Philip "Philo" Germano. Youngsters in the background are playing softball and basketball. The building in the upper portion of the photograph is the John S. Stanton Brewery, which was demolished after a disastrous fire in the mid-1950s. (Courtesy of Jean Turriglio Cavallo.)

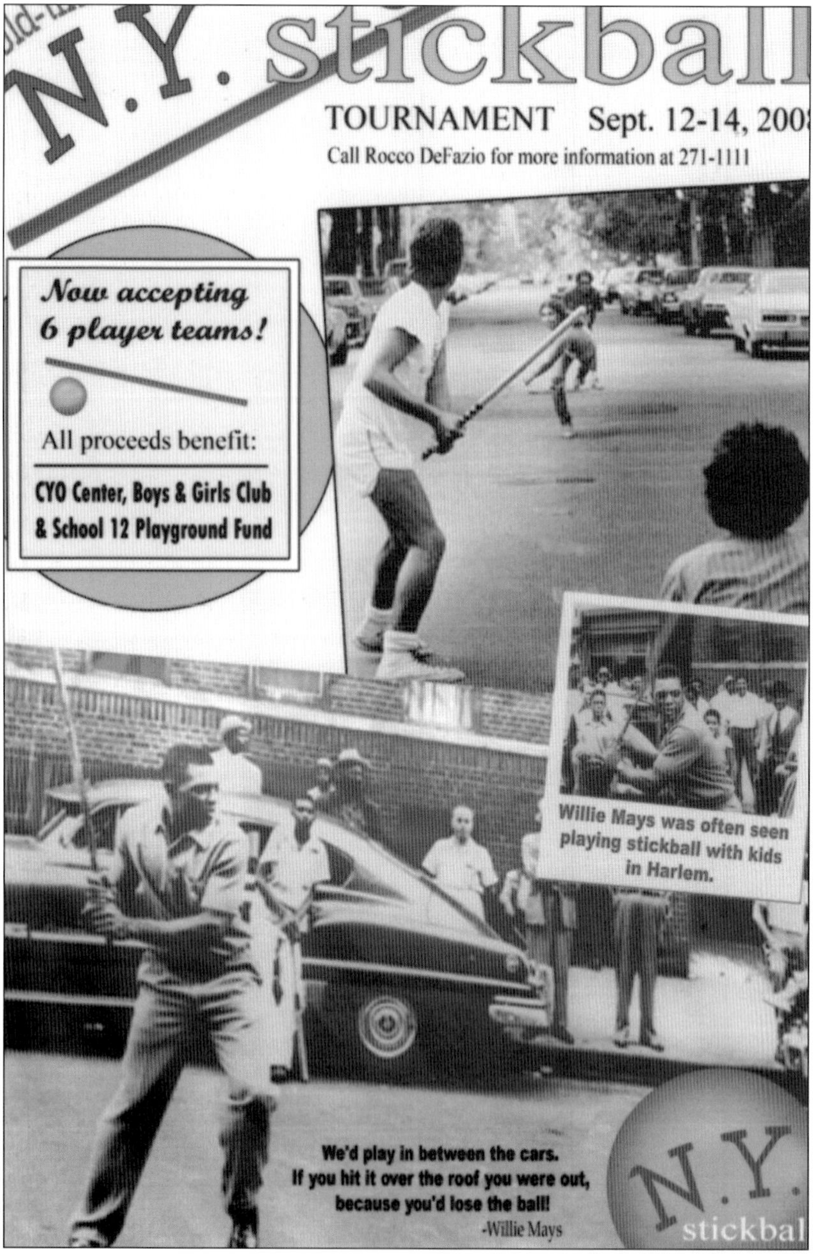

Local entrepreneur Vic Christopher, an enthusiastic supporter of stickball, assisted Fourth Street businessman Rocco DeFazio in organizing the 2008 return of stickball to the market site where locals played in years past. Christopher played the street game as a child in Brooklyn. Stickball was one of the more popular of the inner-city street games. The three basic forms of stickball are traditional fast pitching against a wall, self-hitting, and one-bounce pitching, which is the form used in local tournaments. The annual spring tournaments have raised thousands of dollars in money and canned goods for the local food pantries. The National Association of Letter Carriers, Branch 358, the Association of Retarded Children (ARC), and the Uniform Firefighters Association are among the major contributors and collectors of perishable goods for the event. (Courtesy of Rocco DeFazio.)

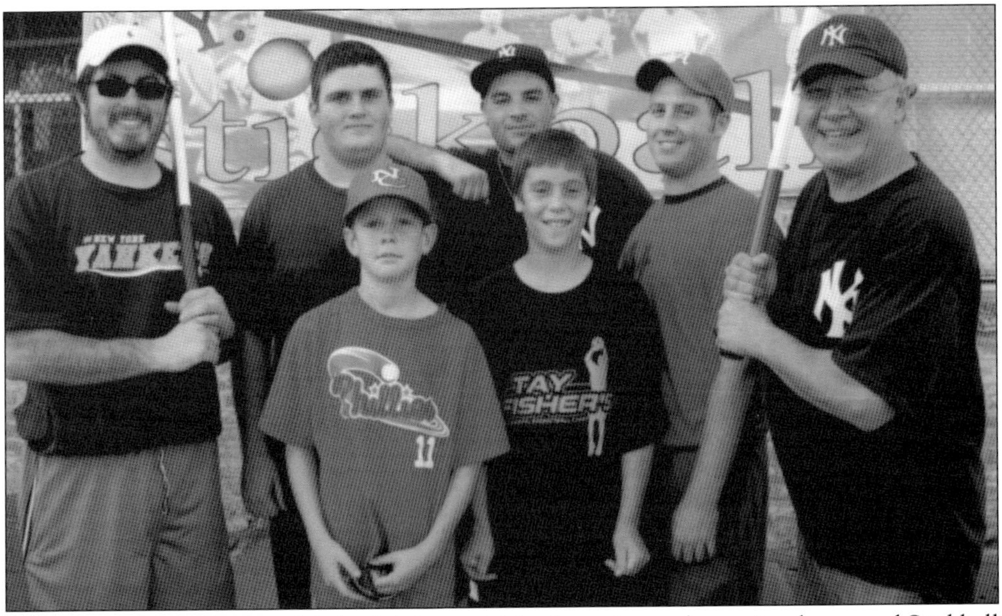

Rocco DeFazio and his sons Michael, John, and Matthew plan and organize the annual Stickball Tournament. High school and college students, local newscasters, nonprofit organizations, local businesses, policemen, fireman, and neighborhood groups all form teams. Team DeFazio members are, from left to right, (first row) Patrick and Connor McCaffery and Matthew and Rocco DeFazio; (second row) Michael and John DeFazio and Michael Butler. (Courtesy of Marion Field.)

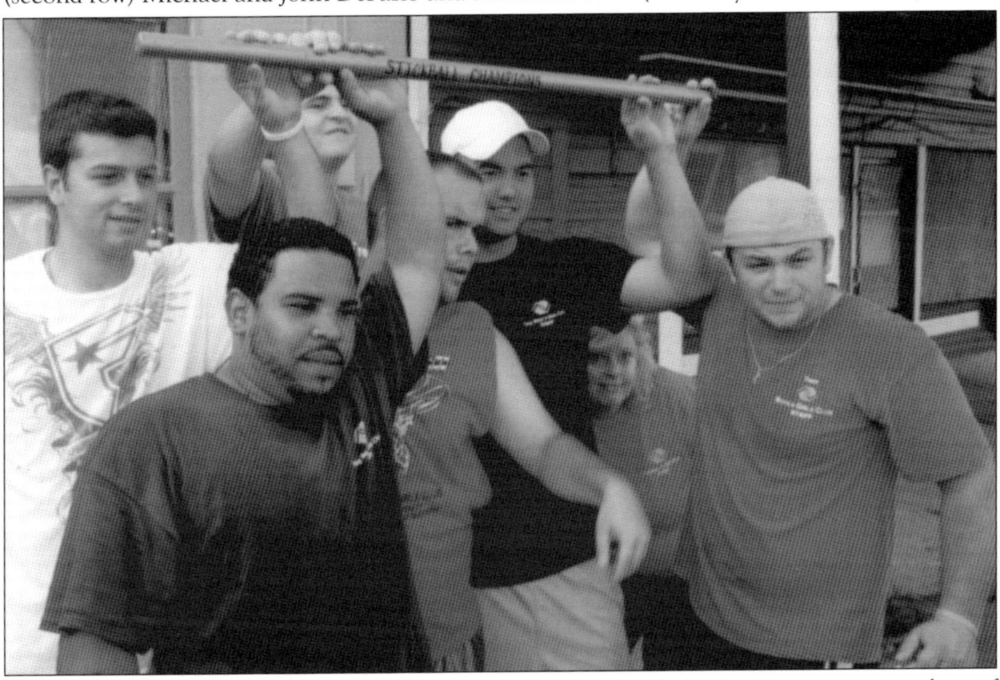

Posing proudly with the Golden Stick bat awarded at the Stickball Tournament are members of the team from the Troy Boys and Girls Club (TBGC), including Patrick Doyle, John Salve, Roger Cuascat, Carlos Maldonado, Nicholas Thomas, Louis Dodge, James Rogers, and Sharon Smith, executive director of the TBGC. (Courtesy of Marion Field.)

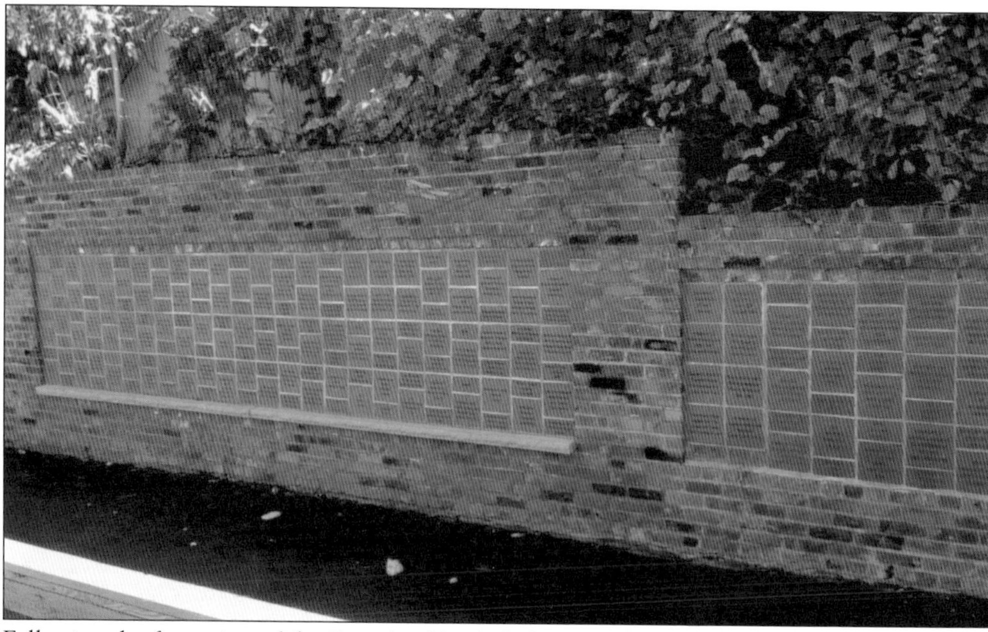

Following the formation of the Friends of Little Italy, an early order of business was a plan for a memorial wall honoring past residents. Rick Sloat of King Fuels donated red bricks from a former South End Troy factory that employed many Italian immigrants and their sons. Troy masons volunteered to set 200 new redbrick tiles, purchased by family members. More than 600 names are inscribed on the tiles. (Photograph by Andrea Daley.)

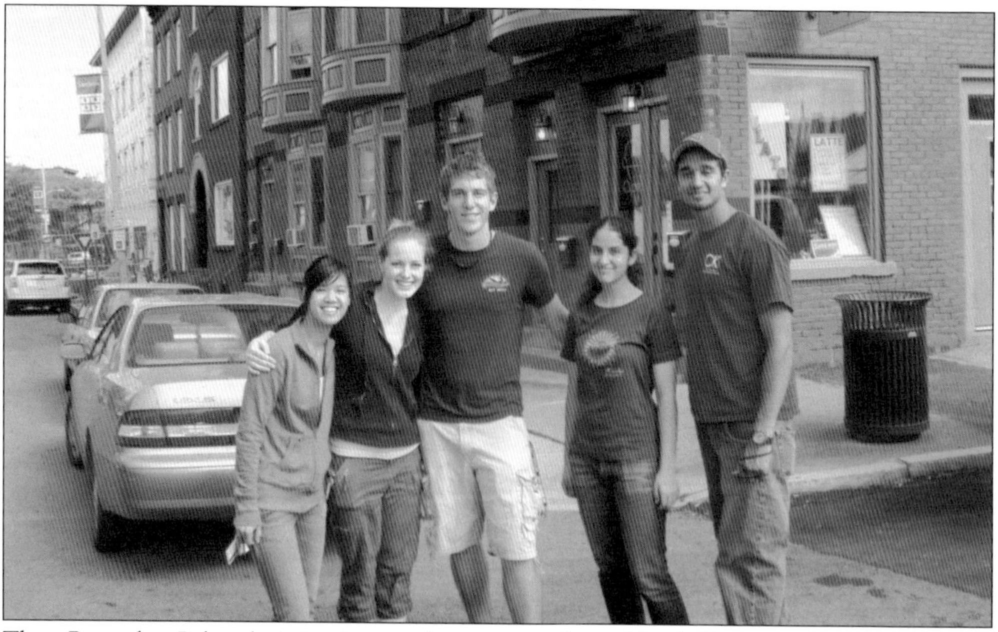

These Rensselaer Polytechnic Institute students are members of Circle K, an international collegiate service organization sponsored by Kiwanis International that promotes service, leadership, and fellowship. The student volunteers work at events in the MarketPlace. They pitch tents, place tables and chairs, install exhibit displays, clean up, paint, distribute brochures, and assist youngsters with arts and crafts activities. (Photograph by Joe Popson.)

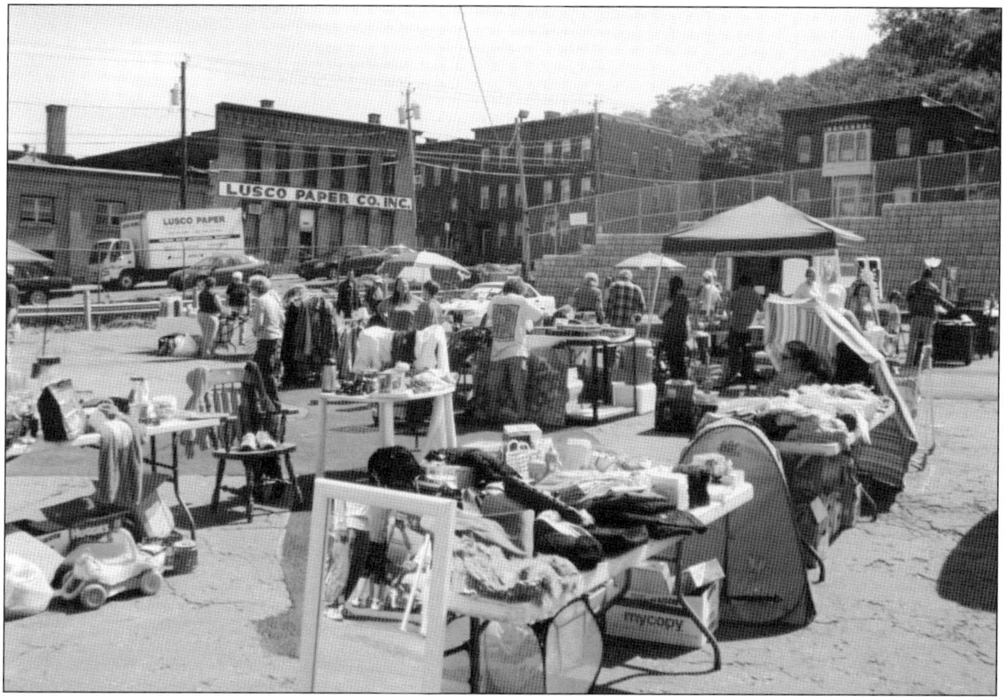

The Hill Street MarketPlace site is a busy place, attracting hundreds of people who attend its family-friendly events, which include popular citywide flea markets and garage sales. Dozens of individual stalls offer everything, from curios and antiques to cut-rate merchandise. (Photograph by Joe Popson.)

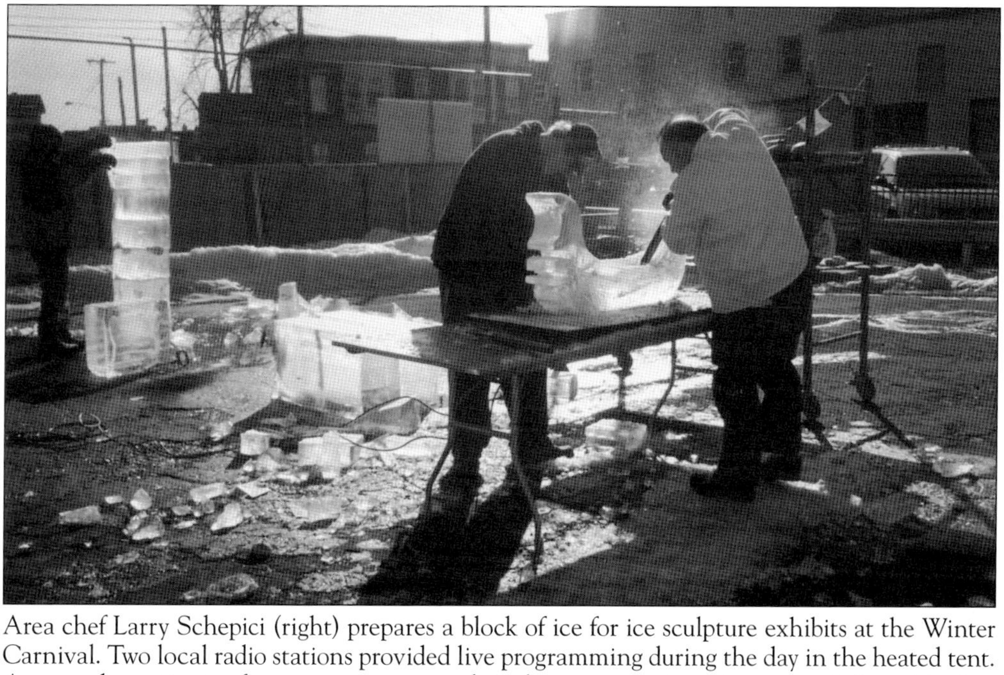

Area chef Larry Schepici (right) prepares a block of ice for ice sculpture exhibits at the Winter Carnival. Two local radio stations provided live programming during the day in the heated tent. Among the activities for youngsters was a short but competitive winter run, followed by hot chocolate and caramel kettle corn. (Courtesy of Marion Field.)

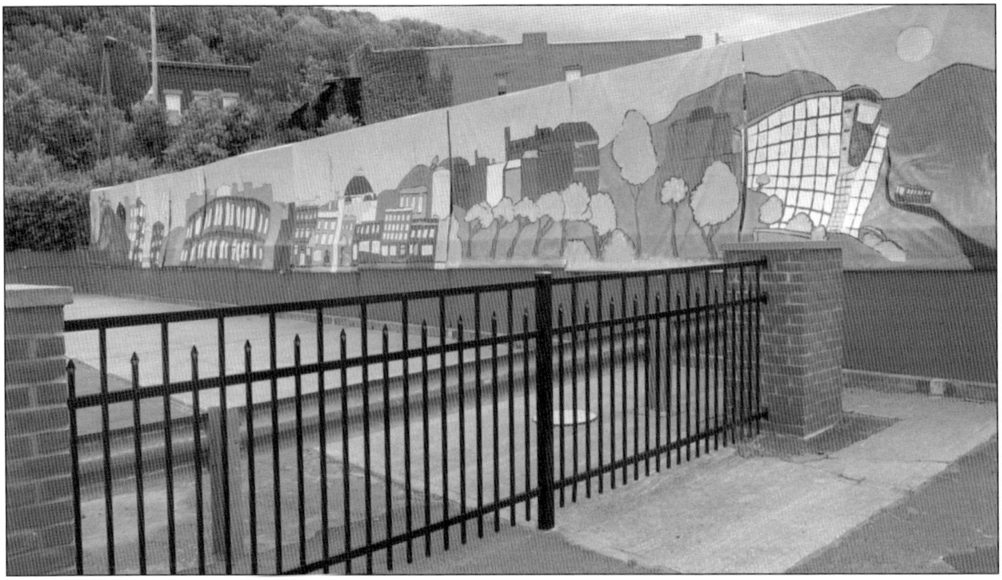

An 88-foot-long colorful mural, designed and produced by students of Questar III, was installed at the Hill Street MarketPlace and depicts Troy's technological evolution from industrial waterpower to current developments in nanotechnology. High school students Ethan Griswold, who conceived and created the design, and Ben Hatch, who organized the transfer of the design to 11 eight-foot panels, worked with other students to complete the project. (Courtesy of Marion Field.)

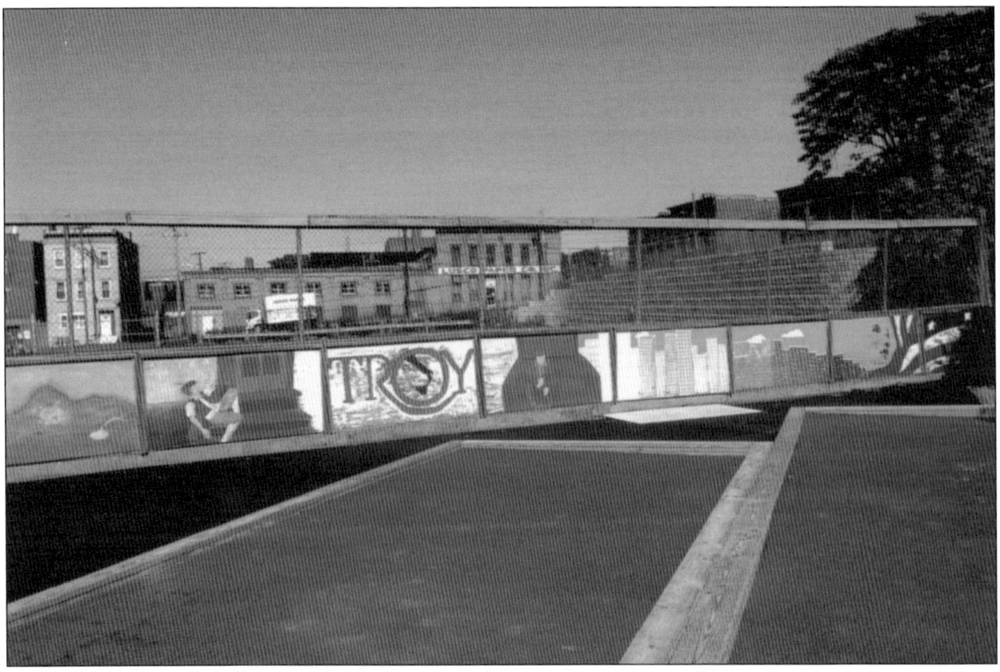

A mural, designed and assembled by nine students from five area high schools and enrolled in the Questar III New Visions Visual and Performing Arts Program, depicts scenes from an Italian neighborhood, including several gentlemen positioning themselves to play bocce, two city skyline panels, and an American flag and a baby. The students were supervised by instructors Peg Danner-Frank, Michael Gerrish, and Joe Mix. (Courtesy of Michael Gerrish.)

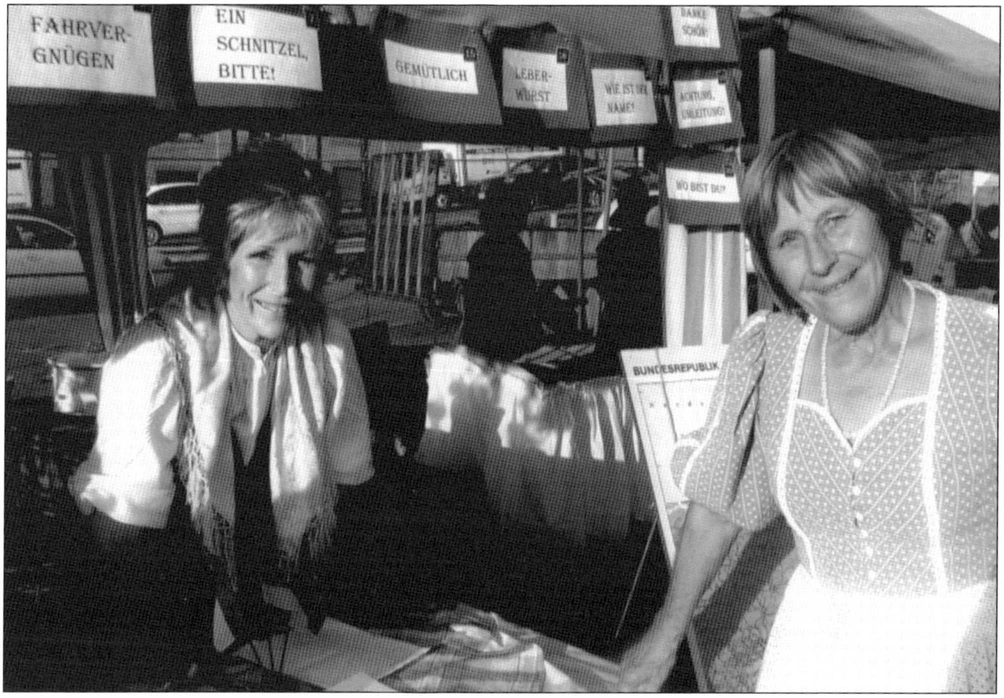

Dressed in ethnic clothing, Andrea Daley (left) and Hannelore Wilfret represented the German American community by providing ethnic food and information on German culture and traditions to people attending the International Festival. St. Lawrence's German Catholic Church was the worship site for German immigrants from 1870 to 1987. The St. Lawrence Academy opened in 1890 and closed several years before the church closed. (Courtesy of Marion Field.)

Fourth Street artist and Little Italy volunteer Andrea Daley designed, constructed, and painted this colorful, life-size plywood stand as part of the German exhibit. Judith (Gerger) Brearton and her husband, former Rensselaer County legislator James Brearton, are photographed behind the display. (Photograph by Andrea Daley.)

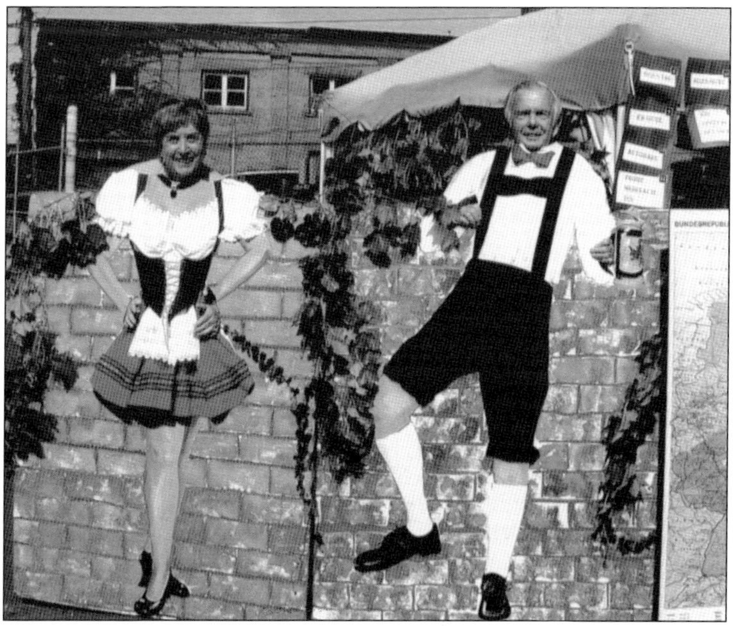

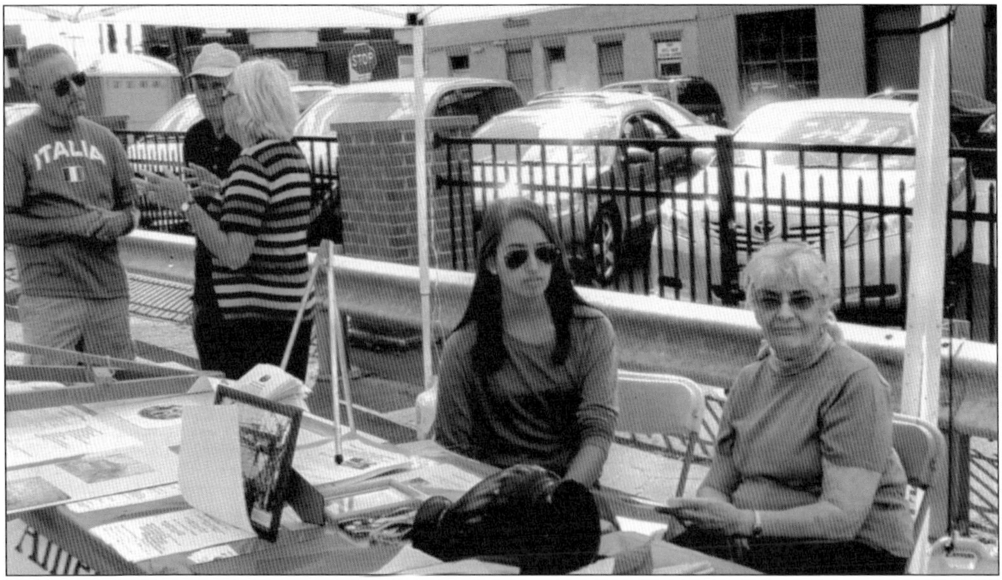

The American Italian Heritage Association (AIHA) was one of several organizations that staffed information stations at the International Festival. From left to right are Philip Maiello, Sandrino Zanetti, Linda Dellea, unidentified, and Rachel M. Anglin. The unidentified woman is Rachel's granddaughter. Founded by Prof./Cav. Philip J. DiNovo in 1979, AIHA maintains a museum and cultural center at 1227 Central Avenue in Albany, New York—one of only a handful in the United States and the largest in the East. (Courtesy of Marion Field.)

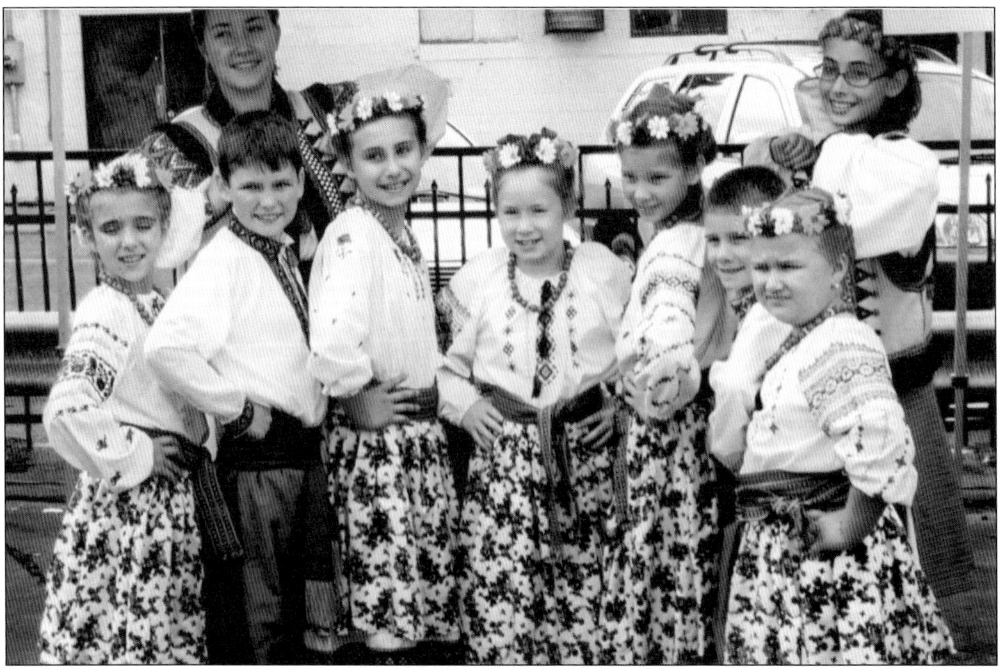

Colorfully dressed youngsters representing the Ukrainian American community gather for a group photograph. Ethnic dance demonstrations are among the most popular attractions at the annual International Festival, held each fall at the Hill Street MarketPlace. (Courtesy of Marion Field.)

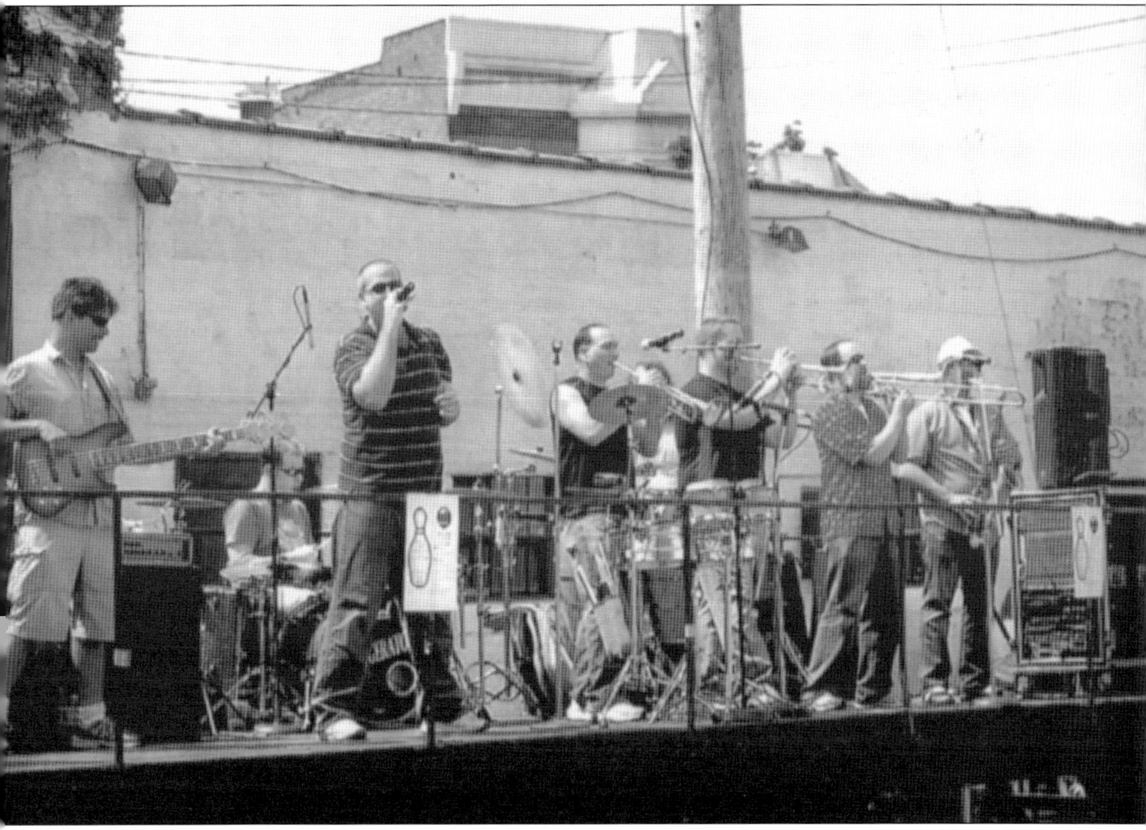

Among the most popular local bands to perform at the Hill Street MarketPlace are The Refrigerators, led by Dave Cerrone. The high-energy horn band was photographed during a performance at the annual Stickball Tournament. The Quality of Life Committee of the Neighborhood Watch works with the city events coordinator Vito Ciccarelli Jr. on plans to bring additional entertainment venues to the MarketPlace, now that several important site improvements have been completed. (Courtesy of Marion Field.)

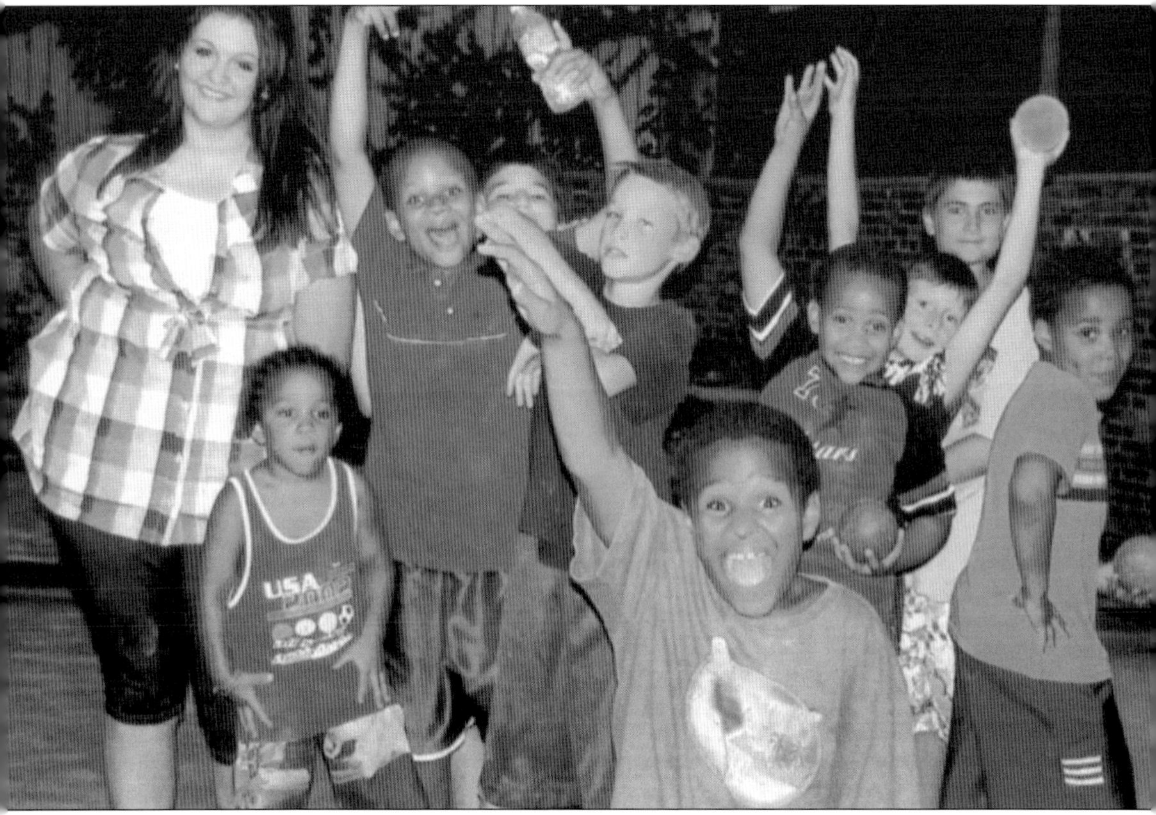

Youngsters attending a National Night Out event, held at the Hill Street MarketPlace in Little Italy, are quite enthusiastic as they practice a game of bocce—the age old sport played and enjoyed by individuals of all ages. The game is popular among Italian Americans and, like stickball, often for nostalgic reasons. Plans are being developed to organize a bocce league and eventually sponsor a charity bocce tournament. Two outdoor bocce courts were assembled by John Fanning, Rocco DeFazio, and his children. Seven-time US National Bocce Champion Michael Nicosia of San Jose, California, attended the opening of the courts on Thanksgiving Day in 2005 while spending the holiday with local members of his family. Several indoor bocce courts are available at the Italian Community Center, located one block from the MarketPlace. (Courtesy of Marion Field.)

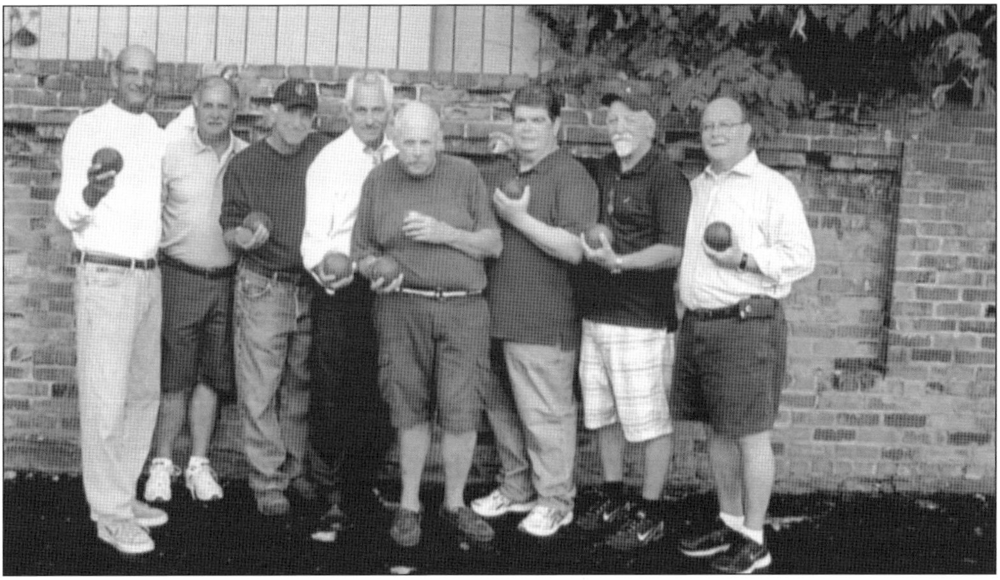

Memories of LaSalle Institute are only part of what brings together these 1968 graduates, who play friendly but competitive games of bocce each week during the warm months. From left to right are Tom Testo, Paul Montarello, D. Thomas Testo, Frank Merola, Dr. J. Kevin Gebert, Tony Magnetto, Michael Esposito, and Paul Santandera. The friends conclude the evening with Italian food, dessert, and beverages. (Courtesy of Frank Merola.)

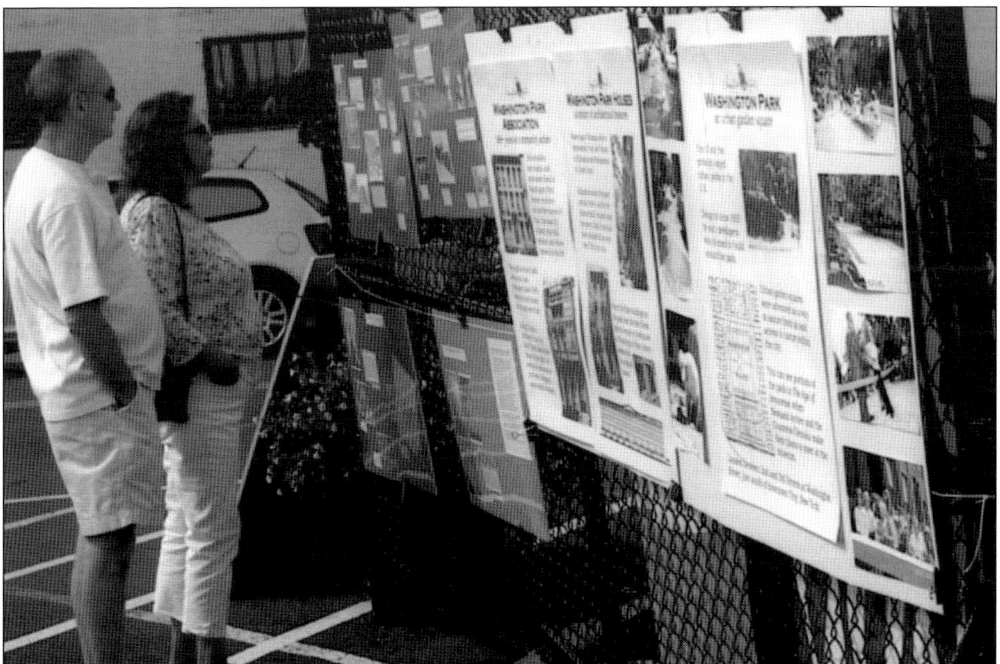

Local history buffs assisted in researching the neighborhood for Troy's quadricentennial celebration. The multi-paneled exhibits included late-19th-century maps, photographs of historic Washington Park residences, photographs and images of worship sites, and brief histories of congregations representing ethnic groups. (Photograph by Dorcas Rose.)

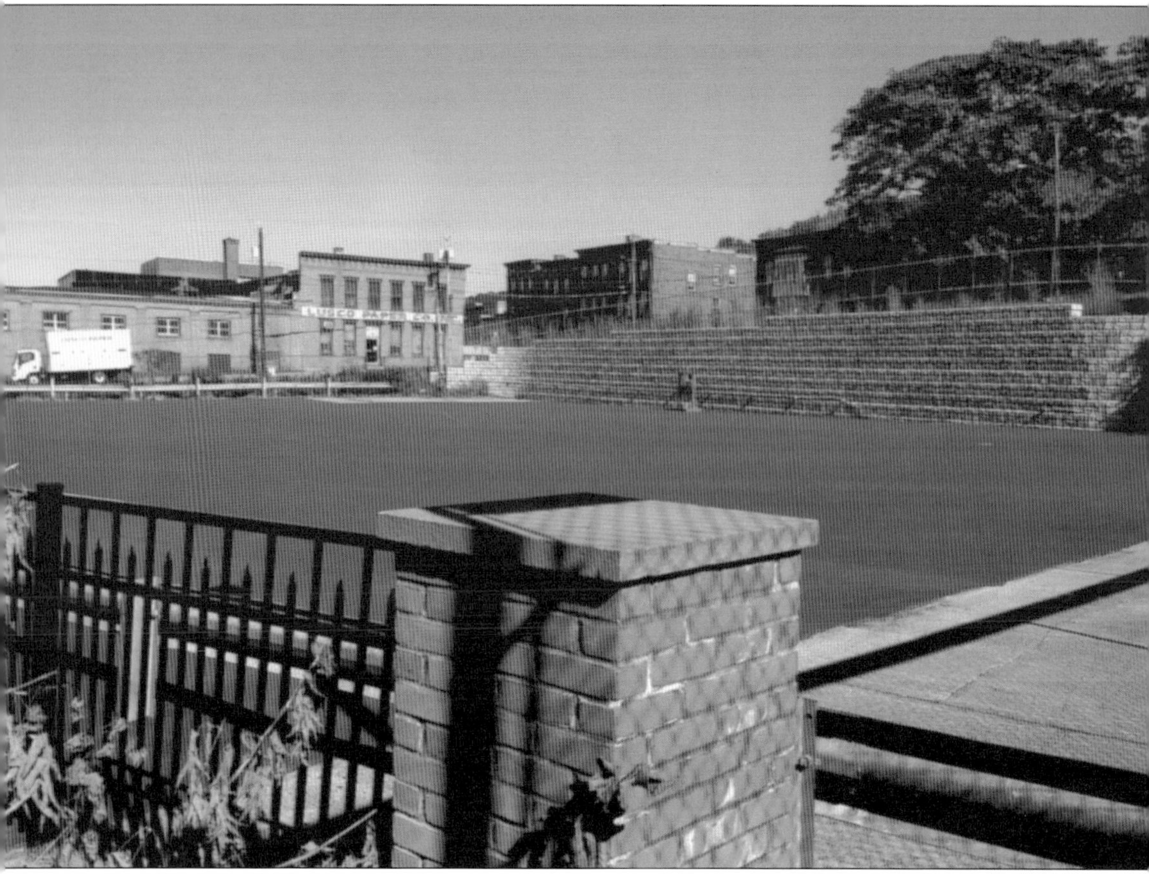

In November 1975, the City of Troy sold the former Hill Street public market site to Troy News Company, Inc. The site was fenced in and used as a company parking lot. Ownership was returned to the City of Troy in 2002 after the Friends of Little Italy proposed plans for the revitalization of the old market. Since then, the city has replaced the deteriorating brick wall with a 170-foot retaining wall of grey block. The 1.2-acre site was resurfaced, and National Grid restructured the bocce courts after remedial work on the site was completed. A 300-foot-long chain link fence was replaced with redbrick posts and black aluminum fencing that resembles traditional wrought iron. Angle parking, bike racks, electrical outlets, and planters for seasonal flowers have been added at the site. (Photograph by Andrea Daley.)

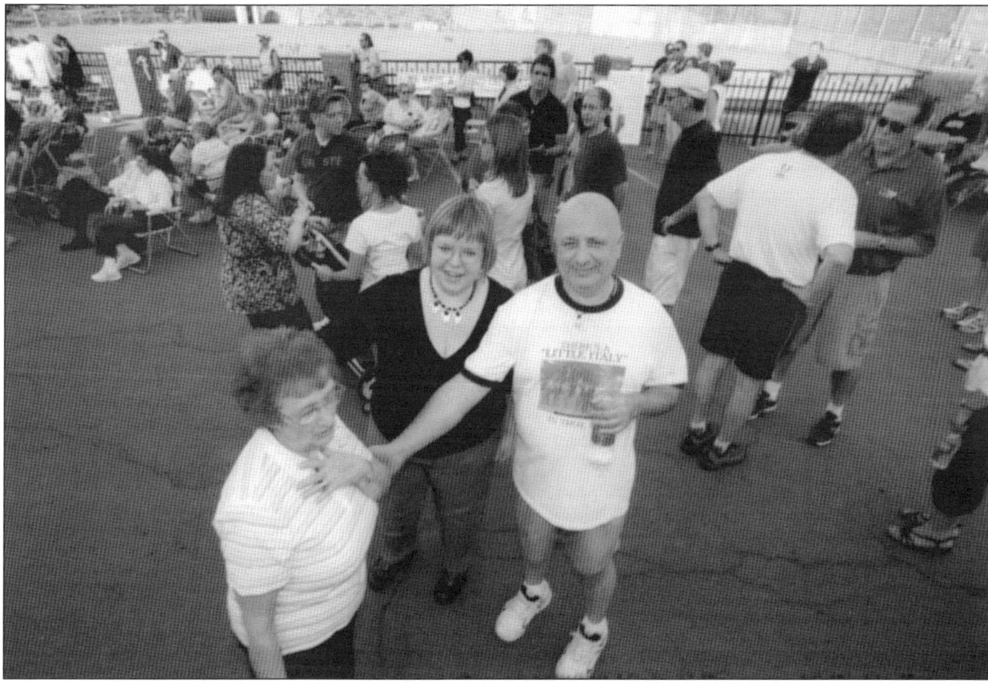

Musical entertainment is always a crowd pleaser at the Hill Street MarketPlace. From left to right are Jean (Turriglio) Cavallo, Cathy Hamel, and Jean's son Joseph Cavallo Jr. (wearing a popular Little Italy T-shirt). Behind the Cavallos are members of the Chiappone family, including Samuel, Joshua, and Jessica Chiappone and their guests. (Photograph by Michael Dzaman.)

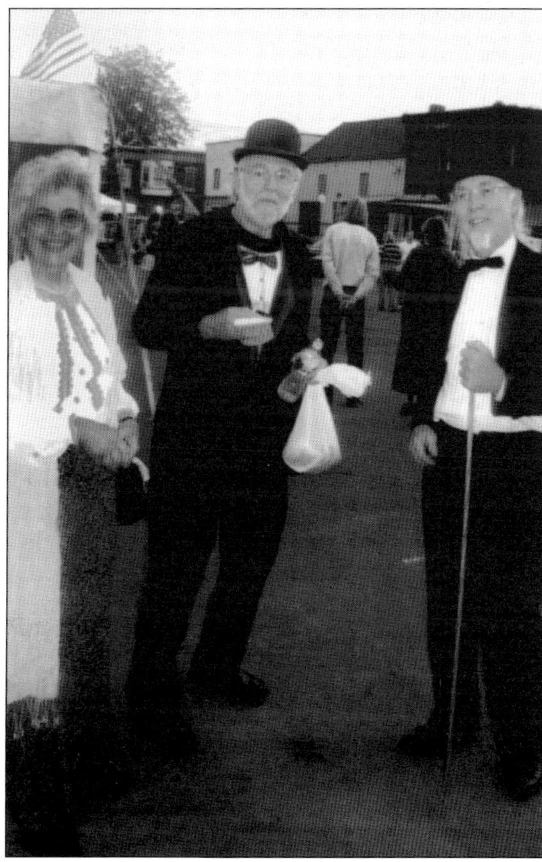

Little Italy volunteers (from left to right) Claire (Porcello) Davis, Frank LaPosta Visk, and David Graham enjoy an afternoon at the City of Troy's quadricentennial celebration, hosted by Troy Little Italy in September 2011. The theme of the event was the ethnic and cultural diversity of the neighborhood, which is now celebrated annually with the International Festival. (Courtesy of Marion Field.)

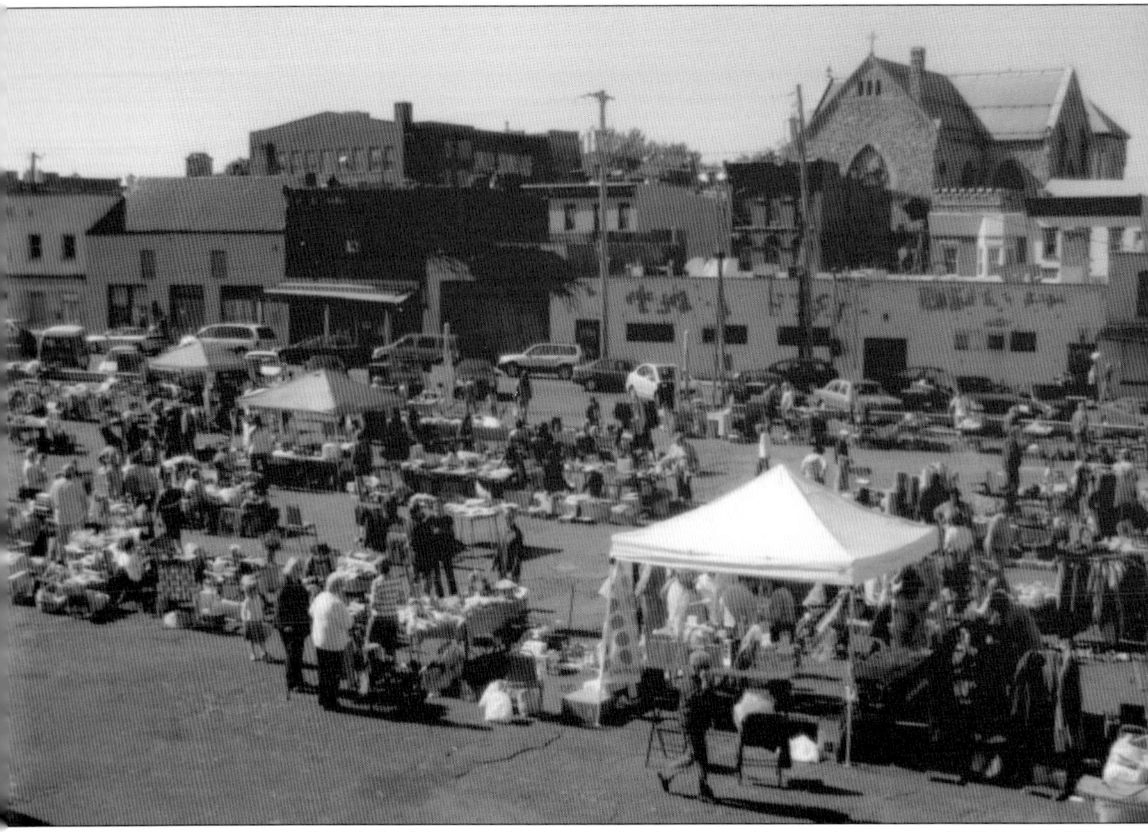

The centerpiece of Little Italy's revitalization is the former public market site on Hill Street. The MarketPlace is the site of the annual spring Stickball Tournament, summer's Cinema Under the Stars, and the fall International Festival. Food and beverages are often available from local restaurants and food vendors. The neighborhood is fortunate to have a huge public space available for community events. The City of Troy, along with area organizations, is a willing partner in assisting Troy Little Italy as cosponsor of events. (Courtesy of Marion Field.)

Six

Catalyst for Change

The neighborhood group Troy Little Italy was organized in 2005, three years after Fourth Street businessman Rocco DeFazio formed the Friends of Little Italy. Dozens of creative and energetic group members work to maintain a healthy and vibrant community on the south side of Troy. Residents and business owners believe that by establishing Little Italy as an ethnic tourism destination, restoring Troy's historic market place, and making the neighborhood safe and clean, it will be a place where people will want to live, work, and visit.

Members of Troy Little Italy and the South Central Neighborhood Watch work within existing city systems and programs to focus on the neighborhood housing stock; support the preservation and adaptive reuse of buildings; cooperate with Troy's Departments of Public Works and Code Enforcement and the Community Policing Unit; identify and encourage ways to attract artists, young professionals, entrepreneurs, empty nesters, and young families to the neighborhood; communicate with other neighborhood groups; and collaborate with community partners.

Programs and events are planned that honor the achievements of neighbors, support local businesses, celebrate neighborhood history and diversity, raise funds for local social service providers, share ethnic culture and traditions, represent Little Italy in a positive way, and continue to maintain a web presence and monthly newsletter. Little Italy neighborhoods throughout America continue to stand the test of time, flourish, and inspire a sense of pride and community.

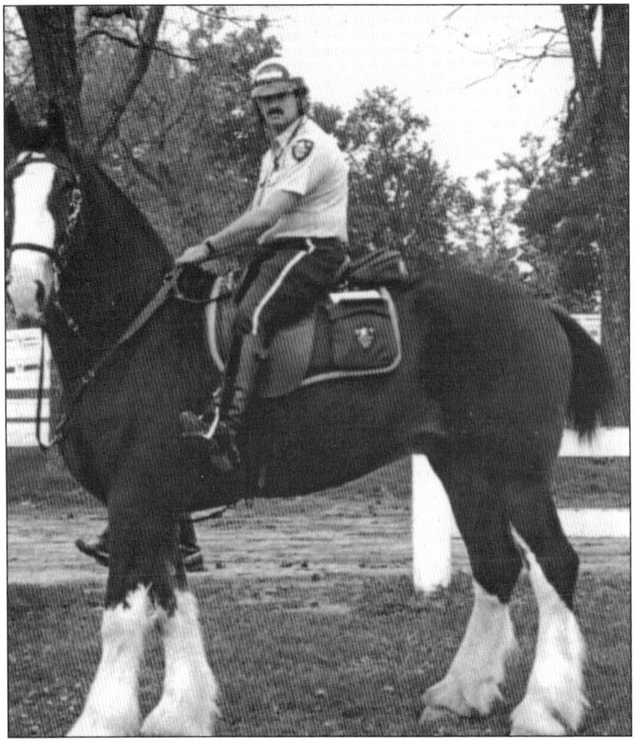

Police horse Big Ben and Sgt. Samuel Carello, members of the Troy Police Department's Community Policing Unit, were welcomed throughout the city at over 150 events. Part of the cost of Ben's upkeep came from donations provided by city residents and business people. He participated in 79 arrests and the issuance of almost 1,500 citations. The beloved police horse died in May 2013. (Courtesy of Marion Field.)

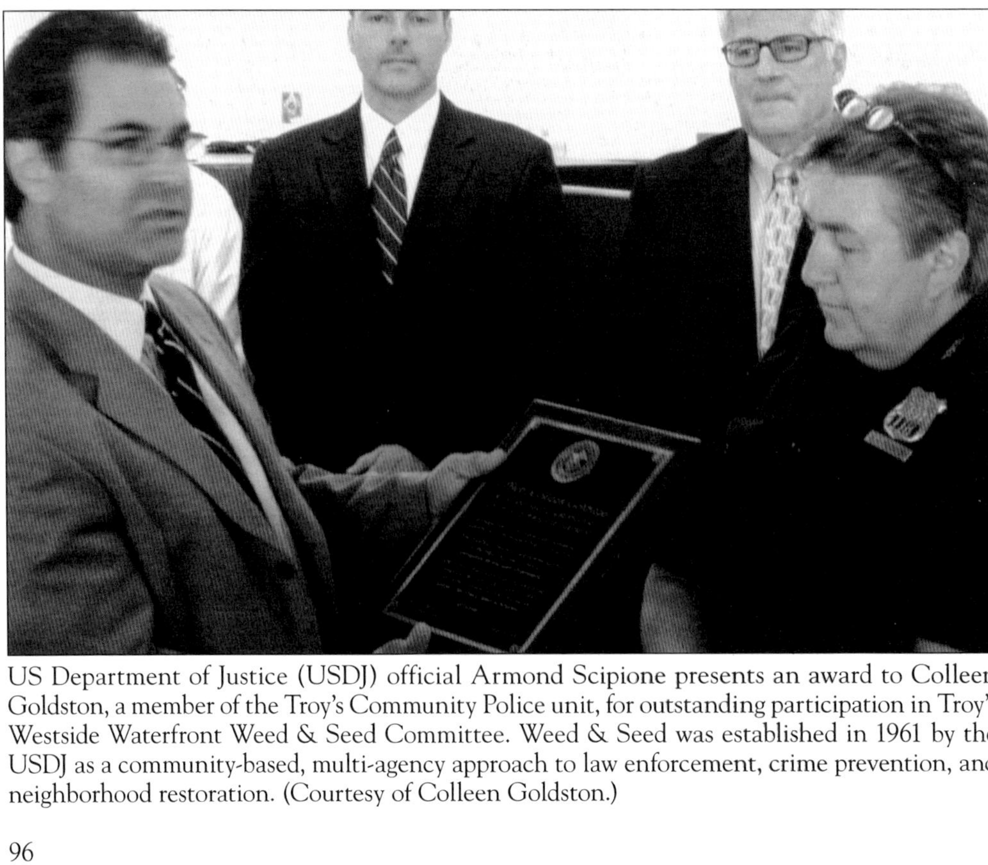

US Department of Justice (USDJ) official Armond Scipione presents an award to Colleen Goldston, a member of the Troy's Community Police unit, for outstanding participation in Troy's Westside Waterfront Weed & Seed Committee. Weed & Seed was established in 1961 by the USDJ as a community-based, multi-agency approach to law enforcement, crime prevention, and neighborhood restoration. (Courtesy of Colleen Goldston.)

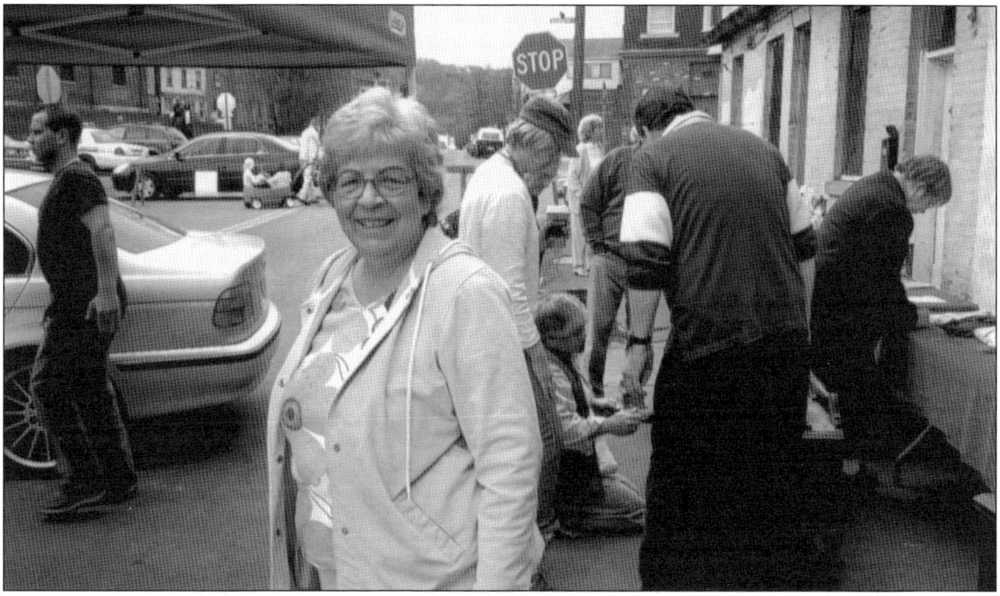

Marion Field, president of Troy Little Italy, is pictured in front of the Little Italy Visitor Center at 37 Hill Street during the group's first garage sale. Marion was honored by Troy Rehabilitation & Improvement Program (TRIP, Inc.) in 2013, as a "Troy Treasure" and by the US Department of Justice in 2014 for her community work in youth services. (Photograph by Joe Popson.)

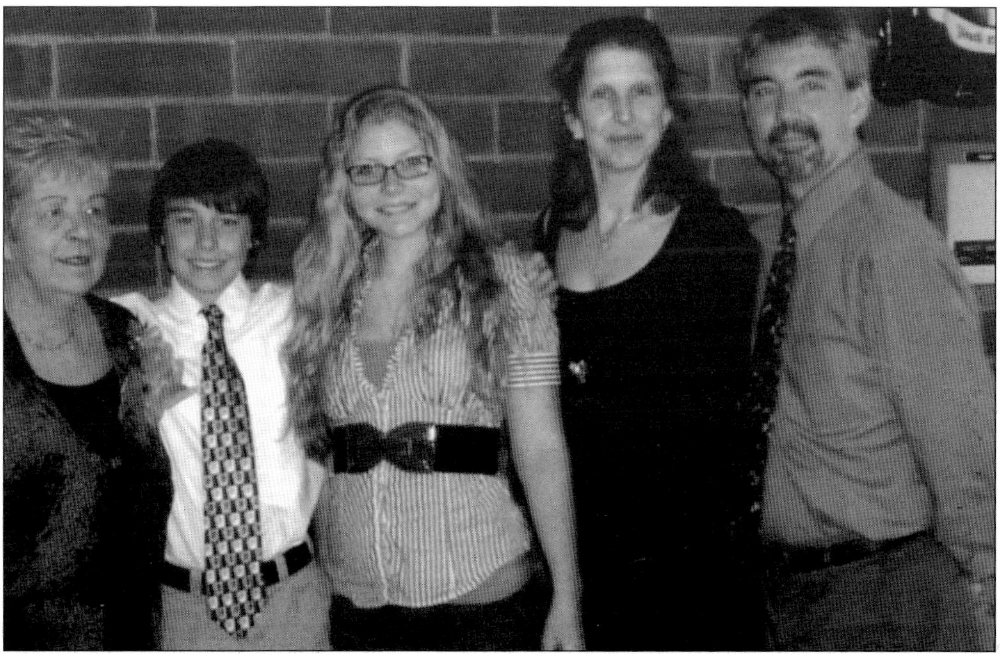

Pictured from left to right are Marion Field, her grandchildren Cameron and Alyssa, daughter-in-law Theresa, and son Frank Cietek attending a 2010 ceremony where Marion, Rocco DeFazio, and the author were awarded the William J. Pascarell Award for Person of the Year, presented by the Troy Youth Association. Marion's grandson Drew was not available for the photograph. (Courtesy of Marion Field.)

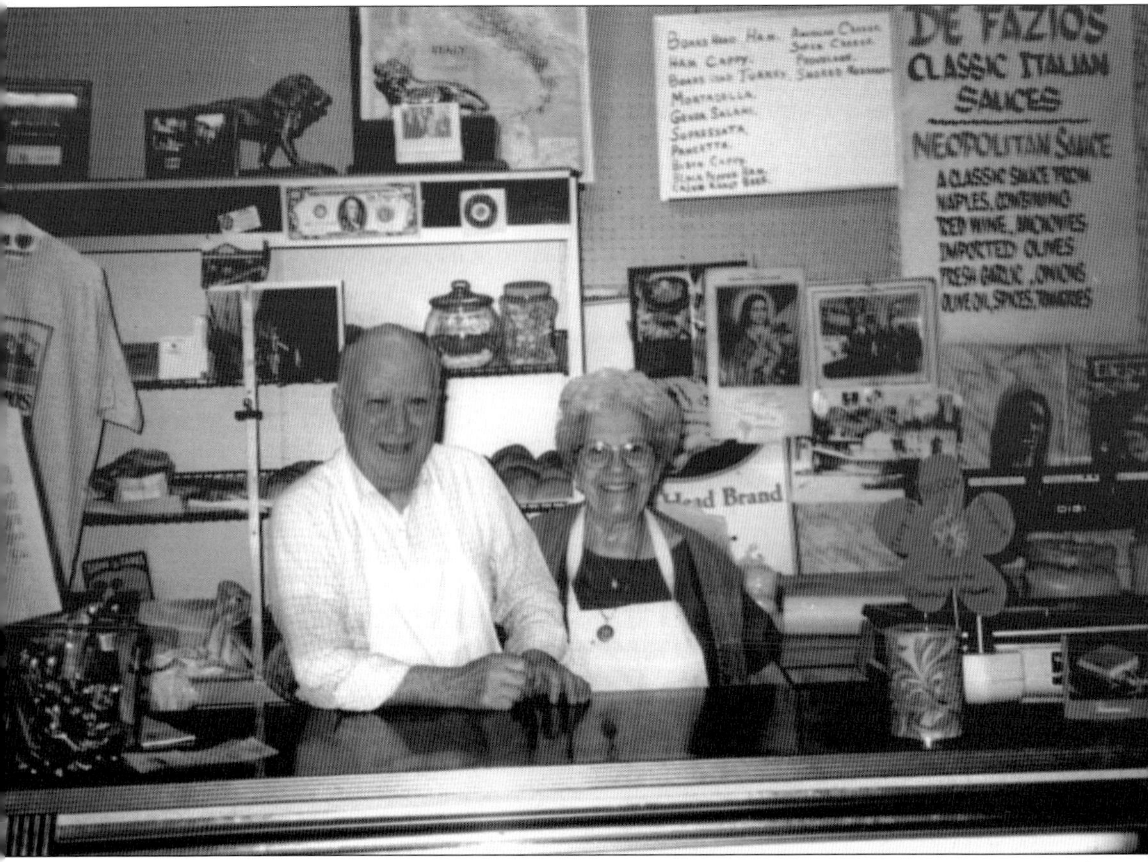

Anthony and Josephine DeFazio stand behind the counter of the Italian import store they opened on Fourth Street in 1951. The DeFazios immigrated to the United States in the 1930s—"Josie" from Cervinara, Campania, and "Tony" from Valle Florita, Calabria. They organized and planned the annual Feast of St. Joseph's Dinner to feed the underprivileged and disadvantaged in Troy, worked tirelessly on fundraisers to aid earthquake victims in Naples and Sicily and orphans in Italy, and organized countless spaghetti dinner fundraisers at St. Anthony of Padua Parish. As members of the American Committee on Italian Migration, they worked to change immigration laws in the 1960s and 1970s. Tony was also active in the Knights of Columbus and the Sons of Italy and was awarded the Cavaliere della Stella Solidarieta Italiana by the president of Italy. He was also instrumental in the development of Troy's Columbus Square. (Courtesy of Rocco DeFazio.)

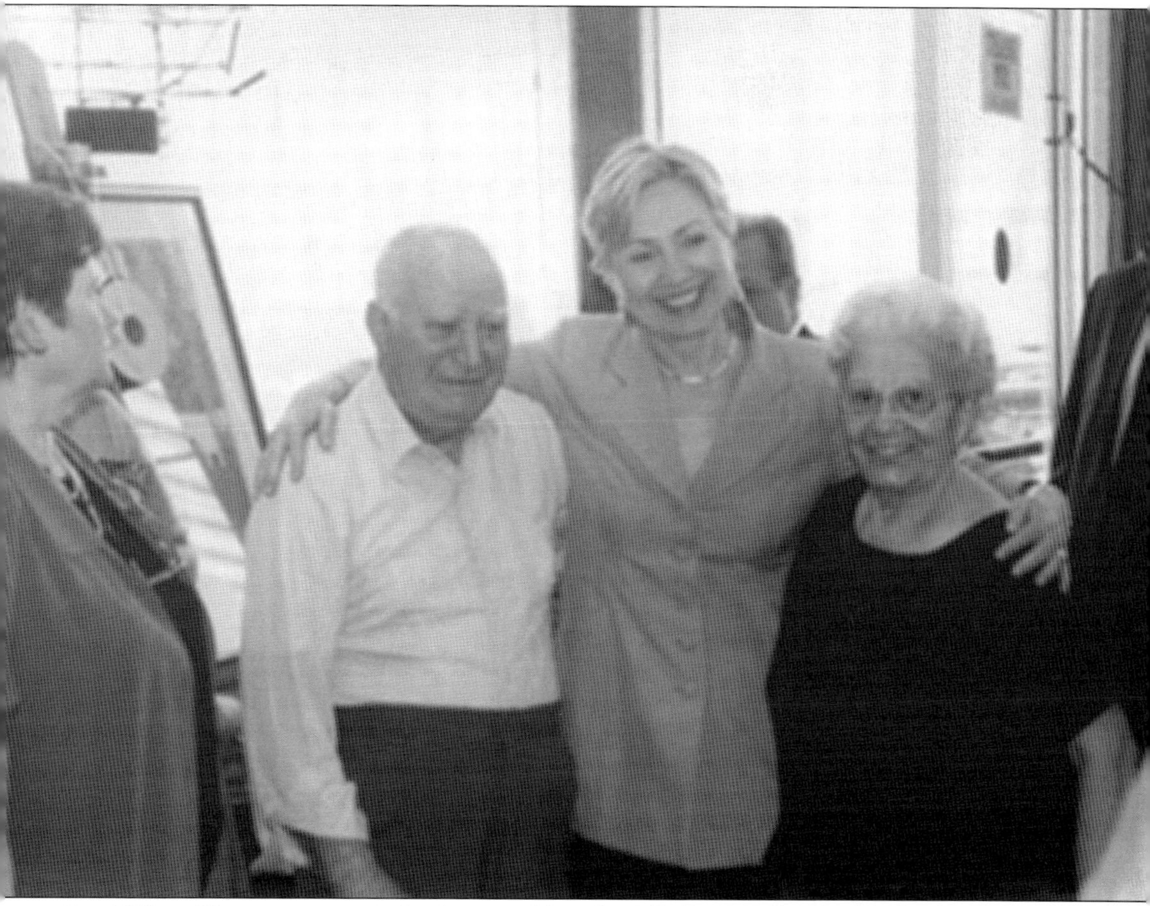

Sen. Hillary Clinton visits with Anthony and Josephine DeFazio at their Italian import store in 2003 while in the neighborhood to review proposed plans for Little Italy's former Hill Street Public Market site. Tony and Josie have been active participants in the Italian American community for decades and, in 2005, were honored by the Rensselaer County Historical Society for their service to the community. (Courtesy of Rocco DeFazio)

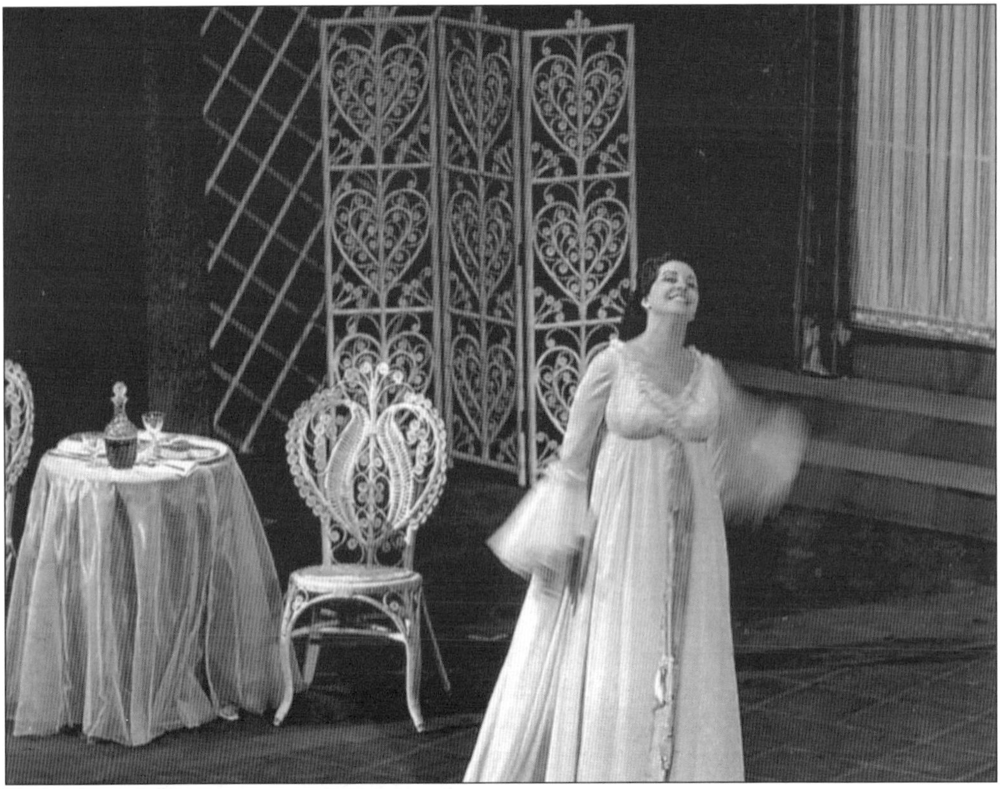

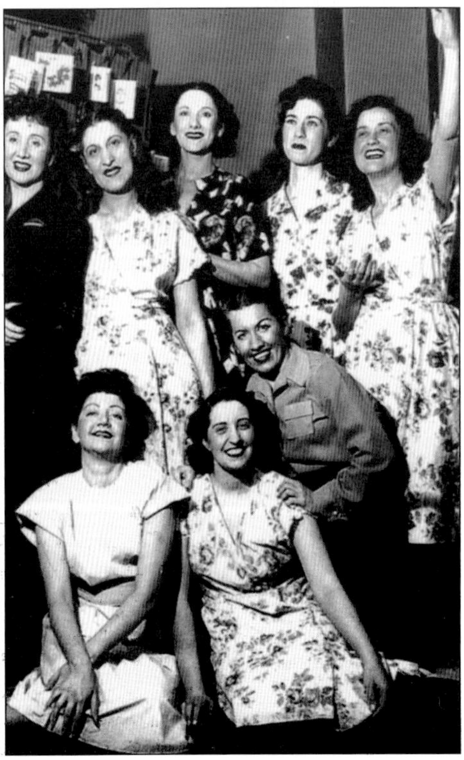

Olivia Bonelli, daughter of Louis and Jenny Riccardi Bonelli, was born on July 2, 1920. The Bonellis were longtime residents of 1454 Seventh Avenue. Possessed of a gifted voice and encouraged by her family, Olivia began voice studies with Charles Pickering, who taught at Troy's Emma Willard School. Her first recital was at the school's concert hall. Olivia is pictured on stage at a performance later in her career. (Courtesy of Peter Bonelli.)

In 1945, after Olivia Bonelli successfully auditioned for the chorus of Radio City Music Hall, she stepped in at the last minute to sing "O Holy Night" at the hall's famed Christmas show. It was a song familiar to the young Troy woman, except this time, she sang while accompanied by a full symphony orchestra for the first time. Olivia is seen sitting in the front row in a flowered dress with members of the Radio City Music Hall chorus. (Courtesy of Peter Bonelli.)

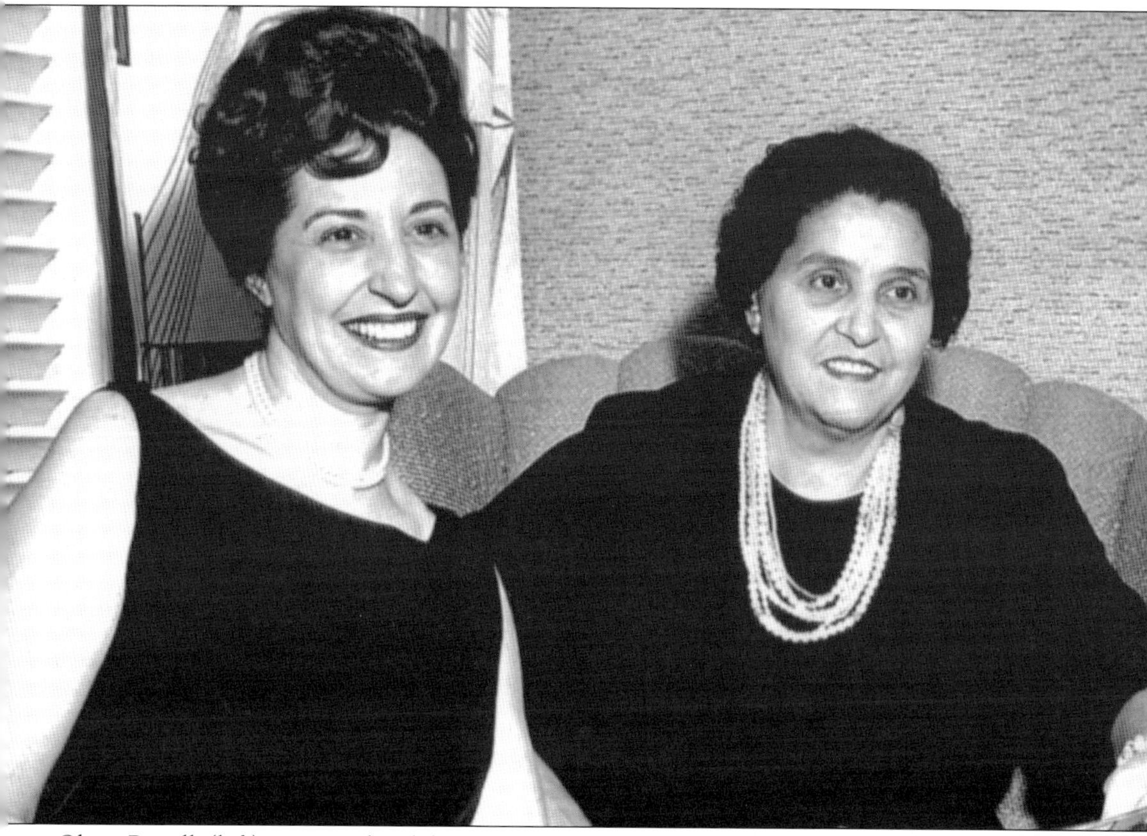

Olivia Bonelli (left) is pictured with her mother, Jenny, at a concert Olivia gave at the Troy Music Hall. Troy's native soprano was heard by opera fans across America during tours, in live televised opera, and for many years with the New York City Opera. Her beautiful, clear, expressive soprano was heard by thousands of opera fans throughout America in roles from Mimi *in La Boheme*, to Gilda in *Rigoletto*, to Michaela in *Carmen*. Early in her career, she toured with the Starlighters, a USO group that sang for wounded service members in hospitals throughout the country. Entertaining wounded service members was the most meaningful experience of her life. In 1950, she married George Ortell, a performing tenor who died in 2005. Olivia died on December 17, 1990. (Courtesy of Peter Bonelli.)

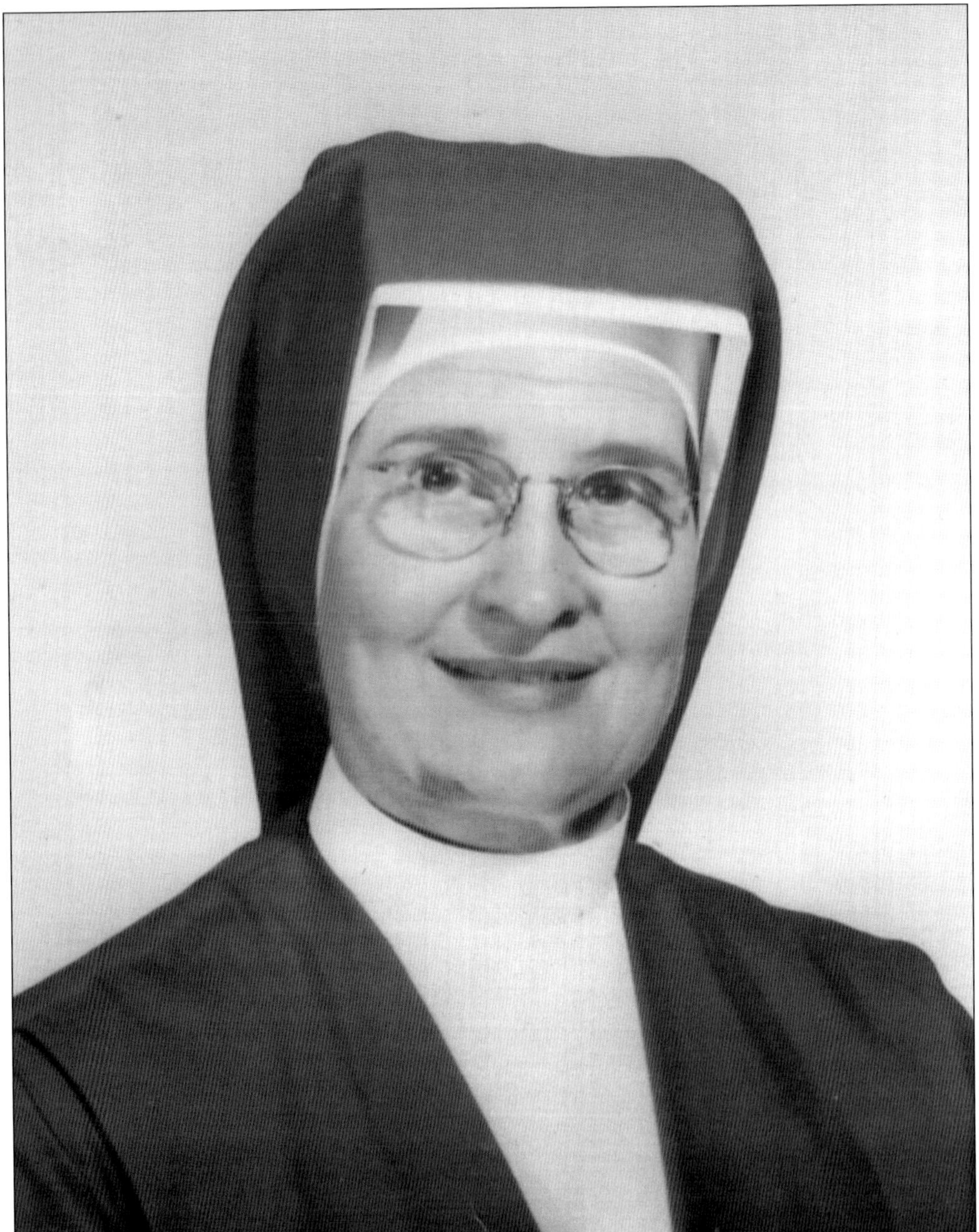

Sr. Carmelite Germinario was born on December 26, 1919, in Molfetta, Province of Bari, Italy, to Maria Luisa Silvestri and Giuseppe Germinario. Sister Carmelite's family journeyed to Troy when she was a year old and lived for many years on Hill Street. Her brother Mauro Antonio died in infancy, and she grew up in Little Italy with her sisters Angela and Sabina and brother Maurice. On Columbus Day in 2013, family members, friends, and neighbors placed a plaque at Sister Carmelite's former home at 63 Hill Street, honoring her 70 years of devotion as a teacher and pastoral caregiver in schools, orphanages, and hospitals. A traveling exhibit containing photographs, newspaper articles, and memorabilia of Sister Carmelite's life was displayed at eight local sites between August 2013 and January 2014. (Courtesy of Louise Germinario.)

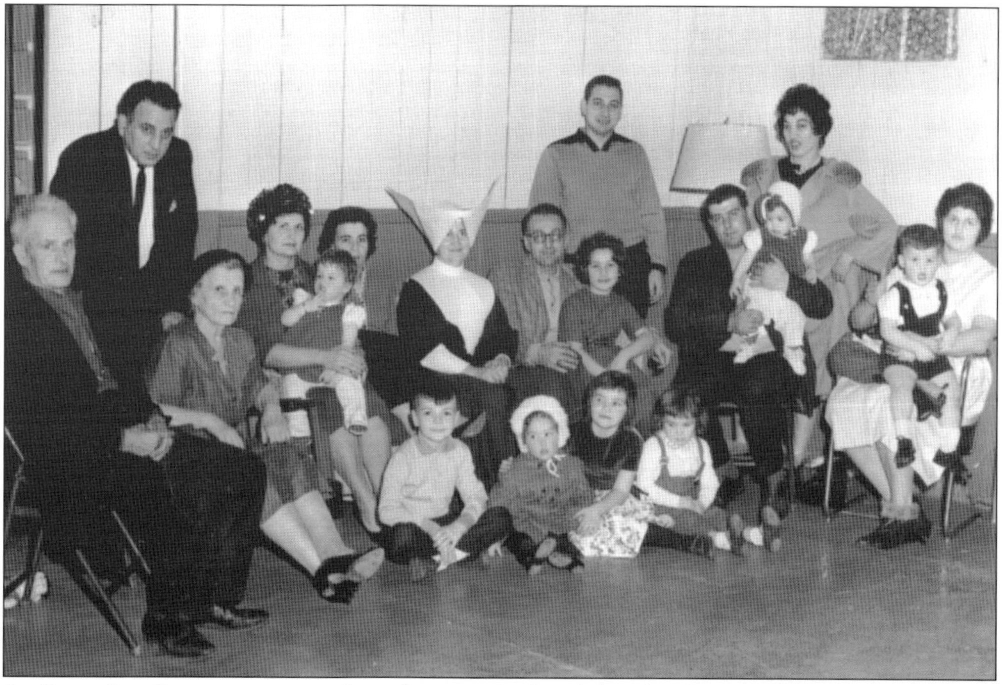

Sr. Carmelite Germinario was often photographed with her family. From left to right are (first row) Giuseppe Germinario (Sister Carmelite's father), Lucretia Francese, Robert Zink, Carmella Germinario, Tina Zink, Maryanne Zink, and Sabina "Bebe" Thomas (holding her son Joseph); (second row) Angela Fazio (holding Rina Thomas), Jay Zink, Sister Carmelite, Ignatius "Iggy" Francese, Louise Germinario, and Maurice Germinario (holding his daughter Maria); (third row) Archie Fazio, James Francese, and Helen Germinario. (Courtesy of Louise Germinario.)

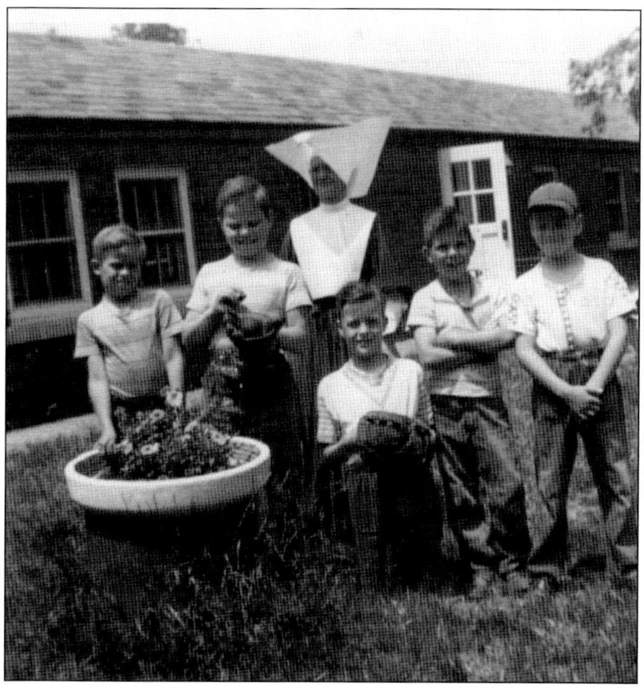

Sr. Carmelite Germinario is surrounded by youngsters at a children's home in central New York—one of her earliest assignments. She entered the Daughters of Charity in 1940, serving as an elementary school teacher, religious instructor, and eventually, principal of St. Mary's School (from 1963 to 1971), which she had attended herself. Sister Carmelite returned to Troy in 1982 and served 25 years as a pastoral caregiver and spiritual advisor at St. Mary's Hospital. She died on November 25, 2010. (Courtesy of Louise Germinario.)

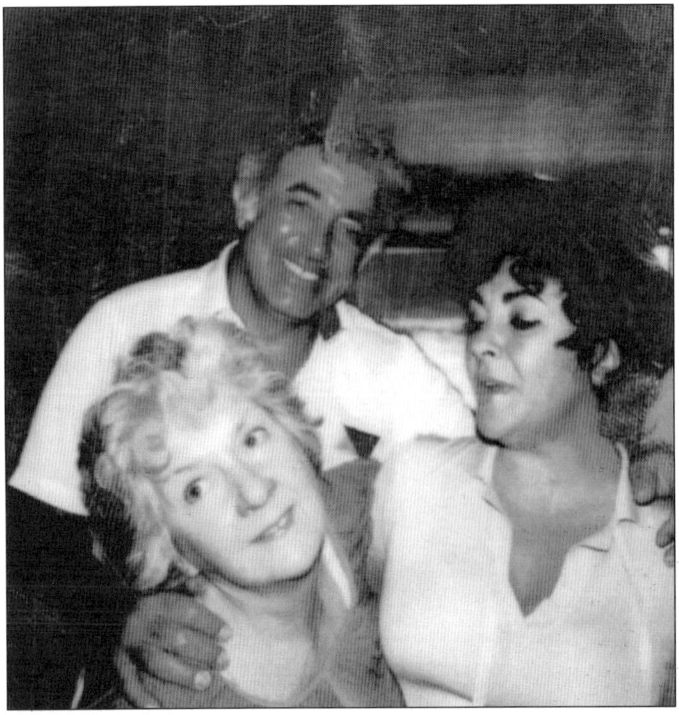

Lois Maureen Stapleton (left), daughter of Irene and John Stapleton, was born on June 21, 1925, into an Irish American family. Maureen and her brother Jack were graduates of St. Mary's School and Catholic Central High School. Maureen's last role on Broadway was in *The Little Foxes*, appearing with her longtime friend Elizabeth Taylor (right). Also pictured is Maureen's lifelong friend Peter Simonian. (Courtesy of Peter Simonian.)

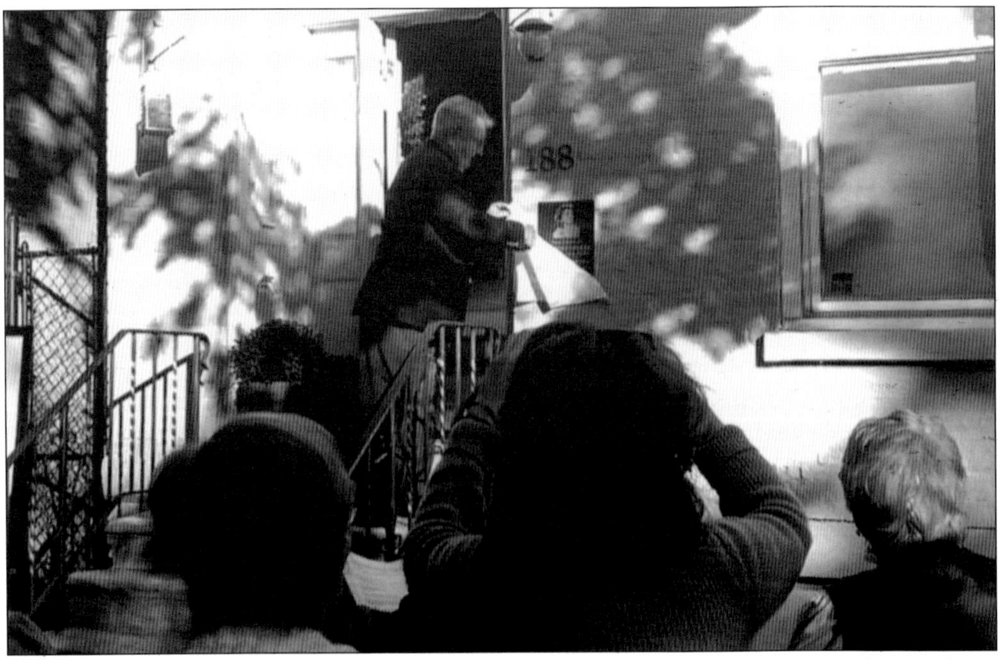

Jack Stapleton, Maureen's brother, is seen unveiling a commemorative plaque on the Stapleton homestead at 188 First Street. Author Jane Scovell, who assisted Maureen in writing her biography, *A Hell of a Life*, shared her memories of Maureen at a program held at the Troy Public Library. Early in her book, Maureen writes: "There's a place called Troy on the east bank of the Hudson River. If you want to know me, you have to know where I came from, and Troy is my hometown." (Photograph by Cassandra Allison.)

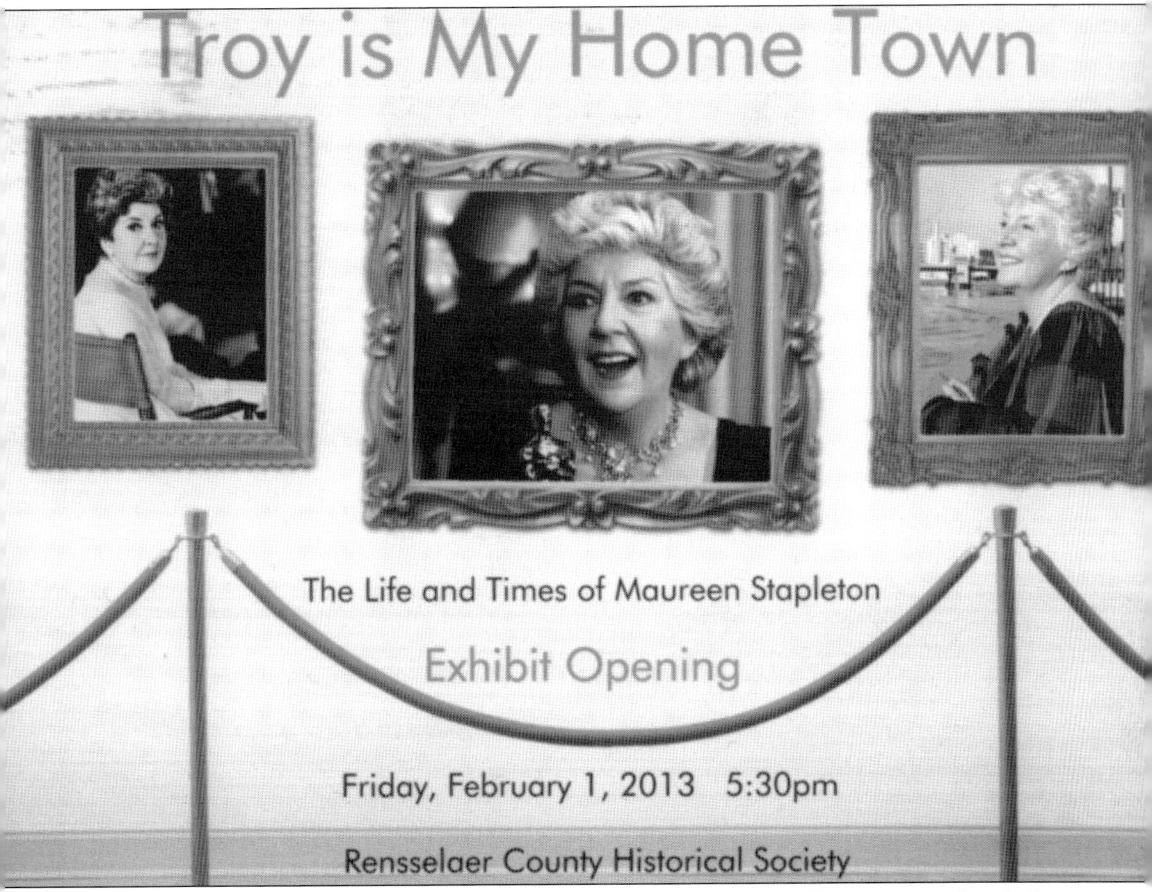

The Rensselaer County Historical Society (RCHS) and Russell Sage College partnered with the neighborhood group Troy Little Italy to honor Maureen Stapleton. The RCHS exhibit included Maureen's Oscar, Tony, and Emmy Awards, along with extensive memorabilia and photographs provided by Maureen's family and local fan William G. Carey. The Theatre Arts Department of Sage College, under the direction of David Baecker, presented a stage tribute to Maureen. Maureen was nominated for four Oscars, six Tonys, seven Emmys, and a Grammy. In 1981, she was inducted into the American Theater Hall of Fame. The Maureen Stapleton Theatre, located at Troy's Hudson Valley Community College, was dedicated in 2000. Maureen died on March 13, 2006. She is survived by her brother Jack, daughter Katherine, son Daniel Allentuck, and grandchildren Alexandria and Max Bambery. (Courtesy of Rensselaer County Historical Society.)

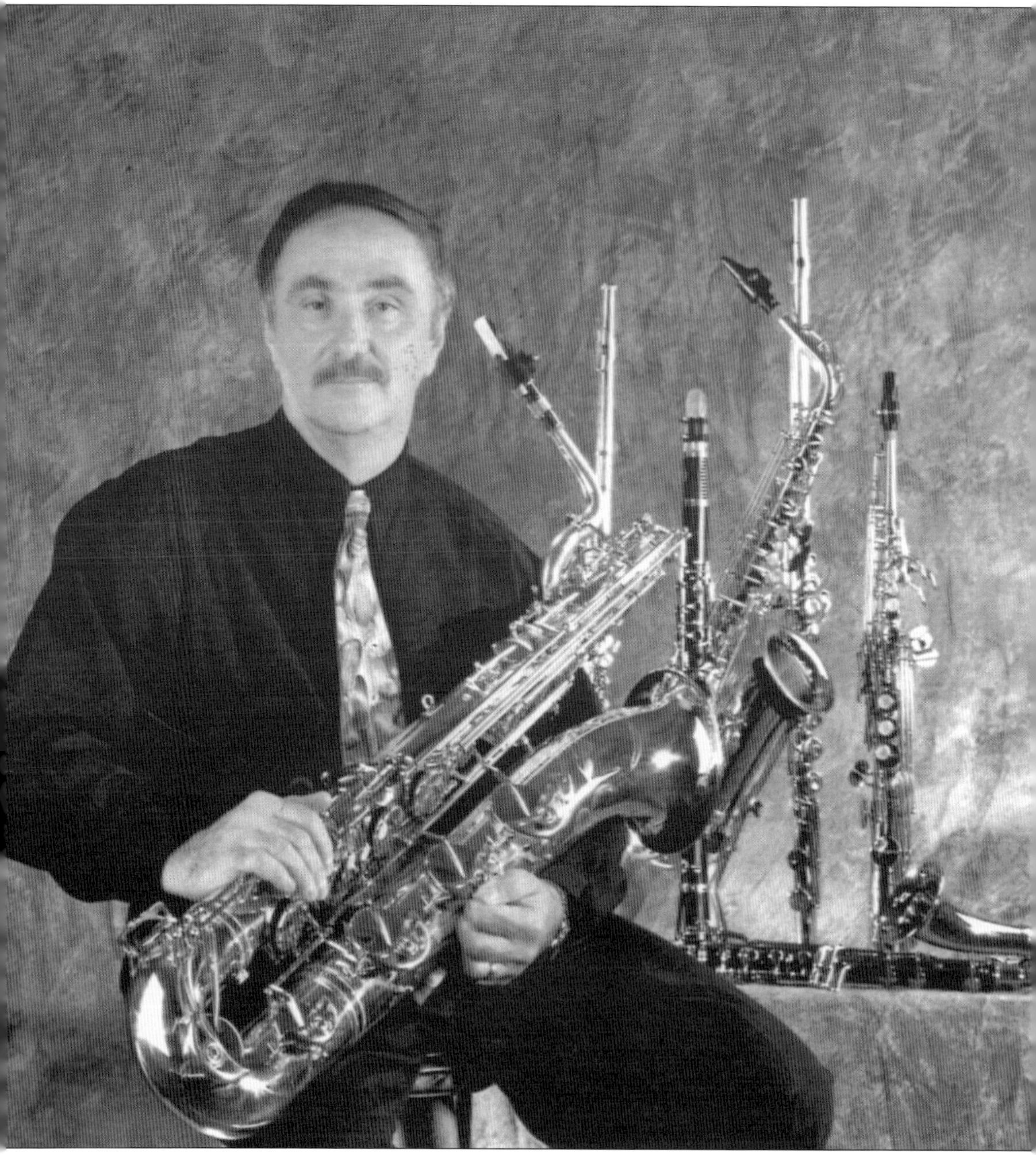

Nick Brignola was born on July 17, 1936, into an Italian American family—the son of the late Margaret (Rubino) Brignola and Dr. Nicholas Brignola. Nick, a 1954 graduate of Troy High School, was the featured soloist for a jazz combo who won the National Jazz Fraternity's 1957 intercollegiate contest and the New York Jazz Critics National New Star state combo contest while he was at Ithaca College. The following year, he won a worldwide contest sponsored by *Down Beat* magazine and was awarded a Benny Goodman scholarship to the prestigious Berklee College of Music in Boston. He toured the world, performing at jazz festivals for over a decade. Nick died on February 8, 2002. He is survived by his wife Yvonne, daughters Jillian Haggerty and Kristin Walker, son Nicholas F. Brignola, and a granddaughter. (Courtesy of Yvonne Brignola.)

Nick Brignola, who was named Best Baritone Saxophonist for many years in *Down Beat* and *Jazz Times*, was nominated for a 1979 Grammy for best instrumentalist with his fourth album, *LA Bound*. Nick was an active member of the International Association of Jazz Educators, as well as teacher and guest artist in residence at many colleges and universities in the United States and Europe. (Courtesy of Yvonne Brignola.)

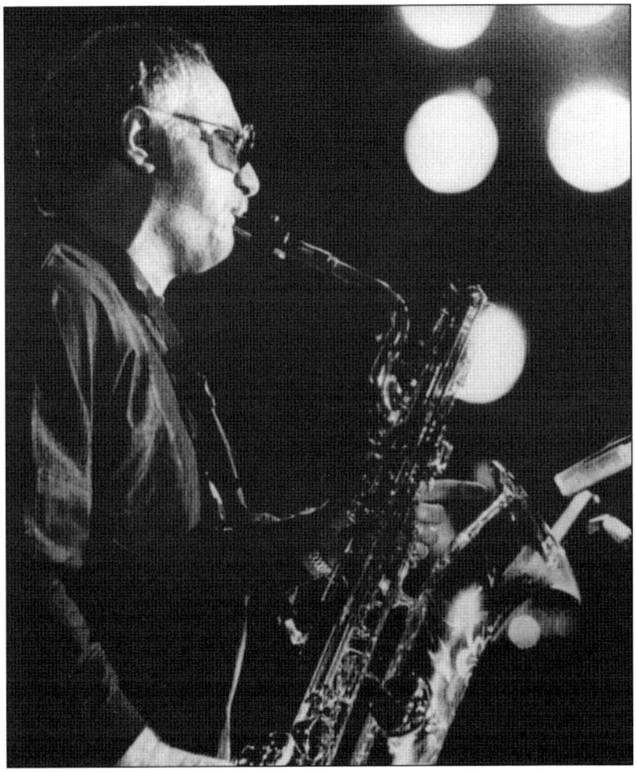

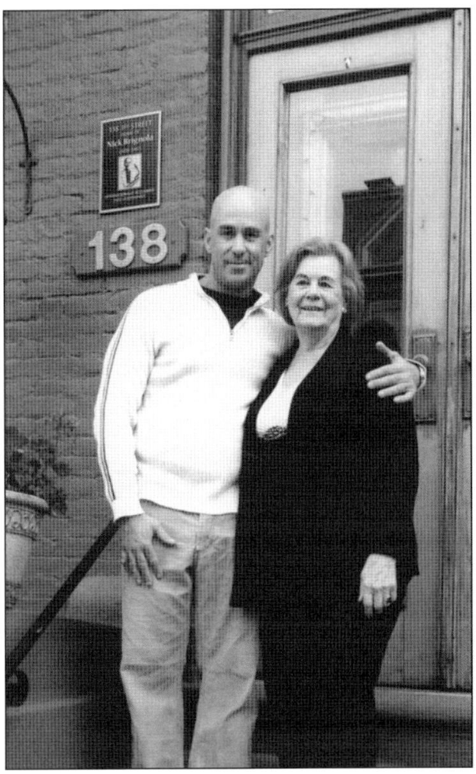

Nicholas F. Brignola and Yvonne Brignola, son and wife of Troy jazzman Nick Brignola, stand near a memorial plaque honoring the internationally known saxophone player. The plaque is located on Nick's childhood home, located at 138 Third Street, is now owned by Troy songstress Patti Melita. In 2011, Troy Little Italy selected Nick Brignola as their first neighborhood honoree for significant career achievement. (Photograph by Andrea Daley.)

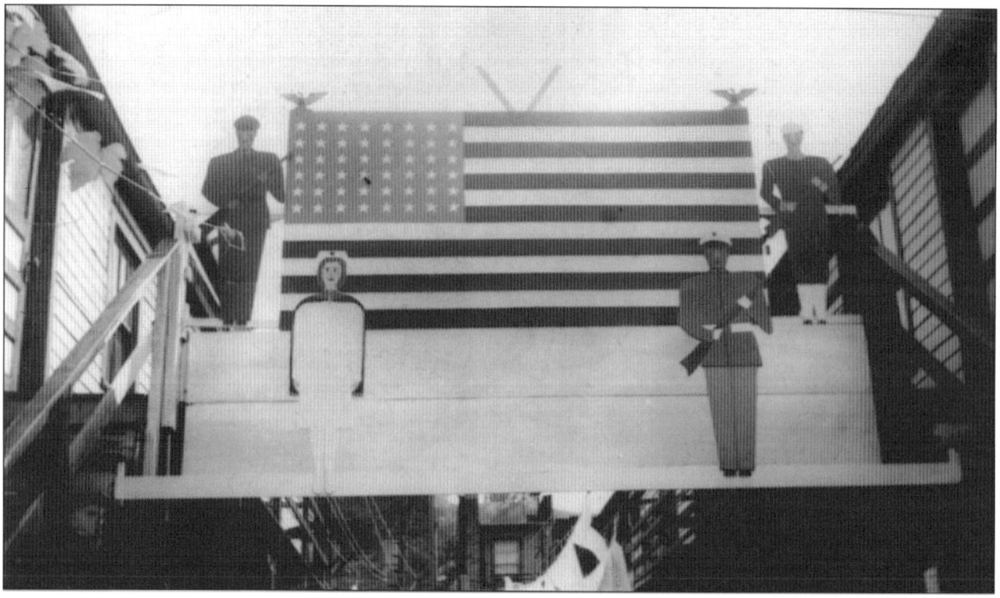

During World War II, a huge patriotic billboard—depicting service members from the Army, Navy, and Marine Corp, as well as a nurse and an oversized American flag—was carved by Fourth Street resident Philip Campana and painted by Michael Bazicki. The billboard, prominently displayed between homes at 256 and 258 Fourth Street, within a few feet of the New York Central's railroad track, was viewed by many train passengers. (Courtesy of C.A. Bieg.)

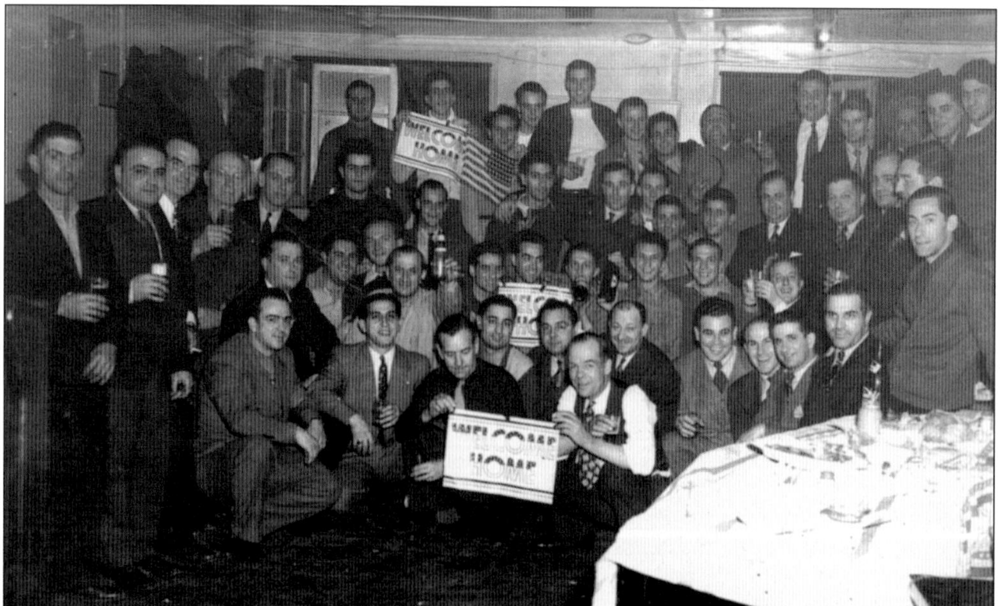

Neighborhood veterans Fiore Testo (holding a sign) and Francis Cardenuto (holding an American flag) are identified at the back of this photograph of a reunion honoring local veterans. Ida Street resident Samuel Chiappone worked with members of Troy's Boy Scouts Troop 502 to form a committee that rallied local businesses to assist with the restoration of two neighborhood World War II memorials. (Author's collection.)

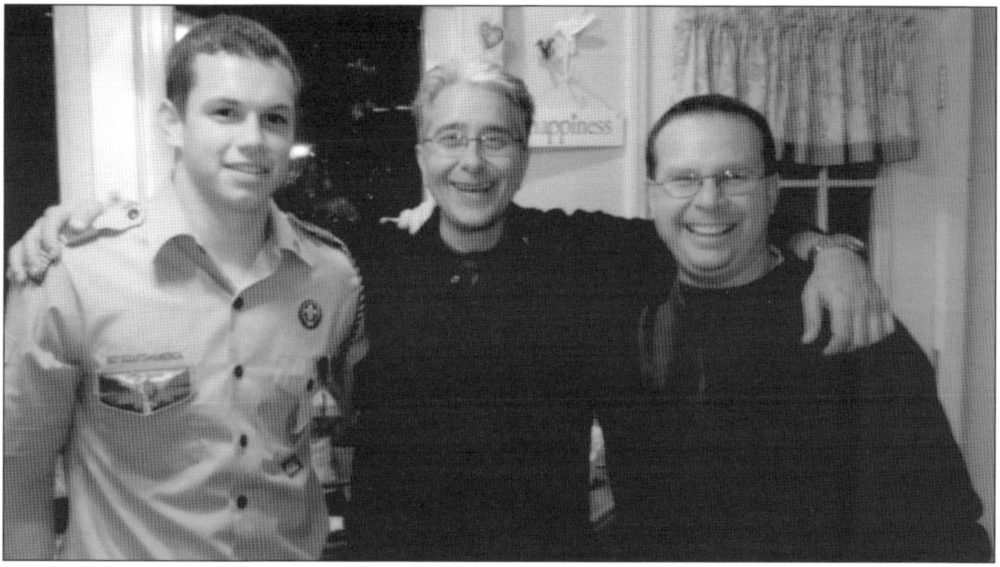

From left to right, Jonathan Carroll, Samuel Chiappone, and Daniel Carroll are pictured at a planning meeting of the Eleventh Ward WWII memorial committee. Jonathan, member of Boy Scouts Troop 502, organized and coordinated the plan for the restoration of the Eleventh Ward memorial working with committee chair Samuel Chiappone and members Brian and Mary Barnes, Judy Brearton, Robert Caprara Jr., Kellie Chiappone, Joshua Chiappone, Jessica Chiappone, Sam Chiappone Jr., Michael Esposito, Barbara McMahon, and Blanche and James Rivers. (Courtesy of Sam Chiappone.)

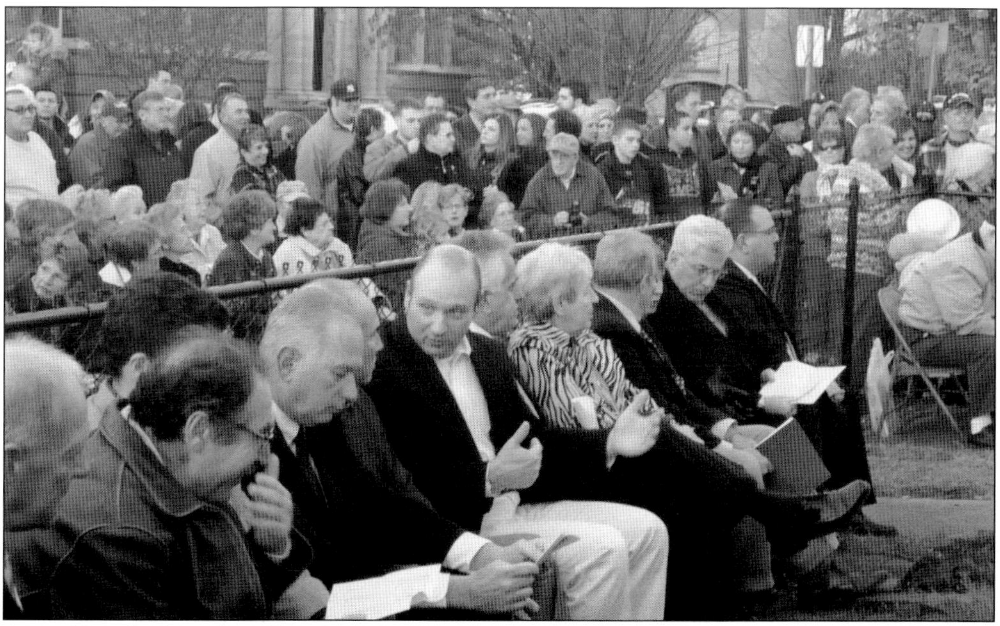

Several hundred people gathered to attend the Eleventh Ward World War II memorial's rededication ceremony on Veterans Day in 2010. On the 2012 anniversary of D-Day, hundreds also attended the First Ward World War II memorial's rededication. Anthony Mancino, Joseph Rodino, and Ignatius DeGenero—veterans from the First Ward—were honored at the ceremony. (Courtesy of Sam Chiappone.)

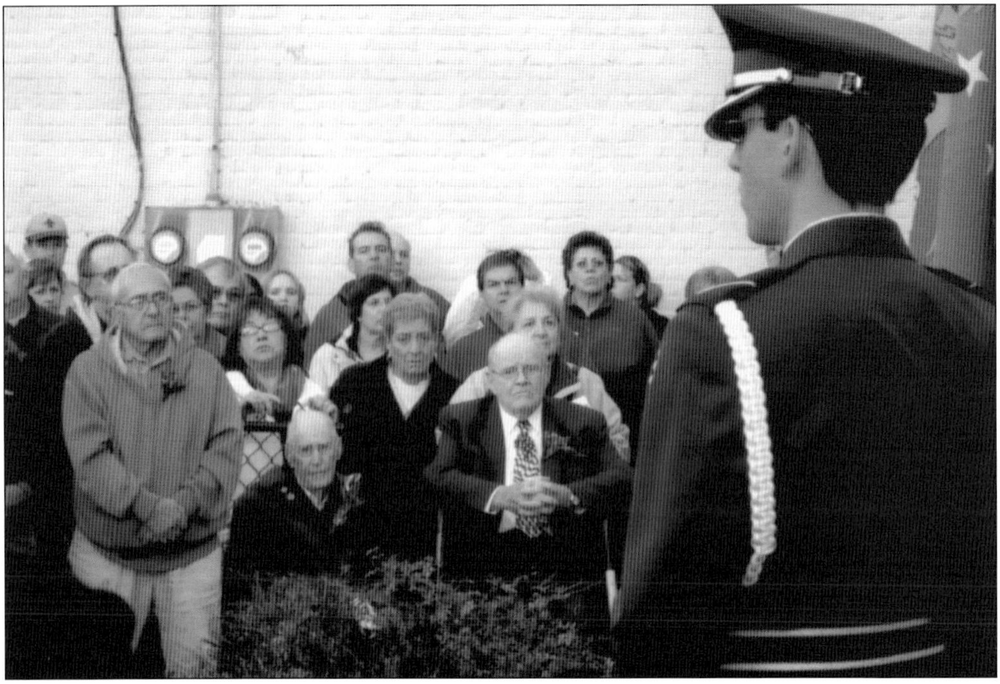

The men pictured in the first row are among the 268 names inscribed on the Eleventh Ward World War II Monument. They are, from left to right Justin J. Kehn, John Zullo, and William Murray. The names were read by members of Troy's Boy Scout Troop 502 at the solemn event, and Rensselaer Polytechnic Institute's Joint Services Color Guard presented the colors. Identified in the background are Sandra Padalino, Joseph Padalino, Louise Columbe, and Edith Novack. (Courtesy of Sam Chiappone.)

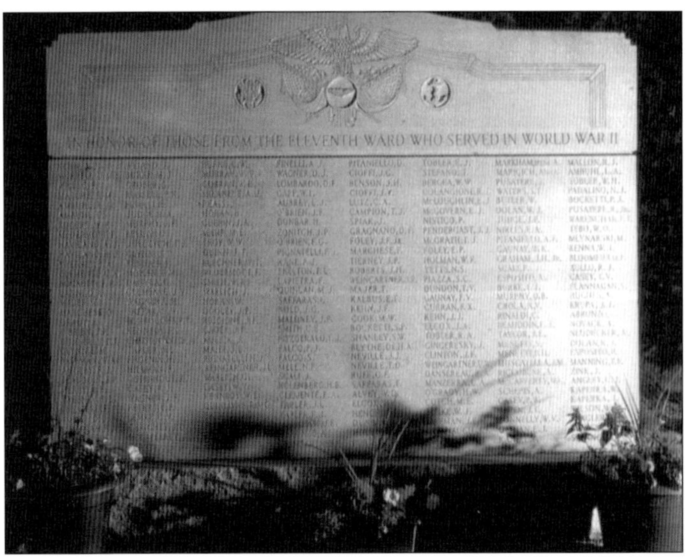

The Eleventh Ward World War II memorial is located on Third Street, three blocks south of the First Ward memorial. Over several years, the two neighborhood memorials were professionally cleaned. Walkways leading to them were repaired; hedges were trimmed or replaced; benches, flags, flagpoles and lighting were repaired or replaced; and fence fabric and poles were either repainted or replaced. (Photograph by Sam Chiappone.)

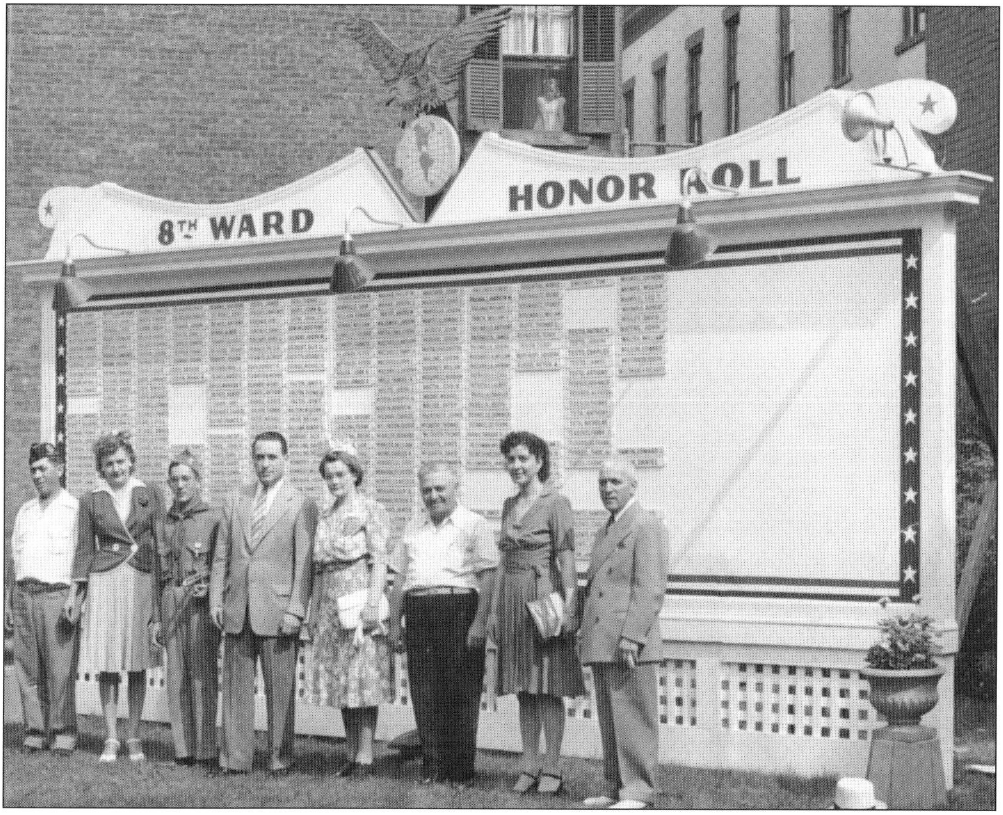

Members of the Eighth Ward World War II memorial committee stand in front of the memorial honor roll located on Washington and Third Streets. Three members of the committee can be identified. Far left is Vito Furciniti Sr. (wearing the service cap), a Mrs. McCarthy is the fifth person from the left, and Celia DeMaria Church is the seventh person from the left. Vito is the father of Pvt. Gerald A. Furciniti, an infantryman killed in action in Belgium on October 15, 1944. (Courtesy of Marion Field.)

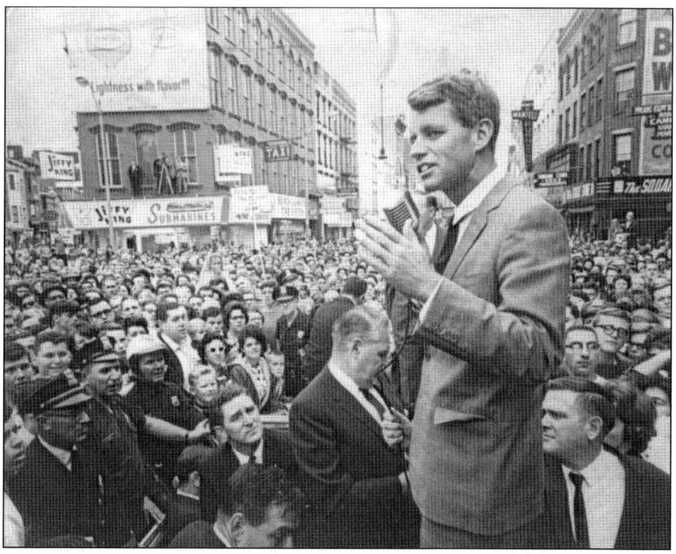

Several hundred neighbors join a crowd of thousands as Robert F. Kennedy speaks from a platform at Franklin Square, situated in the heart of Troy's downtown business district, during his successful senatorial campaign in 1964. The buildings in the background were demolished in the late 1960s. The structures on the left were replaced by a parking garage, and those on the right were replaced by Troy's Riverside Park. (Courtesy of Annette Rizzo Sanders.)

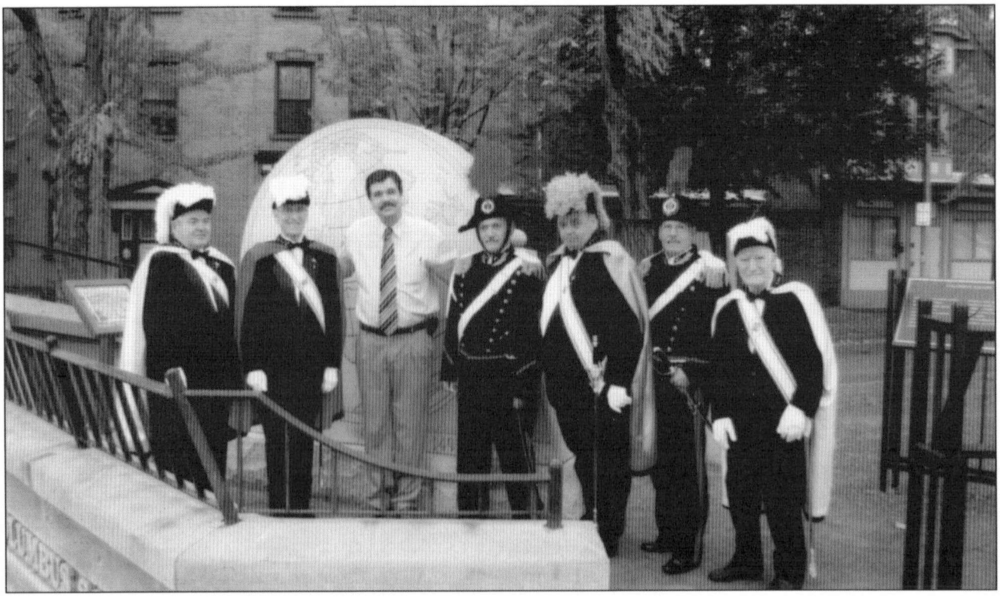

A flag-raising ceremony at Troy's Columbus memorial includes members of the Knights of Columbus (K of C), the Italian Community Center, and Troy Little Italy. From left to right are James Ziegler (K of C), Robert Gallagher (K of C), Vito Ciccarelli Jr. (Troy events coordinator), Martino Tedesco (ICC), Timothy Girvin (K of C), Dominick Mamone (ICC), and Anthony DeFazio (K of C). The memorial, dedicated in 1992, was designed by architect Joe Fama and built with funds donated by Troy's Italian American community. (Courtesy of Marion Field.)

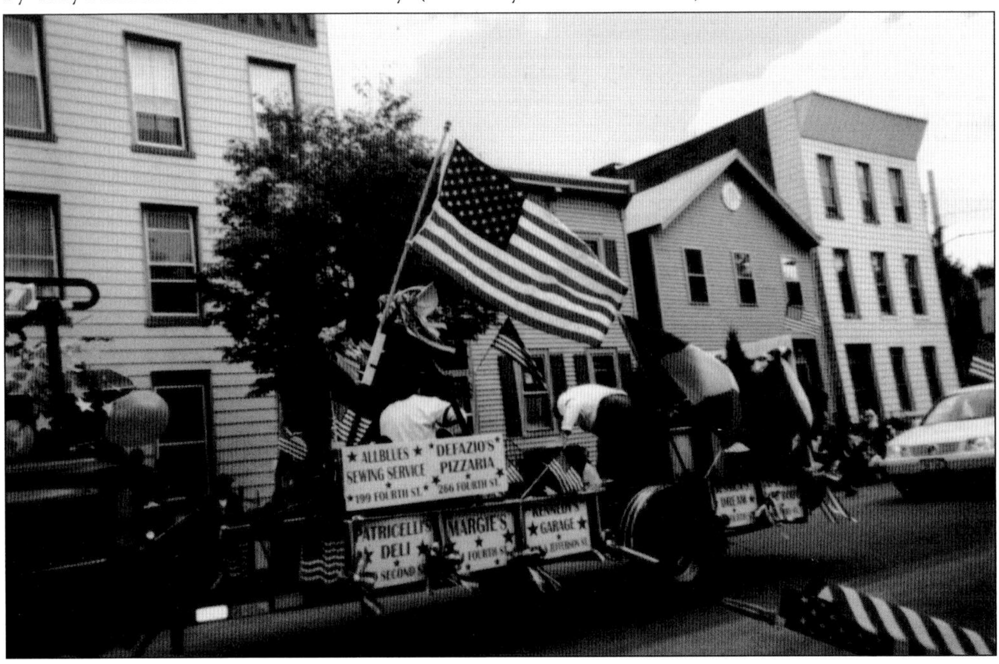

Neighborhood volunteers design and assemble a theme float for Troy's annual Flag Day Parade, enlisting support from local organizations and 19 neighborhood businesses. The primary parade route runs along Fourth Street through Little Italy. James Pasinella, a Marine veteran and retired US postal employee, organized the parade—first held in 1967. (Author's collection.)

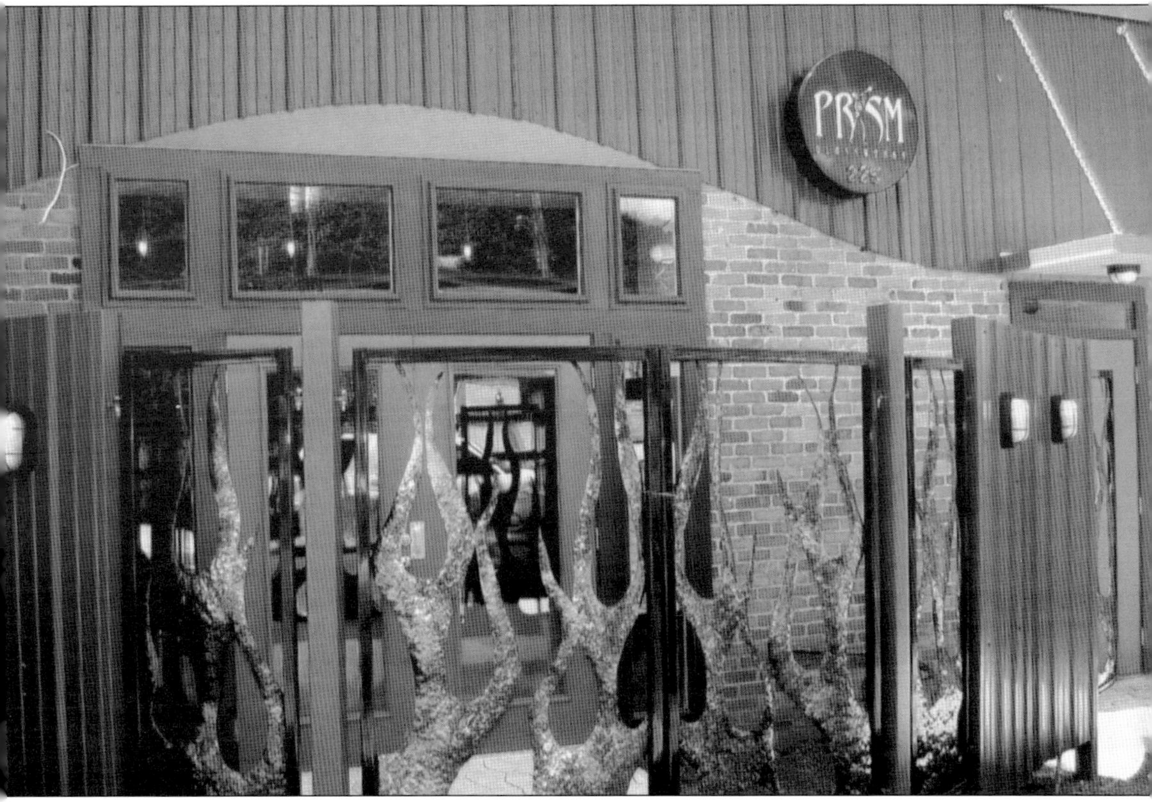

This building was awarded the 2011 Little Italy Best Rehab award. Prism Glassworks, located at 225 Fourth Street, is a combination art gallery, retail space for collectibles and glass products, and glassblowing studio. The site formerly contained a three-story brick building with three apartments. When it was demolished, a two-car garage was built at the site. Several years later, the structure was used as a judo center. Phil Sundling, the talented working owner of the glassworks business, extensively renovated both the exterior and interior of the building. (Courtesy of Marion Field.)

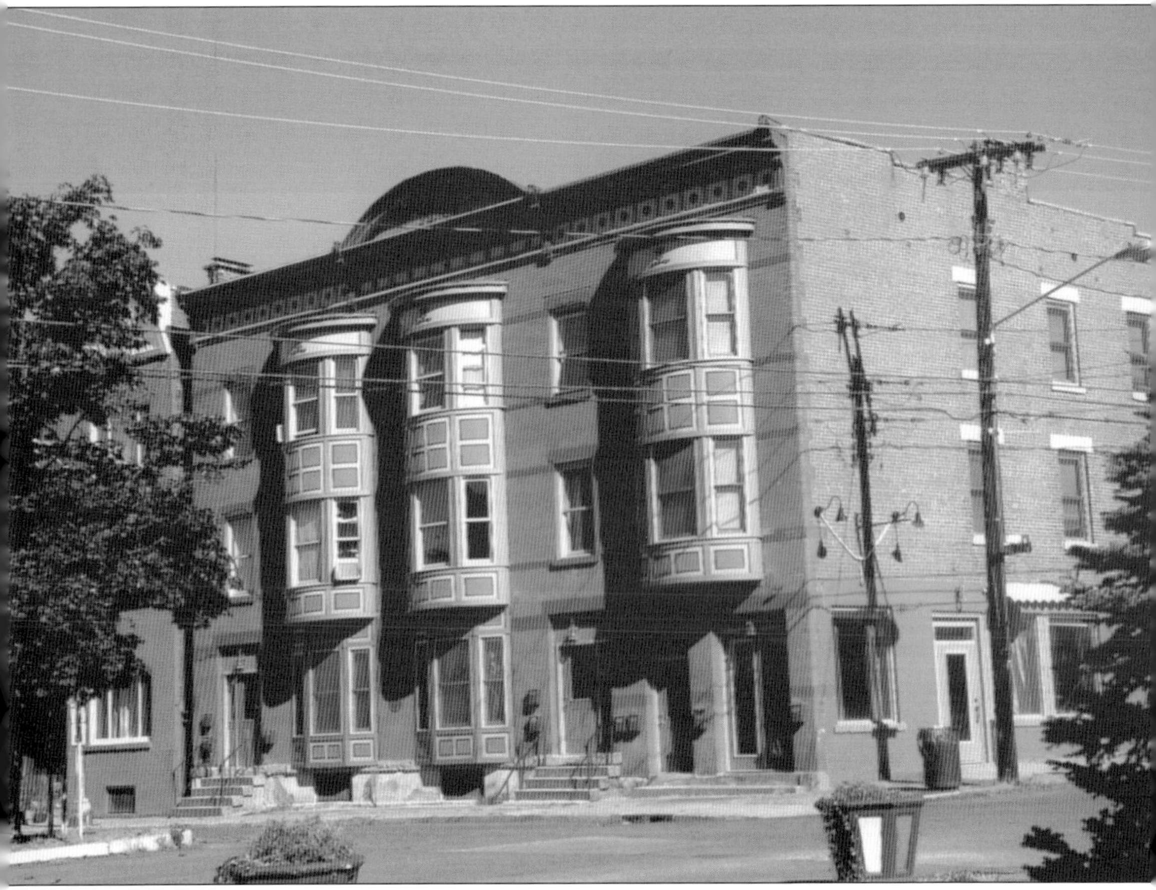

Terry and Lisa Jordan, owners of the three-story apartment complex located at 5, 6, and 7 Hill Street were the first winners of the Little Italy Best Rehab award. It was presented to the couple in 2010 for their extensive restoration and renovation of their property. Their complex, seen here, contains residential apartments and Gelateria Lisa, a gelato and coffee shop, and is located on the corner of Hill and Liberty Streets. Each year, members of the neighborhood group choose a businessperson whose building was substantially rehabilitated. David Graham, board member and secretary of Troy Little Italy, suggested the award. (Courtesy of Marion Field.)

Two unidentified artists prepare plaster for frescoes. Andrea Daley and Janet Murphy were the primary instructors for the 30 artists who learned the technique of painting on freshly applied plaster. The frescoes were on exhibit at business establishments in Troy for several days. They were then displayed at the Italian Community Center's Festa Italiana. At the conclusion of the ICC festa, an awards ceremony was held, and the frescoes went up for auction. (Photograph by Andrea Daley.)

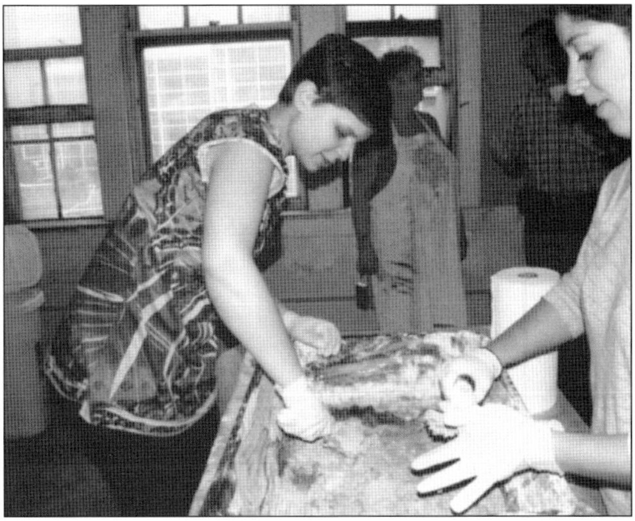

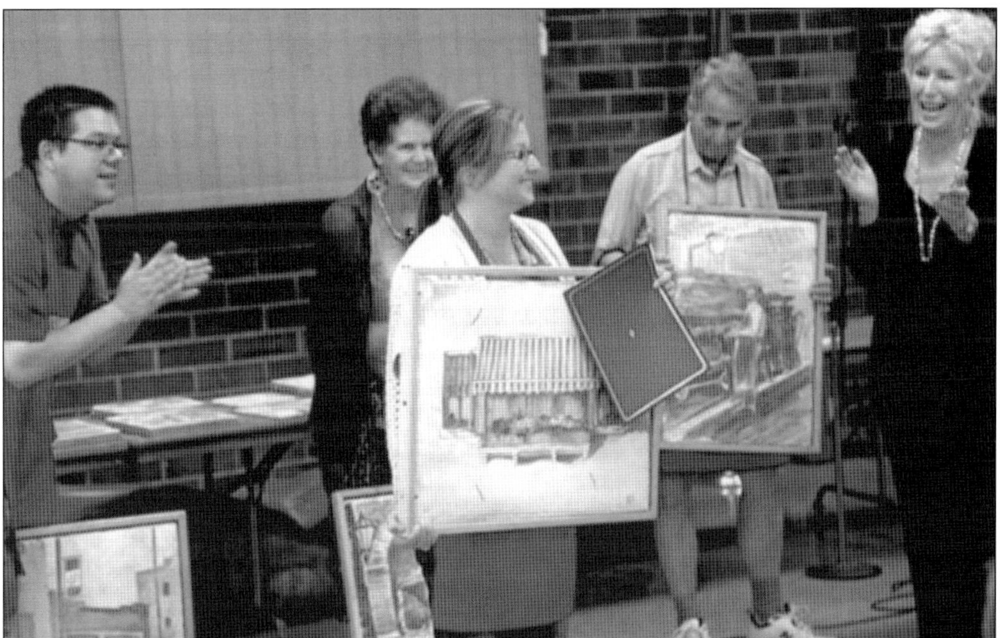

A fresco of a Mediterranean window by Troy artist Kristen Lombard won first place for the best Buon Fresco; it competed with 30 original works of art. From left to right are Patrick Pigott, Jean Tower, Lombard, Michael Brennan, and project leader Andrea Daley. Lombard won of a trip for two to Italy. (Courtesy of Bill Daley.)

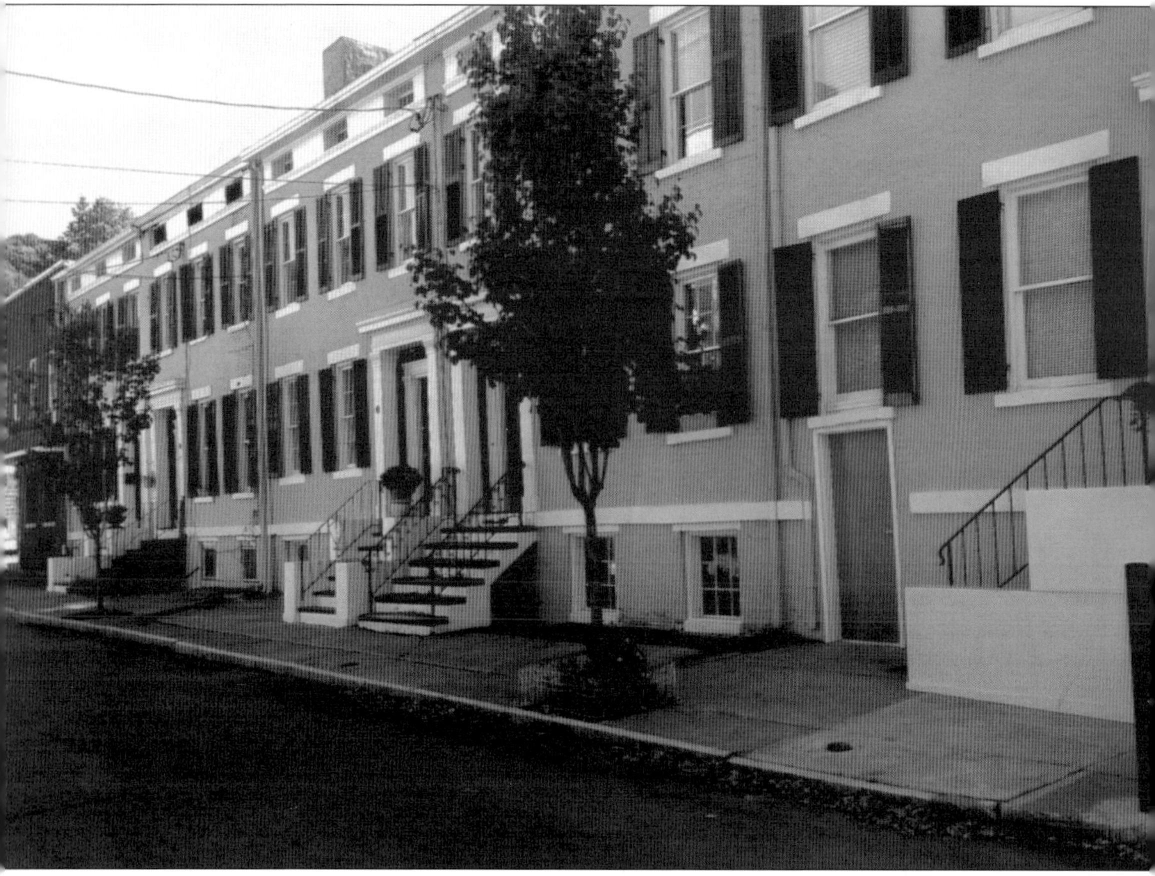

Shown here are several Greek revival row houses located on Franklin Place, adjacent to Liberty Square. Craftsmen, who worked on the Washington Place mansions opposite Troy's Washington Park, constructed the buildings in 1838. The lots at Franklin Place are 20 feet wide by 70 feet deep. During the past several years, homes on Franklin Place and several other streets throughout the neighborhood have been carefully restored and renovated, which contributes to the city's historic character. (Photograph by Andrea Daley.)

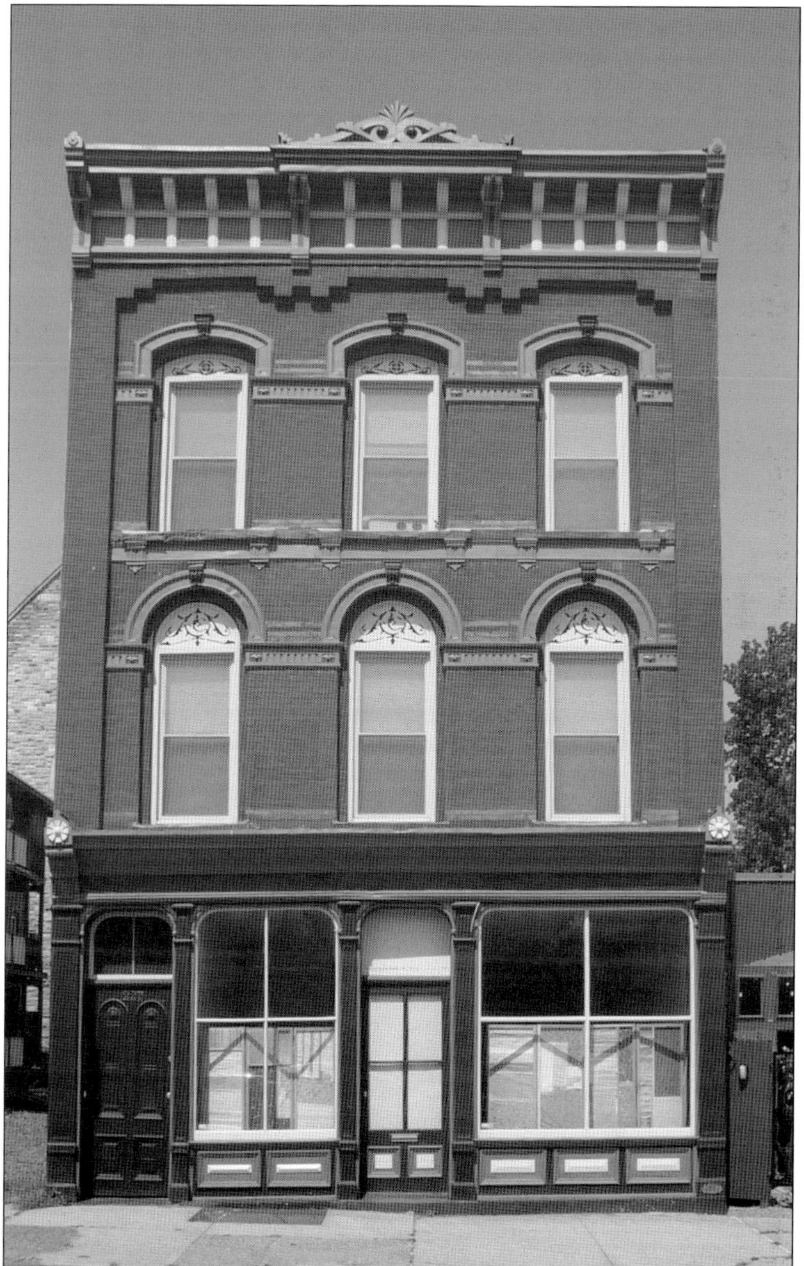

In August 2014, artists Denise Saint-Onge and Andrea Daley organized a tour of several restored and renovated properties in Little Italy. Both artists are property owners in the neighborhood. The tour, attended by 200 people, provided an opportunity to showcase six residences and commercial buildings along Fourth, Hill, and Adam Streets, including the 277 Fourth Street building in this photograph. The building was selected as the 2014 Little Italy Best Rehab. Saint-Onge recently purchased the three-story brick building, which has an iron front on the first level. Her art studio is located on the first floor of the building, and the two upper floors house residential apartments. Previously, the first floor was home to Sheeran's Printing for more than 80 years. (Photograph by Denise Saint-Onge.)

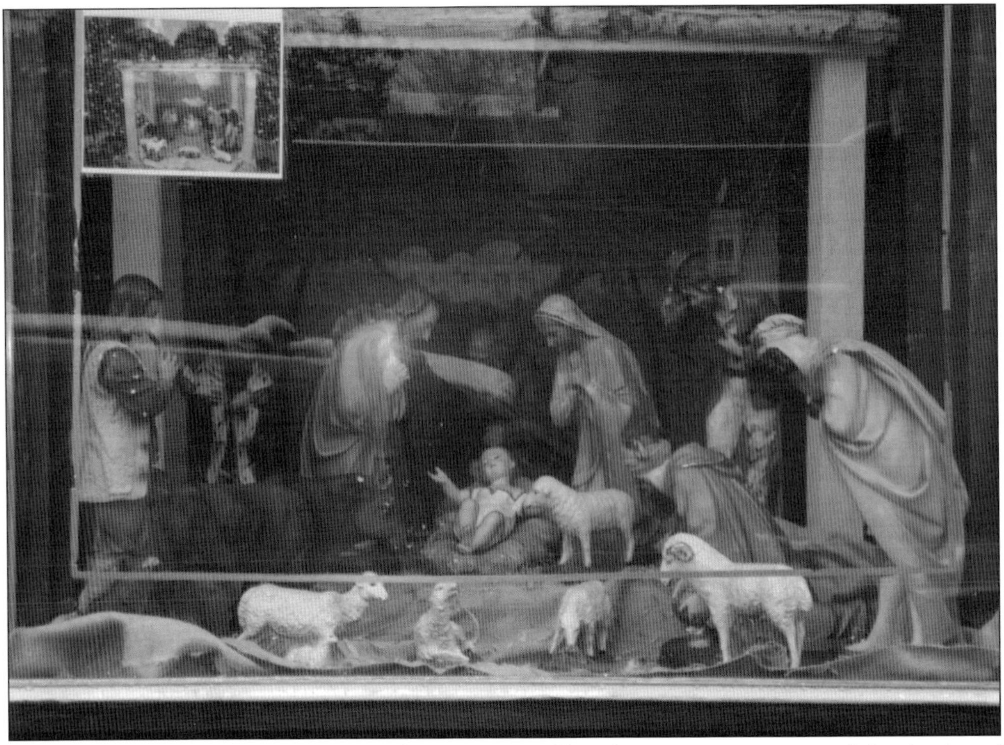

The Chiappone family, caretakers of the St. Mary's Church nativity set, arranged the display of the crèche in the window of the USA Track & Field building, located at 233 Fourth Street. The church closed in 2010, but the nativity is out on display from early December—just in time for the neighborhood's Christmas in Little Italy event—until the Feast of the Epiphany. (Photograph by Sam Chiappone.)

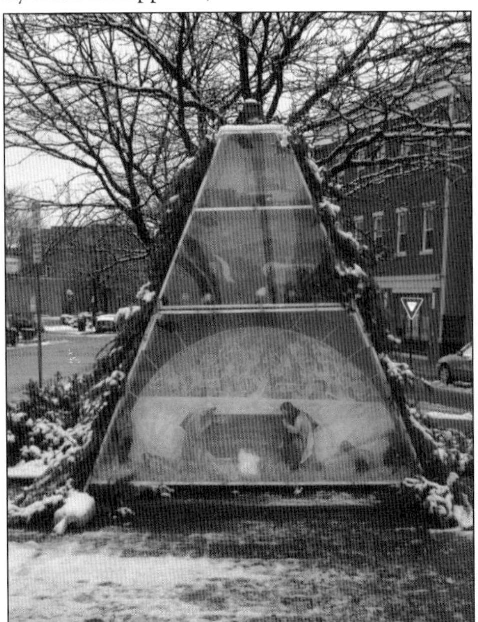

The structure photographed is a *ceppo*, an eight-foot high, three-tiered pyramid of wood. It was designed and constructed by Joseph Mix, Anthony DeFazio, and members of the woodworking class at Questar III. The *ceppo* has its origin in the Tuscan region of Italy. The shelves contain a Nativity set and greenery, fruits, nuts, and presents representing the gifts of the Earth and man. (Courtesy of Marion Field.)

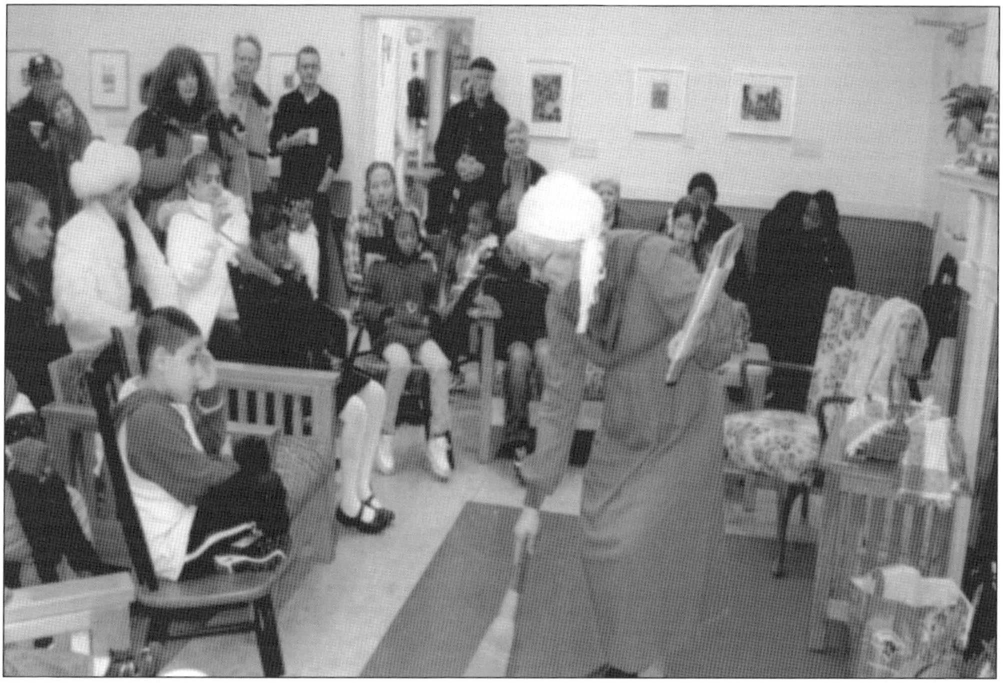

Claire (Porcello) Davis is seen at the Christmas in Little Italy event, presenting the timeless Italian Christmas folk legend of LaBefana as she reads from Tomi DePaola's book *The Legend of Old Befana.* The event also includes a reenactment known in Latin-speaking countries as Las Posadas. It symbolizes Mary and Joseph's search for shelter on the eve of the birth of Jesus. (Courtesy of Marion Field.)

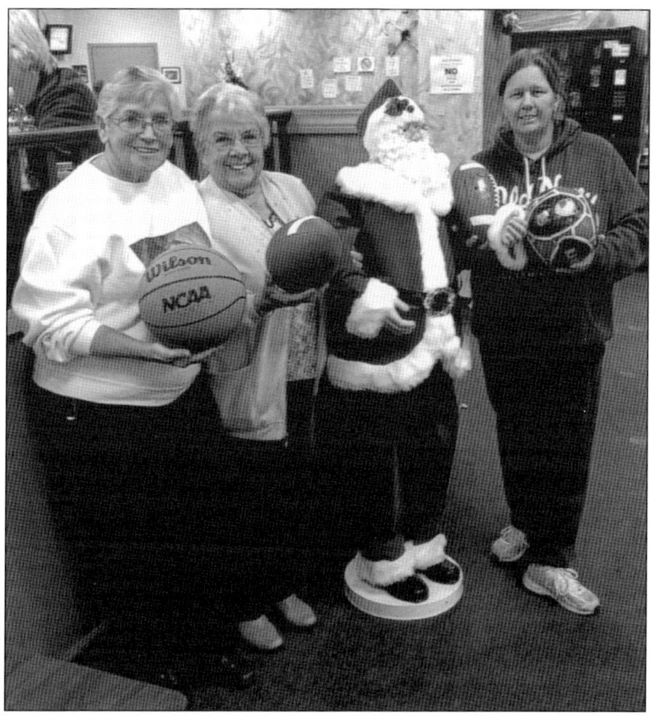

Volunteer workers and bingo players from the weekly games sponsored by St. Anthony of Padua Parish and Troy Little Italy hold a silent auction to benefit Adopt a Family, which raises funds for clothing and toys for families. From left to right are Jeanne Brahm, Rose Mary Kotansky, and Sandra Anselment, bearing toys for families in need. (Courtesy of Marion Field.)

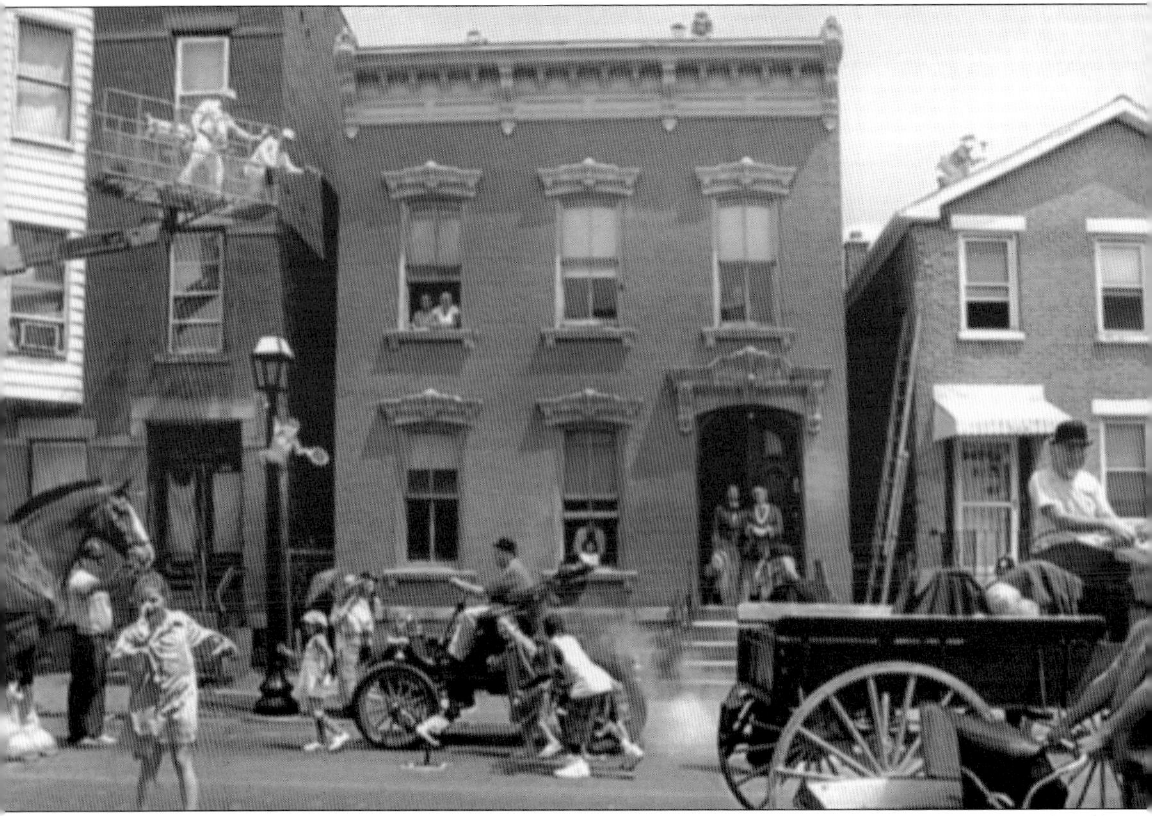

One of the most ambitious volunteer events organized by Troy Little Italy was Norman Rockwell Comes Alive in Troy, New York, held in June 2008. Norman Rockwell was a frequent visitor to Troy. Linda Pero, curator of the Rockwell collection at the Norman Rockwell Museum in Stockbridge, Massachusetts, stated that Rockwell chose Troy because it was the nearest big city to his home. Stephanie Plunkett, deputy director and chief curator of the museum, was the keynote speaker. Little Italy residents David Graham and Andrea Daley led the planning process. The central idea was to reenact a Rockwell illustration that was originally commissioned by the Ford Motor Company for a calendar celebrating 50 years of auto manufacturing. (Photograph by Andrea Daley.)

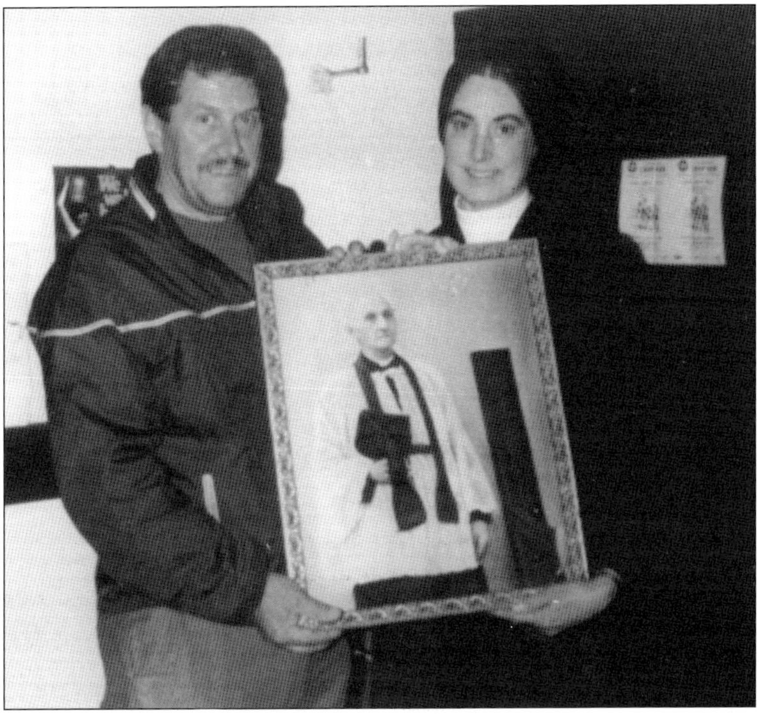

Andrew Van Den Corput, great nephew of Rev. Peter Havermans, visits with Sr. Mary Madeleine Drennan of St. Mary's Parish. They hold a framed print of Reverend Havermans that was included in an exhibit on the priest who founded and served as first pastor of St. Mary's Parish. (Courtesy of Sr. Mary Madeleine Drennan.)

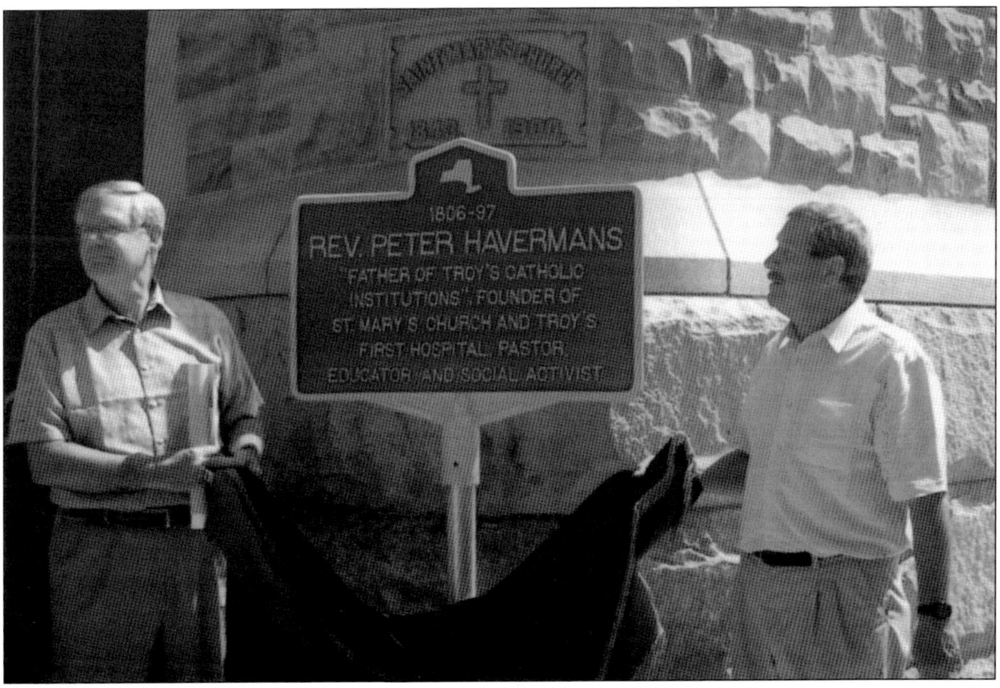

James Conroy (left), a St. Mary's Parish council member, and Andrew Van Den Corput unveil the Reverend Havermans historic marker at the dedication ceremony, honoring the man who is known as the father of Troy's Catholic institutions. This was the first of four historic markers installations, which were cosponsored by Troy Little Italy and the Hudson-Mohawk Gateway. (Photograph by Clement Campana.)

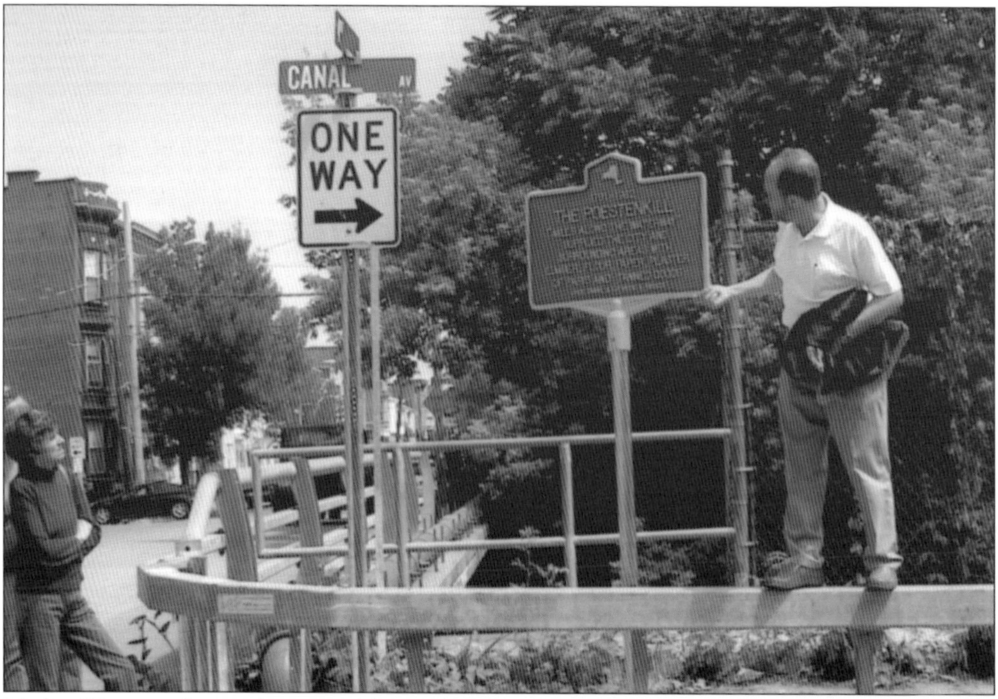

Michael Barrett, deputy director of the Hudson-Mohawk Gateway, references the historic marker at the Fourth Street bridge site along the Poestenkill as he speaks on the importance of waterway industries between 1671 and 1962. Mills supplied the city and surrounding areas with lumber, flour, paper, plaster of Paris, and tanned goods. The last of these was owned Andrew Ruff and Sons, which opened in 1873 and closed by 1930. (Photograph by Dorcas Rose.)

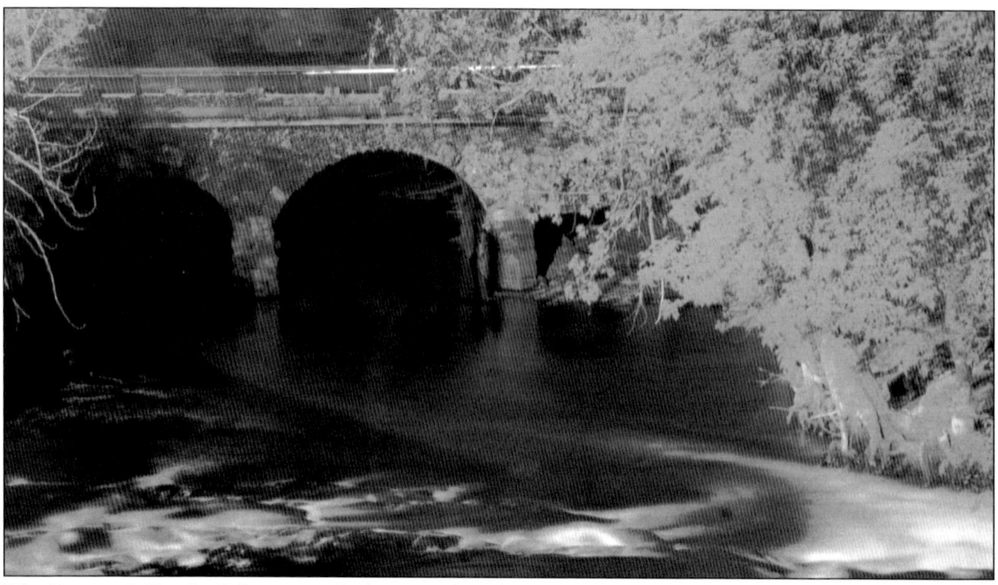

The Poestenkill, which begins at Dyken Pond in the Rensselaer County community of Poestenkill, meanders for 28 miles through several towns and steep gorges in the city of Troy, producing an impressive waterfall before emptying out in the Hudson River. Poestenkill Gorge was added to the National Registry of Historic Places on March 8, 1978. (Photograph by Anasha Cummings.)

Three generations of the Sage family unveil the historic marker at the Gasholder House, located on the corner of Fifth Avenue and Jefferson Street. From left to right are William Sage, grandson Cody, and son Kevin. C. Thomas Carroll, executive director of the Hudson Mohawk Gateway, described the cutting edge importance of the facility. Sage Brothers Paint Company purchased the historic building in 1969. (Photograph by Dorcas Rose.)

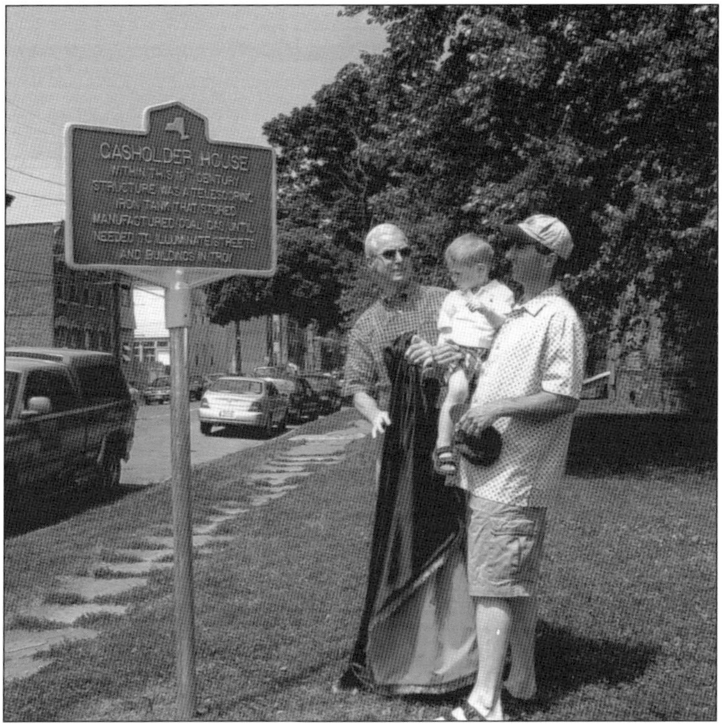

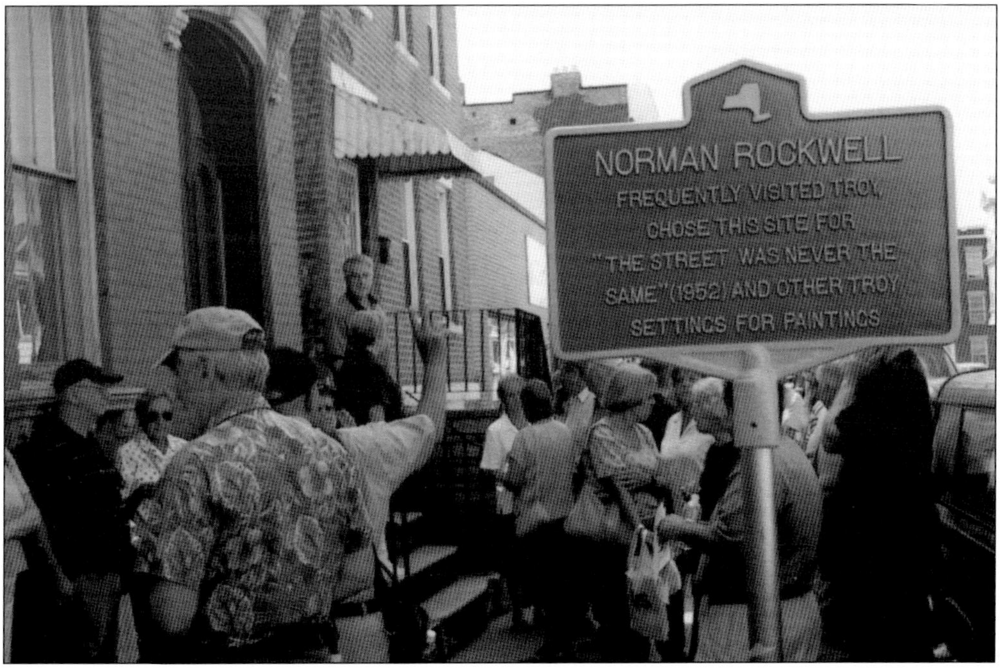

This historic marker was placed at 296 Fourth Street, celebrating a Norman Rockwell illustration commissioned by the Ford Motor Company. "The Street Was Never the Same" is a scene set in 1903. Three Troy scenes by Rockwell were *Saturday Evening Post* covers: "Homecoming GI" (May 26, 1945), "Saying Grace" (November 24, 1951), and "Walking to Church" (April 3, 1953). (Photograph by Dorcas Rose.)

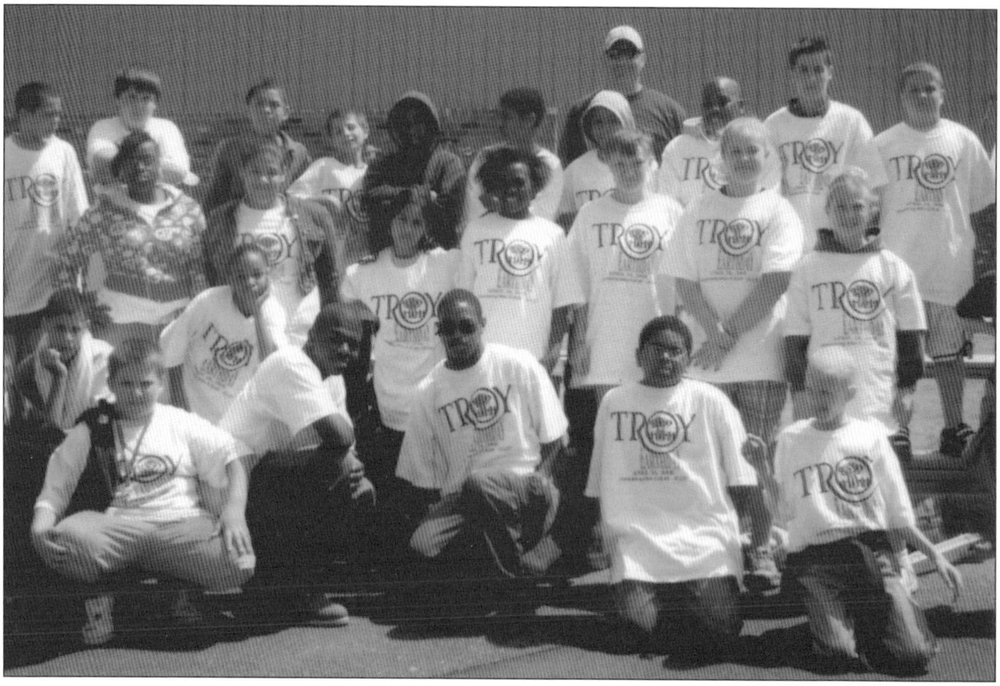

Youngsters wearing their Earth Day T-shirts pose for a group photograph following a successful neighborhood cleanup. Earth Day, organized in 1970 by peace activist John McConnell and supported by US senator Gaylord Nelson, is considered the birth of the modern environmental movement. (Courtesy of Marion Field.)

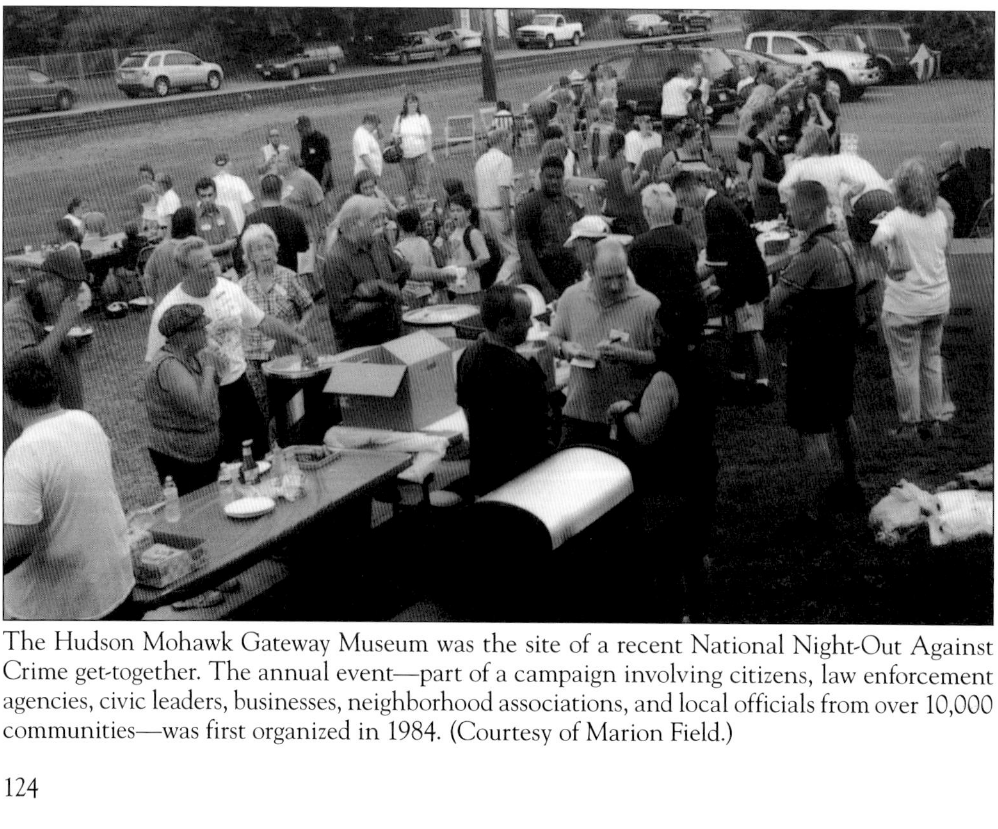

The Hudson Mohawk Gateway Museum was the site of a recent National Night-Out Against Crime get-together. The annual event—part of a campaign involving citizens, law enforcement agencies, civic leaders, businesses, neighborhood associations, and local officials from over 10,000 communities—was first organized in 1984. (Courtesy of Marion Field.)

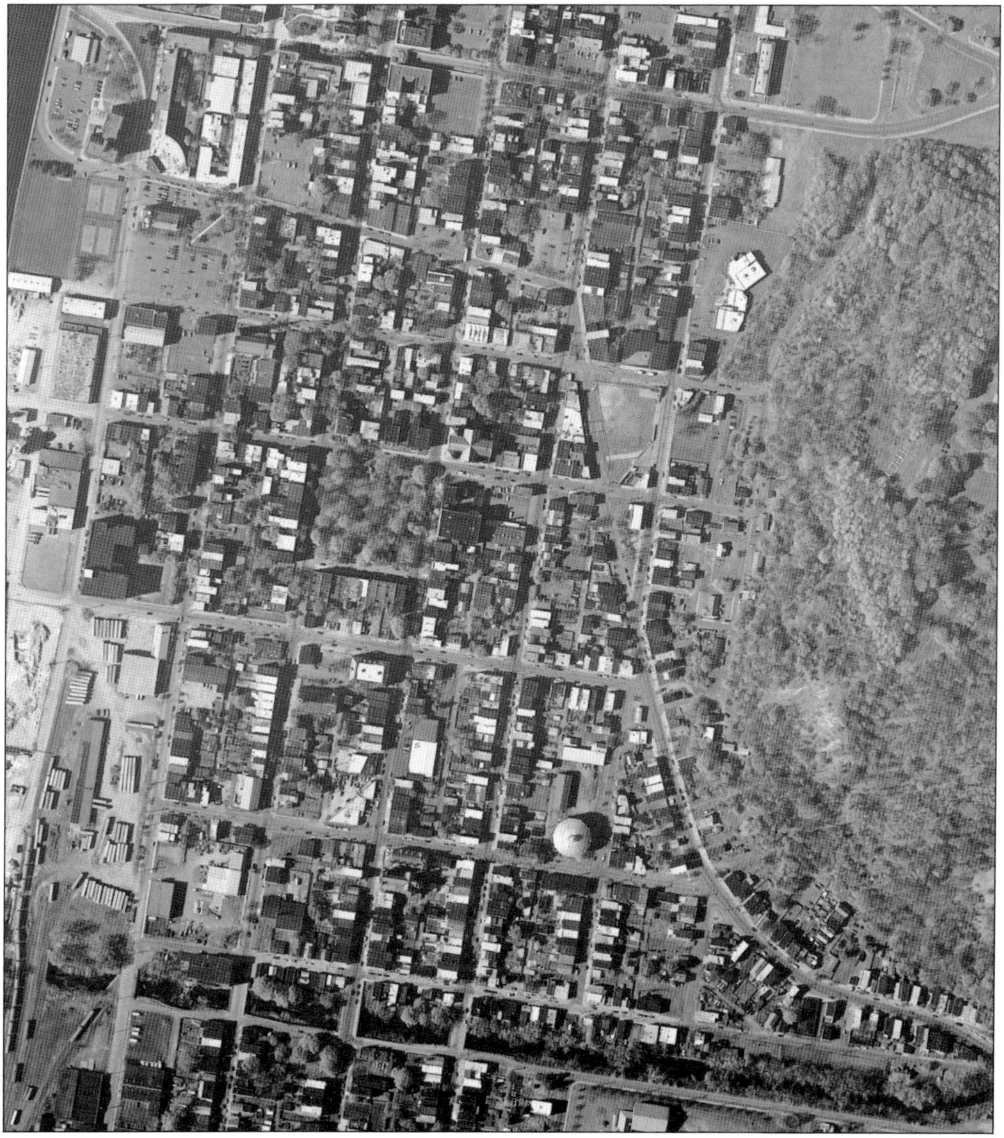

The 40-block area pictured in this aerial view is South Central Troy. From top to bottom are Ferry, Division, Liberty, Washington, Adams, Jefferson, and Ida Streets. The diagonal street is Hill Street, and from left to right are River, First, Second, Third, Fourth, Fifth, St. Mary's, and Havermans Streets. The geographic center is beautiful Washington Park, a privately owned two-acre green space. Washington Place is located on the south side of the park. Little Italy is the 20-block section stretching from Ferry Street on the north to Ida Street and the Poestenkill Canal along the length of the western slope of Mount Ida (Prospect Park). By choice or by chance, these were the blocks settled by Italian immigrants in the 1890s. (Courtesy of the New York State Geographic Information Systems.)

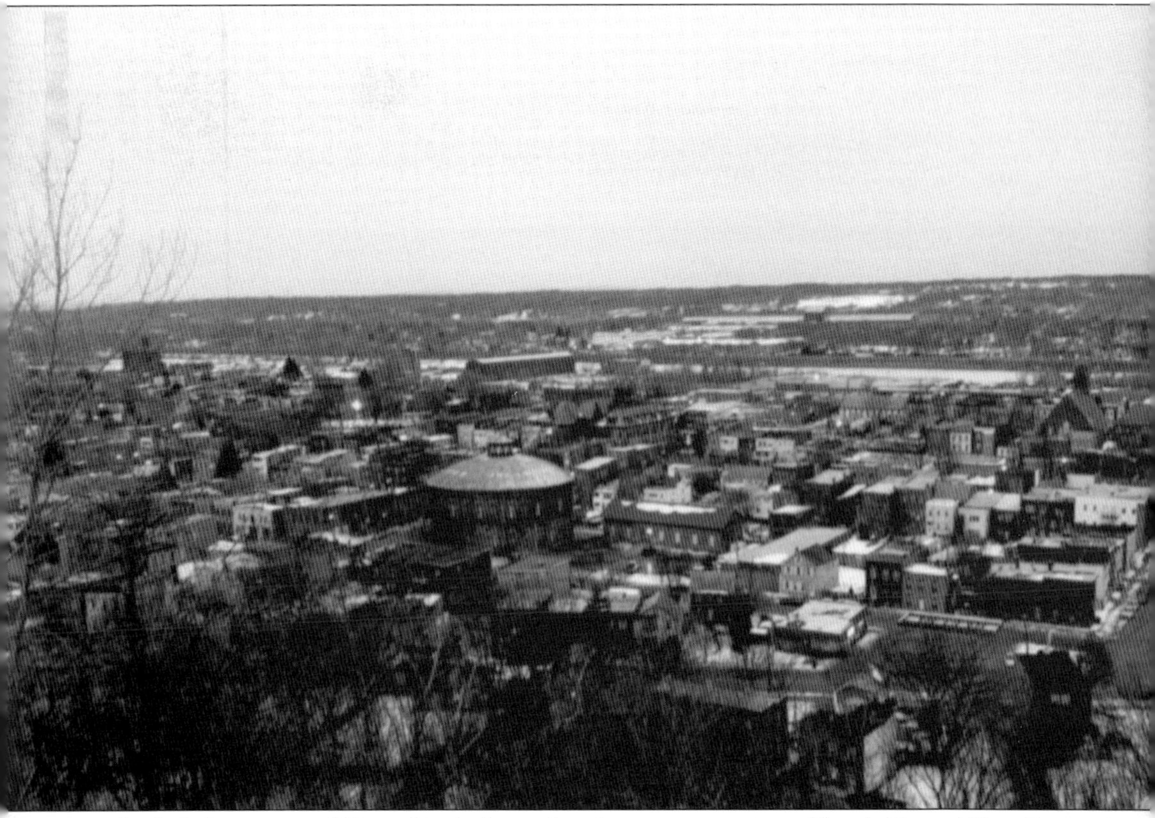

Little Italy consists of 20 city blocks located in the eastern portion of South Central Troy. Pictured is a view of Little Italy from Prospect Park. The circular building in the center is the historic Gasholder House. The neighborhood is adjacent to Troy's historic downtown and the Washington Park Historic District, which is a showcase of Greek, Gothic, Italianate, and Classical revival architecture. The campuses of both Russell Sage College and Rensselaer Polytechnic Institute are within blocks of the neighborhood. The western slope of the Mount Ida's Prospect Park borders the length of Little Italy. The Central Troy Historic District boundary now includes much of the Little Italy neighborhood. (Photograph by Anasha Cummings.)

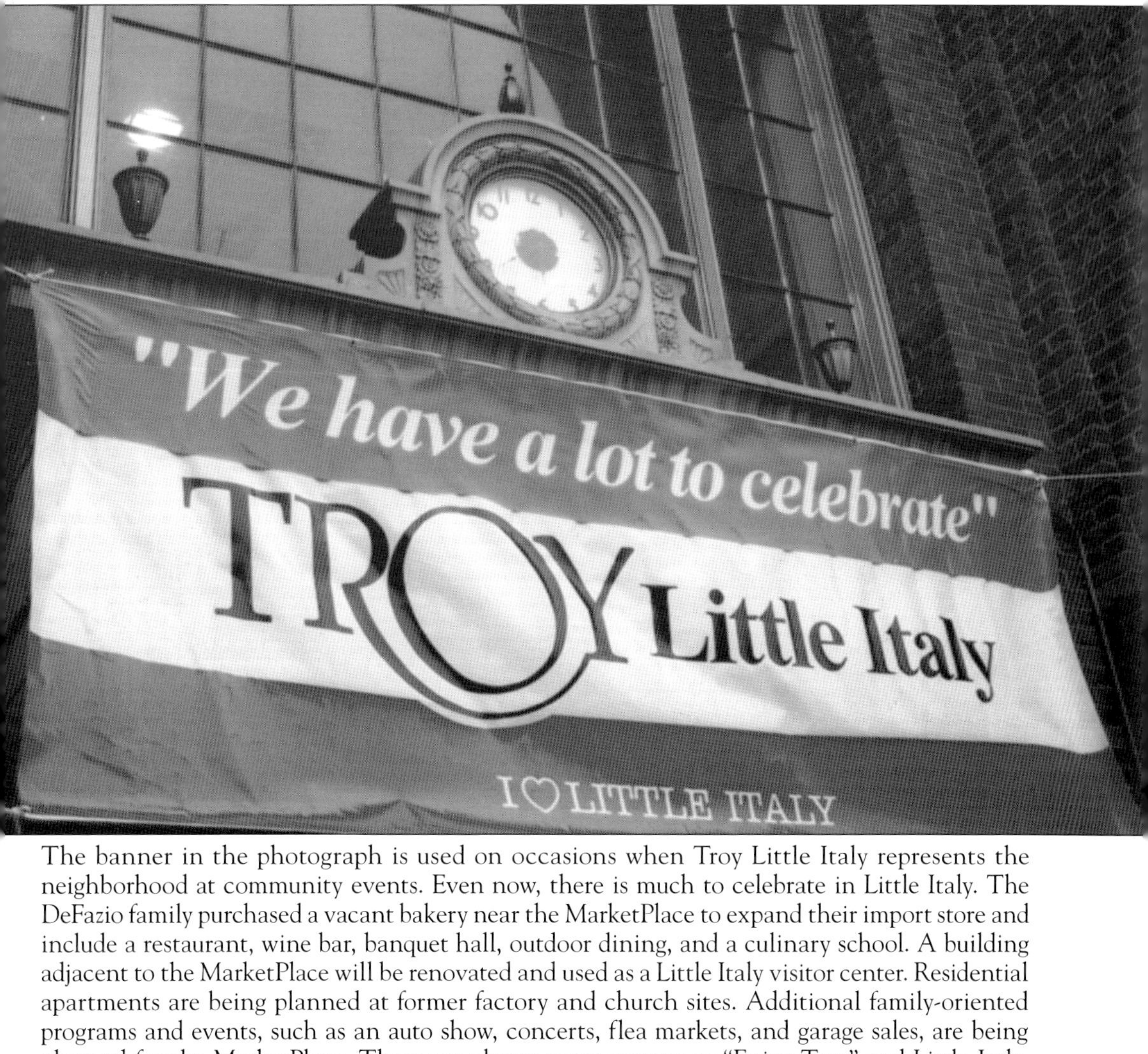

The banner in the photograph is used on occasions when Troy Little Italy represents the neighborhood at community events. Even now, there is much to celebrate in Little Italy. The DeFazio family purchased a vacant bakery near the MarketPlace to expand their import store and include a restaurant, wine bar, banquet hall, outdoor dining, and a culinary school. A building adjacent to the MarketPlace will be renovated and used as a Little Italy visitor center. Residential apartments are being planned at former factory and church sites. Additional family-oriented programs and events, such as an auto show, concerts, flea markets, and garage sales, are being planned for the MarketPlace. There are always more reasons to "Enjoy Troy" and Little Italy. (Courtesy of Marion Field.)

Discover Thousands of Local History Books Featuring Millions of Vintage Images

Arcadia Publishing, the leading local history publisher in the United States, is committed to making history accessible and meaningful through publishing books that celebrate and preserve the heritage of America's people and places.

Find more books like this at
www.arcadiapublishing.com

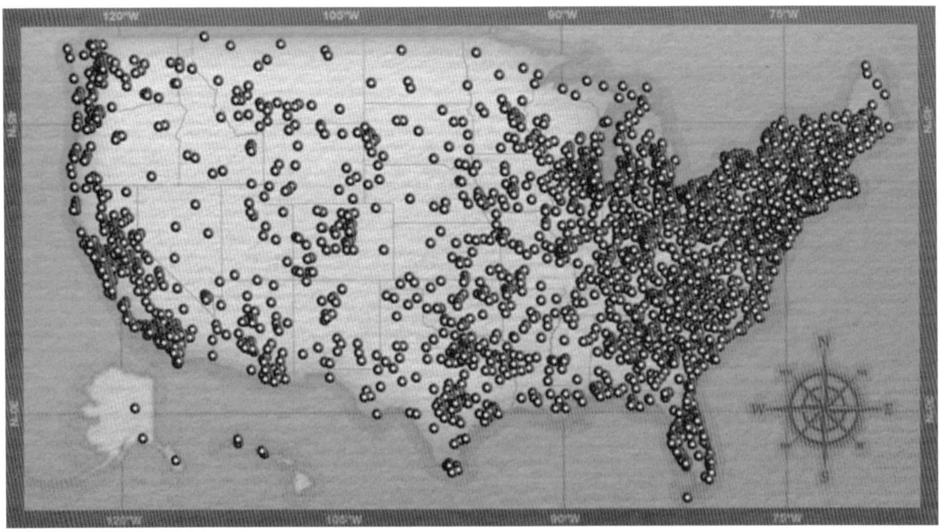

Search for your hometown history, your old stomping grounds, and even your favorite sports team.

Consistent with our mission to preserve history on a local level, this book was printed in South Carolina on American-made paper and manufactured entirely in the United States. Products carrying the accredited Forest Stewardship Council (FSC) label are printed on 100 percent FSC-certified paper.

MADE IN THE USA